Women-at-Law

Lessons Learned Along the Pathways to Success

Phyllis Horn Epstein

with a Foreword by Martha W. Barnett,
Past President of the American Bar Association

ABA **LAW PRACTICE MANAGEMENT SECTION**
MARKETING • MANAGEMENT • TECHNOLOGY • FINANCE

Commitment to Quality: The Law Practice Management Section is committed to quality in our publications. Our authors are experienced practitioners in their fields. Prior to publication, the contents of all our books are rigorously reviewed by experts to ensure the highest quality product and presentation. Because we are committed to serving our readers' needs, we welcome your feedback on how we can improve future editions of this book. We invite you to fill out and return the comment card at the back of this book.

Cover design by Gail Patejunas.

Reprinted with permission and used by arrangement with author: excerpts from *How to Save Your Own Life* by Erica Jong, New York: Signet Books, New American Library © 1977.

Philadelphia Bar Association statements and model policies in Appendices A–G reprinted with permission from the Philadelphia Bar Association.

Library of Congress Cataloging-in-Publication Data
Women-at-Law: Lessons Learned Along the Pathways of Success. Phyllis Horn Epstein: Library of Congress Cataloging-in-Publication Data is on file.

ISBN 1-59031-354-2

08 07 06 05 04   5 4 3 2 1

Discounts are available for books ordered in bulk. Special consideration is given to state bars, CLE programs, and other bar-related organizations. Inquire at Book Publishing, American Bar Association, 321 North Clark Street, Chicago, Illinois 60610-4714.

Contents

Dedicated to Earl and Charles

Acknowledgments

I could not have completed this book without the love and support of my family and friends. When I voiced my intention to write a book, not one of them confronted me with the obvious question: When was I going to do it? I practice law during the day, and have a son to raise, a husband, and a house to keep. Did I really want to spend my days interviewing and my nights typing, researching, and editing? The other gift my family and friends gave me was never doubting I could break out of my box and write a book. To them, there was simply no question that I would pull this off. For their blind faith in me, I am profoundly grateful.

Without the love and encouragement of my husband from the day we first met, I never would have realized my full potential as a lawyer, as a mother, and as a woman. He has been my mentor and my friend. He has also been my willing researcher and editor, even when the reality of a finished book seemed distant. I want to thank my son, Charles, whose enthusiasm for this project and for life has been a great source of happiness and encouragement. He has never stopped believing in me and I am grateful for his love and his shining face. I thank both my husband and son for accepting reduced standards of orderliness at home, late laundry, and hastily gathered meals these past few years. I thank them for my time at the computer, for sharing the printer, and for their creative ideas.

I want to thank my parents for giving me a happy childhood, and for always believing in me and for telling me so. I have always had the gift of their love and support, without which nothing is possible. To my mother—for teaching me the nuts and bolts of juggling work, school, and raising three children, all at the same time, and for reading and editing countless versions of my work. To my father—who encouraged me to be anything I wished and to be the best I could be, and who always made it obvious how proud he was of me. I believe his love of history has been handed down to me, as shown by my choice of major in college and now by the writing of my own history. To my brothers Burton and Ivan—who have been my best friends in life, keeping me sane and sharing so much that I have never been lost for long in this world. To my sisters-in-law Joan and Lynn—who are so special to me, as I grew up with only brothers. I am glad to include them in the small circle of family and friends that keeps me secure and feeling part of something.

My niece Abigail Horn was a great reader of an earlier version of this book. She is at Yale Law School today, and I hope that I had some small part in that. Abby's comments were particularly valuable, going beyond the standard suggestions to add a comma or move a paragraph. She was considering law school when she read this book and had just completed four years at Duke University. Her comments were insightful and she encouraged me to contribute more of myself. My cousin Nomi Eve is a wonderful published author herself. When I first expressed the idea of writing a book, Nomi could not have been more generous in her support of writing and the business of getting published. Thanks also to my cousin Lauren Rosen for putting me in touch with the women in her law school class of 2002 at Temple University. Sara Kimmel, a young woman who recently earned her doctorate and someone I call friend, aided my research by putting me in touch with Psychdata Online Services, an online research company that allowed me to expand my contributors to women lawyers across the country.

My law partner Boris Shapiro contributed to my consciousness-raising by displaying in his office the *ABA Journal* with the cover that says, "I Don't Think That Ladies Should Be Lawyers." I thank him for years of partnership and for never practicing what those words were preaching. To the contrary, he has been a supporter, mentor, and

equal-opportunity partner these many years. The women in my office, Jacqueline Heffron and Annette Davis, encouraged me from the start and helped with the printing and mailing of transcripts and letters. They are more than my backup—they are my cheering section.

A few years back I had a temporary crisis of life, and just at that moment my friend Frank Conlin stepped into my path and invited me for a cup of coffee. As we spoke, Frank floated the idea of my writing a book. For all the cups of coffee and for all the good, friendly advice, I owe one to Frank.

My friends Cheryl Kritz, Jayne Spangler Weiss, and Joan Lerner Volinsky have been behind me every step of the way. Cheryl and I met in law school. Over many lunches, we discussed the versions of this book. She is a contributor and fellow traveler through this journey of work, family, and whatever else we have time for. Jayne and I also met in law school, and I am very pleased to say we still are pals, even though our lives are so busy. I value most highly the women I call my friends, and I am pleased to include Joan in that small circle. Aside from her eternal good cheer and loyal support—to say nothing of her endless supply of good coffee—Joan has always been there to offer thoughtful reflections about life. My friend Janice Ocko was a lifesaver last summer when she agreed to read a chapter and offer her advice. I was experiencing a crisis in confidence, and Janice, a writer herself, took the time to read something I wrote and set me back on my feet.

I want to thank the women at the American Bar Association who helped bring this work to light, including Beverly Loder and Judith Grubner, who read, edited, and presented it for publication. There would be no book without them. Thank you Bev for your enthusiastic endorsement of this project.

I want to thank Martha Barnett for her eloquent and interesting foreword. Martha is a veteran trailblazer for women in the legal profession. In her foreword she relates her own personal experience in those early years, with what is in retrospect a humorous account, about becoming accepted, albeit begrudgingly at first, in the society of male lawyers. Not only was she accepted, Martha excelled, becoming a partner in her law firm, and then President of the American Bar Association. Martha continues to be an exemplary role model and mentor to other women lawyers, in both the professional and personal spheres. I am grateful to her for her contribution.

Many sincere thanks to Gerry Spence for his eloquent contribution. I feel privileged to be the beneficiary of his valuable advice. I wish to thank Justice Ruth Bader Ginsburg for her inspiration and kind words of encouragement and also for sharing with me writings of her own.

Last, there would be no book without the women who participated in sharing their views on work and life. I interviewed many in person. Others contributed online, in writing, and by telephone. All of these women lead very full lives and I appreciate the time they took to be part of this project, even before I could claim to have a publisher. I thank them for what they have given me: a feeling of community, a sense of belonging to a sisterhood of working women, wisdom, and perspective. I was warmed by their level of sharing and their generosity of spirit—to me and to the people in their own lives. Meeting these women and speaking with them has been an entirely uplifting experience. There is a Talmudic teaching that as long as there are ten righteous men in the world, God will not destroy the earth again. Well, I think there is room to amend that saying to include women, and I can attest that the world is not at risk of destruction.

Phyllis Horn Epstein

. . . *a diamond is the last and highest of God's mineral creations, as a woman is the last and highest of God's animal creations.*

From Acres of Diamonds
by Russell Conwell, founder of Temple University

Foreword

In the thirty years that I have been practicing law, I have seen dramatic changes in the legal profession. Many of them are reflected in my own firm. I was the first woman that Holland & Knight ever hired. Looking back at it now, I think it was probably a bit more traumatic for the law firm than it was for me. But they handled it well, and we all survived and even prospered. Several years later I had occasion to look at my personnel file and there was my résumé, complete with several notes stapled to it. I couldn't resist the temptation—I had to look at what someone thought was important enough to attach to my résumé when I was interviewed.

There was a copy of an article from the *Wall Street Journal* about a large international law firm being sued for "sex discrimination" (this was even before "gender" was the accepted term) and a handwritten note from the associate who reviewed résumés for the firm's recruiting partner (and a former law school classmate). The note said, "If we have to hire a woman, let's hire this one." Today, we hire as many women as we do men.

In the years since, Holland & Knight has continued to evolve, and I have as well, both professionally and personally. The practice of law has provided me with opportunities that simply would not have been there otherwise. Law, in fact, was not my original calling. After earning my bachelor of arts degree at Tulane University, I planned to enroll in a graduate program in social work. My experience volunteering at Project Head Start programs had instilled in me a strong desire to work with underprivileged children. But, one day, my husband, who is an architect, said, "Martha, if you really want to help people, why don't you become a lawyer?" And I did just that, not realizing at the time the daunting challenges and deeply satisfying rewards I would experience—and continue to experience—throughout my career.

My early years as the lone woman associate were filled with unexpected challenges—everything from having a client refuse to let a woman work on his cases to representing a former state governor on a pro bono matter. I worked hard and quickly learned that the biggest challenge of all was how to find the right balance among my professional and personal ambitions and responsibilities. While I am sure I will never master that particular challenge, I have loved every minute I have been a lawyer. I really enjoy my work. I respect lawyers and the role we have in insuring that the Rule of Law is preserved. I became the first woman partner at Holland & Knight. I have remained with the firm to this day for many reasons, chief among them the constant support for my involvement in the firm, in the community, and in bar activities. In each area, I was encouraged to assume leadership roles, culminating in my election as the second woman president of the American Bar Association in 2000, and as the first woman to chair my firm's Directors Committee.

But my family has been even more important to me. I have had the joy of sharing a life and raising two beautiful children with a man I adore, a man who has been my partner, my friend, and my protector. His support has been the key to my success in achieving an acceptable balance in my life.

I am just one woman who has found great fulfillment in the practice of law. The pages of this book are filled with stories from so many others who have come to the law with aspirations of contributing to society in meaningful ways. Author Phyllis Horn Epstein has made it her mission to gather these stories and share them with women who are interested in learning how others have fared along their own "pathways to success." But this is not simply a collection of personal anecdotes; rather, the author has used the voices and experiences of these women to highlight and discuss the issues that women lawyers care about most. Phyllis set out to write the ultimate insider's handbook for young women lawyers and "lawyers to be," while offering the rare opportunity for seasoned women lawyers to read about their peers, connect, and recognize that they are not alone.

The result is an illuminating resource filled with advice and wisdom from women lawyers who, in the last half-century, have in very individual ways confronted—and overcome—obstacles to their self-fulfillment. We hear from lawyers in private practice in firms of all sizes, as well as from judges, public officials, and law school professors. They are of many generations and backgrounds from all over the United States; some are just starting out, others are in the prime of their careers, and some are now retired. Every woman lawyer can find someone to relate to in this book.

To share one's personal experiences is at the heart of mentoring. Women considering the law, and those already fully engaged in their work, can only benefit from the perspective of others who have been down similar roads. Successful women lawyers can leave no more important legacy than to inspire others to create lives that are satisfying both professionally and personally. I hope you will find the inspiration you need to make for yourself the kind of life that will fulfill your own dreams of success, whatever they may be.

Martha W. Barnett
Past President, American Bar Association

Martha W. Barnett is a partner in the law firm of Holland & Knight LLP and serves as chair of the Directors Committee. She is the past chair of the Public Law Department of the firm. Her primary areas of practice are administrative and governmental law, public policy, and state and local taxation.

Ms. Barnett is a member of The Florida Bar and the Bar of the District of Columbia. She has worked extensively with the American Bar Association and The Florida Bar. She was President of the American Bar Association in 2000-2001. She also served as the Chair of the American Bar Association House of Delegates, the first woman to serve in this position.

Ms. Barnett graduated *cum laude* from Newcomb College, Tulane University of Louisiana with a bachelor of arts degree in 1969, and earned her J.D. *cum laude* from the University of Florida in 1973. She is a member of Phi Kappa Phi and Phi Delta Phi, and was an editor of the *University of Florida Law Review*. She is married to Richard R. Barnett, an architect. They have two children, Richard Rawls, Jr., and Sarah Walters.

Introduction

The new millennium occasioned many to reflect inwardly, not only about the passing year, but the larger picture of life. I came to this work from a very personal perspective after musing about the passing century. In the year 2000, I had been out of law school for twenty years and was practicing law as a partner with Epstein, Shapiro & Epstein. I was married to my law partner, living in suburbia. Our son was ten years old. Who I was and how I had reached this place as a woman, mother, wife, and lawyer occupied my thoughts. I was curious to know how I measured up in my accomplishments. Being a partner in a small firm, with one of the other three partners being my husband, was a bit isolating. I believed somehow that my personal and professional experiences might not be unique and might indeed fit into some larger context for women lawyers. To confirm my hunch, I wanted to reach out to my law school classmates and find out just what had become of them. My twentieth class reunion was sparsely attended. Where were the women and what had been their achievements? How had they applied their law degrees that were so hard won?

What began for me as a quest for information and a reaching out to my peers expanded naturally into a larger examination of the history of women lawyers generally and the evolution of women's roles in the last half of the twentieth century. I did not wish to retell the entire story of women lawyers so amply related elsewhere, although some retelling is required to place our role in history into perspective. I also did not wish to recite mere statistics, although they are here and are important in telling the whole story.

Although a few good histories of women lawyers are available, most stop about sixteen years ago.[1] Yet, in the past two decades, significant changes have occurred for women lawyers, as supported by available surveys, statistics, and a journal article here and there. For example, on March 26, 2001, a *New York Times* article reported that by 2002, it was likely the majority of law students would be women.[2] Clearly, something was happening. Simply looking around any law office or courthouse reveals a landscape that has changed to include more women.

Fortuitously, in 2001, the ABA Commission on Women published a revised edition of its report *The Unfinished Agenda: Women and the Legal Profession,* and a manual, *Balanced Lives, Changing the Culture of Legal Practice,* prepared for the commission by Deborah L. Rhode. Both publications are based upon original 1990 public hearings and interviews, as well as more-recent surveys of various-sized law firms and interviews with lawyers and managers of those firms. *The Unfinished Agenda* claims to be no less than "the most comprehensive contemporary review of the status of women in the American legal profession and justice system." The manual seeks to address the needs of lawyers "who seek a better balance between their personal and professional lives." My classmates had already responded to my questions before I stumbled upon the commission's publications, and I was fascinated at how my thoughts and my classmates' stories mirrored the findings of the commission.

At this same time, a nonprofit research group named Catalyst completed and published a research project, also based upon extensive surveys and interviews with lawyers across the country.[3] The report provides reflections upon the practice of law and the balancing of work and personal lives. It is also a good source of statistical information for the status of today's women lawyers. Closer to home, I had membership surveys conducted by the Philadelphia Bar Association in five-year intervals from 1990 through 2000. (An earlier survey was performed in 1984 with less comprehensiveness, and therefore was not appropriate for in-depth comparisons.) The Women's Commission of the Pennsylvania Bar Association began issuing annual "Report Cards" in 1995, the year of its inception, and these proved to be an invaluable source of information about the evolution of women's growing presence in the profession. To me, they were evidence of women's increased self-awareness about their place in this profession. The state of Washington commissioned an extensive analysis of its legal professionals in the year 2001, and the National Association of Law Placement issues reports and statistical summaries annually. These reports and others, along with more than one hundred interviews, provided me with the foundation for my writing.

It is hard for me to fathom, but I know it is true that there are women in the world—successful women—who believe they have "made it" on their own without a nod to the feminist movements of the nineteenth and twentieth centuries, or the solitary acts of courage by women who struggled in previous decades. Not all women rode the coattails of the sixties into the legal profession. Many I interviewed graduated from law school well before the feminist movement of the sixties. But ultimately, their participation in the legal profession, I am certain, gave inspiration to those who engineered the cause of women.

For a woman, becoming a lawyer was—and is—a hard-won privilege. In 1873, the U.S. Supreme Court refused to recognize the right of women to become lawyers under the Fourteenth Amendment of the Constitution. As women enter the legal profession in larger numbers today, and as sexual harassment and discrimination in the employment process is less visible, it would be so wrong to point to the exemplary firsts among women lawyers and conclude that our work is done and the environment for women lawyers to achieve is, and always has been, welcoming. It is easy to be lulled into believing that women lawyers have always enjoyed the presumption of competence and a choice of employment opportunities within the law.

If we fail to learn the history of women in the legal profession, we risk turning a blind eye to all that has been and has yet to be achieved. Women lawyers face many obstacles related to their gender, not the least of which is creating a balance between work and family. Though most women lawyers have fashioned their own individual compromises, we have yet to arrive at a place where society is part of the solution.

In my long saga of interviews and research for this book, I met many women who were not lawyers but asked me to include something about women in their particular professions. I was asked to write about women who are doctors, accountants, and corporate professionals. I agree that there are more books to be written and that women lawyers will find much in common with their sisters in the working world. I was not equipped at this juncture to write those stories, and chose instead to write about the profession I know first-hand. I hope that the advice and wisdom within these pages will resonate with all women in the working world.

The women who participated in this book generously opened their lives to me and I was rewarded with amazing pearls of wisdom that I have shared with the reader. One of the most valuable bits of advice garnered from my talks was to toss out completely the traditional image of success as the highest rung of a tall ladder. I have learned to appreciate the horizontal nature of a woman's life, without an end zone. A woman lawyer's life is a journey—a continuum of experiences with shifting priorities and manifold rewards.

ENDNOTES

1. Karen Berger Morello, The Invisible Bar, The Woman Lawyer in America: 1638 to the Present (1986).

2. Jonathan D. Glater, *Women Are Close to Being Majority of Law Students*, N.Y. Times, Mar. 26, 2001, at A-1.

3. Catalyst, Women in the Law: Making the Case, Executive Summary (2001).

A Note from Gerry Spence

Women are as intelligent and as powerful as men. They can argue as well. Better. I have been married to my darling for these nearly thirty-five years and I have never won an argument yet. My record in intramural arguments is zero. Hers is 100 percent. This averages out to be 50 percent for each, which, I suppose, is how it should be.

The problems women have in court fall into two categories. One is skill, and the other the preconception of many of the "old school" that women are not as powerful as men. Sadly, women lawyers often adopt as true this extravagant falsehood.

Man or woman, it takes years to become a successful trial lawyer: years in the arena, years in the struggle. We emerge from law school, men and women alike, knowing nothing about trying cases, about being real, about being human, about telling the truth, about caring. What we learned in school about trial lawyering we must unlearn. And we divest ourselves of what we learned in a very slow, painful, and insidious process, like learning Chinese while being boiled in the cannibal's kettle. In short, it takes at least ten years, more likely twenty, of continuous exposure to the rigors of war in the courtroom for any lawyer, male or female, to become a real trial lawyer.

Many of either gender are in their early thirties by the time they begin practicing. By the time they have put in ten or fifteen years in court, they are approaching forty. Many are past forty by the time they've begun to be proficient. It is at this juncture that the true trial lawyer takes shape. He or she has to make a lifetime decision: Do I stay in the law? Has it been fulfilling? Am I really cut out for this? Is there anything better to do with my life? Indeed, am I disappointed now that I know what I know? These kinds of questions hit hard at midlife. Some men leave the profession.

But the timetable for men and women is not the same. Many women who have given up motherhood for the law now must decide: Will my child be the courtroom or the little girl I've always dreamed of? Will my future—my old age—be in the company of the books and judges and juries I did not choose, or will I have that little boy I've always wanted? Nature intervenes and nature is vicious. I know many women who try to compromise, to have their families and their profession as well. But it is harder for women.

I grew up when the man made the living and the woman made the home. I don't argue that times are better. It depends on one's agenda and one's perspective. But I have always believed, perhaps wrongly, that children need mothers more than fathers. Their nurturing instincts are different and perhaps better suited to the needs of the child. Parents together can do a better job, but that inserts another variable into the equation—the willingness, the skill, and the availability of the father to take part in parenting.

This business of mothers in the courtroom is complicated. However it comes out, it takes its toll—on the mother, the child, or the marriage. And how this all translates into trial skills and the utter devotion of the lawyer to her client's cause is problematic.

I am asked repeatedly how I raised six kids and did a pretty good job in the courtroom as well. The answer is that I had a lot of help from my wives and I was not a particularly good father—not one that would pass muster today. When it came time for me to decide whether I took the kids fishing on a Sunday or got ready for the Monday trial, the trial came first. I know about this idea of quality time versus quantity time. Given that quality time prevails, it is nevertheless hard to give quality time to your kids with the worries of Monday's trial on your mind. Your kids want to fish. Your client wants to live. Somehow this gets weighed in as well.

The problem of preconceived views of women lawyers is not as pervasive today as it was a decade ago. There are many fine and famous women lawyers. We see them fictionally and in real life on television. But many women themselves do not have a clear view of what is expected of them in the courtroom. After whom should they model themselves? Some chose Marcia Clark, who presented herself as a mixture of a sexy vixen and a TV wrestler in high, tight skirts. Others model themselves after mothers who fuss over everything and everybody, or female schoolteachers who know all the answers and expect everyone to abide by their rules. Some want to ply their sexuality to the judge or the jury. Some come off like prison guards. But this can be said about men as well, who take on roles specific to their makeup and visions of themselves.

In short, the rule is the same for men and for women. The great power of the lawyer is authenticity. Be yourself. Be honest. Be real. Care. Let your feeling be seen. Feel more than you think. Be, instead of pretending. The woman who is real in the courtroom gathers credibility. She has been able to say when she was afraid. She has been able to cry when it was appropriate. She has a sense of humor. She can admit she has made a mistake or that she is confused or lost. The woman who comes into the courtroom as a whole person will win against any pretenders, men or women.

Clothes, as well as everything else about the lawyer, speak. I think a woman should downplay her sexuality, but not her femininity. Sex should not become an issue in the courtroom. If jurors get the idea that a woman is using it for an advantage, it will backfire every time. Every time. I think men and women alike should dress as Shakespeare suggested: "Rich, not gaudy." The richness should not be in money's worth but in simple good taste. The courtroom is a place where lawyers work. They should come prepared to work and dressed to work.

In the end, the skill of the trial lawyer is communication. To communicate effectively, one must be on the same wavelength as the jurors and the judge. One must be real. The jurors are real. They can and will very soon identify those who "put on." One does not need to be an orator to win in the courtroom. One needs to be a person. That is the goal. The ultimate, exquisite goal.

Chapter One

Diamonds Are Forever

I don't think that ladies should be lawyers.

Special Report on Gender Bias and Women in the Law
Cover story for the *ABA Journal, The Lawyer's Magazine*
December 1, 1986

Since the day it arrived in the mail, my law partner has had the December 1, 1986, edition of the *ABA Journal* prominently displayed in his office, always on top of more current materials. In bold red capital letters against a black background, it reads, "I DON'T THINK THAT LADIES SHOULD BE LAWYERS." I have always maintained a sense of humor about my partner's display, knowing that he does this only to "needle" me, and yet there it has rested, on a table by the door in his office, for the past sixteen years. You can't miss it. On occasion, I have retaliated by placing the cigar butts he leaves on my desk in his coffee cup.

This edition of the *ABA Journal* was published only six years after I graduated from law school and, for me, it was one of the first articles to touch upon the subject of gender issues for women lawyers. It was enlightening. The quote that emblazoned the cover is from a Chicago judge speaking to a twenty-seven-year-old female lawyer:

I am going to hear the young lady's case first. They say I'm a male chauvinist. I don't think that ladies should be lawyers. I believe that you belong at home raising a family. Ladies do not belong down here.[1]

It is very possible that facing the cover of the *ABA Journal* every working day for sixteen years had its effect on my subconscious and destined me to examine the progress of women lawyers. The cover that shouted in stop-sign red letters that "ladies should not be lawyers" was a daily reminder that because of my gender, my participation in the profession was strongly opposed by some lawyers and judges, with the same spirit as it was more than a hundred years ago. I hoped my research would show that attitudes had finally changed.

My research began with attempts to contact fellow women classmates by letter. I was aided in this endeavor by Matthew Konchel, Esquire, Director of the Office of Alumni Affairs and Development at the James E. Beasley School of Law of Temple University. Many generously shared their time and opened their lives to me.

As I began conducting interviews, I found that I required a better perspective on my starting point, 1980. I knew I would have to backtrack and seek women who preceded me in the legal profession and could give me a better perspective. My classmates may have been among the first wave of women lawyers to graduate in greater numbers, but we most certainly did not secure the beach. I spoke with a number of women who graduated from law school in the fifties, while I was just entering grade school. Their experiences, as well as their reactions to the new wave of women lawyers, proved fascinating to me. Because of the courage of this handful of women who broke stereotypes by entering a traditionally male occupation, the women of my generation were able to cast aside societal expectations of dependency, homemaking, and "acceptable" occupations. I also interviewed a number of women across the country who had unique practices and approaches to the law. They shared their thoughts about achieving in a male-dominated profession and its impact upon their personal lives.

I began contacting my classmates in the summer of 2001. The women of 1980 comprised about one-third of the class. Out of approximately one hundred women, I received responses from fifteen. I can only hypothesize about the reasons why not all—or at least no more than fifteen—chose to respond to me. I recognize that everyone is very busy and that taking time to reflect seriously upon events that happened more than twenty years ago can be a chore. On one occasion, I bumped into a colleague at the supermarket and she expressed her refusal to answer in these words: "My life stinks." For those who did not respond, I searched the index of the *Martindale-Hubbell Law Directory* to see if they were still employed as lawyers. Many were missing. I know of two classmates who died of illnesses in the years after school, while they were practicing law: Lisa Heyman and Mary Lou Darsigny. They were bright and strong. I'll never forget my first day of law school when I met Lisa and she insisted with fierce determination, "I'm not here to get ulcers, I'm here to give them." That was Lisa.

The women of the Temple Law School class of 1980 came from a diverse array of experiences. Many, like the tale told by Temple's founder Russell Conwell, represent the "acres of diamonds" found in Philadelphia's own backyard. Some worked in the years between undergraduate school and law school, and others had been home raising families. Some went to law school straight from undergraduate school, some were married, and some had young children. They make a diverse group, traveling different roads to law school and different roads since graduating.

I chose not to limit my ever-increasing fascination with women's progress to my own city, and embarked upon online interviews of women lawyers across the United States and Canada. The response I received was overwhelming. Women from California to Florida, New Hampshire to Texas, and Canada to Utah offered their experiences, wisdom, and insights into the practice of law. I am grateful to the women who have been our mentors, our friends, and our role models (albeit many times unwittingly) for sharing their journeys.

I now believe there is a common experience for women lawyers and that we share similar challenges and conflicts. I thought this book could help us learn from one another and support one another. Perhaps some of us could offer the wisdom of our experiences to younger women who are contemplating careers in the law. It is also my hope that by sharing our experiences and understanding the struggle of all women lawyers over the past 150 years, we might unburden ourselves from unwarranted, self-defeating blame for successes that elude us and take pride in our personal achievements. Let me also confide that I know some readers will disagree with some of my conclusions and find points that I missed. In my defense, let me say that every individual with whom I spoke had something new to offer to the dialogue. I could go on interviewing for a very long time, gathering new insights with each conversation and never losing interest. I see this book as a starting point for women to meet, talk, and continue the discussion.

Let me offer another comment before plunging further along. Some women spoke to me or wrote to me on the condition that they remain anonymous. Some allowed the use of only a first name, to avoid being identified. I respected those wishes and apologize to the reader who wonders why some women are referenced only by a first name or no name at all.

More Than a Matter of Gender

Women belong to many communities beyond their common gender. Their self-perceived identities extend beyond being female. Over the course of this project, I interviewed—in person, by telephone, or in writing—more than one hundred women. In addition to being women and lawyers, many also defined themselves as being Jewish, Christian, African-American, Cuban, Greek-American, Hispanic, lesbian, city folk, country folk, northerner, or southerner; and sometimes as members of multiple communities.

Although I have directed the spotlight upon gender and the experiences of women lawyers as *women*, I cannot discount the unique experience of each woman as a result of her multidimensional background. If women have to try harder, African-American women have to try even harder. If Hispanic women fill a double minority slot, a Cuban or "Cuban-American" woman may experience bewilderment from employers about how to define her ethnicity. Cuban? Cuban-American? Hispanic? Professor Alice Abreu of the Temple University School of Law was born in Cuba and emigrated to this country at the age of nine. She reported being chastised at her undergraduate school for checking the "Hispanic" box for ethnicity, and similarly singled out by her future employer, Temple University School of Law, for *failing* to check the "Hispanic" box identifying her ethnicity. Both experiences honed her sense of identity:

> Although I am now an American citizen and I value that status, I am still Cuban. I have absorbed a tremendous amount of American culture, and I am grateful for all it has given me, but I am still Cuban. My children, who were born in this country, are to me, the real Cuban-Americans, but I am Cuban.[2]

A woman who is Jewish may observe the festival of Sukkot in prayer and observe the Sabbath. Her employer must be willing to accommodate the unfamiliar idiosyncrasies of her schedule. When I entered the work force in 1980 in Philadelphia, I was directed by some lawyers to interview at the "Jewish" firms, such as Wolf Block Schorr & Solis Cohen—firms that had their genesis in the climate of the anti-Semitism of the "blue blood" firms in Philadelphia. There are prejudices, biases, and preferences in our communities and in our law firms that persist even though they have become unspoken.

These multiple dimensions of women's character oftentimes result in specific approaches to the law—a desire to advocate civil rights or battle discrimination based upon a personal experience, a sense of justice, a desire to help others, or a sensitivity to the outsider in society. Women of dual minorities may be groundbreakers in their practice areas not just on account of their gender. To paraphrase the words of Professor Abreu, our gender may no longer be a factor holding us back, but our "race or ethnicity" may still create expectations regarding how "we are expected to use our talents." She writes:

> I have been told that I should not waste my time on tax but that because I am Latina, I should devote my professional life to areas of the law which bear a more direct relation to the Latina/o condition. I have rejected that advice. I have as legitimate a claim to being a tax lawyer as any white American male and neither my gender nor my ethnicity should stand in the way. My experiences in Cuba and later as an exile have no doubt shaped my view of the role and importance of tax policy, just as they have shaped other aspects of my identity, but even if I could see no connection between my experiences as a Cubana and my interest in tax policy, it would still be legitimate for me to be a tax lawyer.[3]

Women of color may surmount the barriers of gender to face those of their race. Just as women in the prior two centuries were stereotyped as being fit for representing children, women, and criminals, women of color may feel they are expected to devote their careers to championing civil rights. Some may follow such a path, but other fields must also be viewed as legitimate regardless of color or ethnicity or other defining dimension.

Charisse Lillie, a former Philadelphia city solicitor, felt that not being a member of the Philadelphia establishment, rather than being an African-American, was her biggest impediment to being hired in some firms in the city. Today, Charisse Lillie believes that gender and race positively affect her career as she advises Fortune 500 companies on ways to avoid discrimination lawsuits. Others share her impression that being a minority and/or a woman is now a benefit rather than a drawback in securing large corporate clients who feel the need to demonstrate to their shareholders their nondiscriminatory hiring practices. But another successful African-American woman lawyer commented recently to me that others would nudge and wink at her, saying her path would be greased because of her double minority status. She shakes her head and says this has not been her experience.

A hyphenated identity can affect a career and a life in other ways as well. Professor Marina Angel of the Temple University School of Law writes that she felt compelled to choose between having a career and a family partly because of her experience as a Greek-American:

> Coming from a traditional Greek-American background it had also been made clear to me that the roles of wife and mother were difficult and time-consuming.[4]

Her experience with motherhood and marriage in the Greek-American community was a contributing factor in her decision to forgo taking on what she perceived as the burden of those roles. Her decision was affected by her gender as well as her ethnicity. Our sense of womanhood is largely affected by our religion, our sexual orientation, and our ethnicity. These influences are probably more crucial to our sense of self and our career decisions than any feminist literature.

The women who speak to you in these pages represent diverse communities, fairly representative of the American melting pot. They are women, mothers, wives, single women, daughters, Jews, Christians, White, Hispanic, Cuban, Greek-American, African-American, hyphenated and unhyphenated, twenty to eighty years old, lesbian, straight, northerners, southerners, city folk, and country folk. They are lawyers, and they are all of us.

ENDNOTES

1. Nancy Blodgett, *I Don't Think That Ladies Should Be Lawyers*, A.B.A. J., THE LAW. MAG., Special Report on Gender Bias & Women in the Law, Dec. 1986, at 48.

2. Alice Abreu, *Lessons from LatCrit: Insiders and Outsiders, All At the Same Time*, 53 U. MIAMI L. REV. 787, 799 (1999).

3. *Id.* at 808.

4. Marina Angel, *Women in Legal Education: What It's Like to Be Part of a Perpetual First Wave or the Case of the Disappearing Women*, 61 TEMP. L. REV. 799, 815 (1988).

"A DAY IN THE LIFE"
MICHELE LELLOUCHE, A LAWYER WORKING IN THE EMPLOYEE BENEFITS AREA WITH A LARGE SOFTWARE COMPANY IN JACKSONVILLE, FLORIDA

In my position, I write the legal language for retirement plans. I answer a lot of phone calls—we do phone consulting for our clients (which are mainly lawyers, CPAs, TPAs, insurance companies, and banks). And I have been called "sweetie," "dear," etc., too. I also write the plans and modify them for individual clients. I've given seminars and written educational materials as well. It's really consulting work. I love the job—it's an odd niche—we're the biggest thing in what we do. I wear jeans to work (we are completely business casual—even more than we used to be. Now if you wear a suit, everyone thinks you're on an interview). It's 8:30 to 5:30 unless we're very busy. I'm one of five lawyers out of two hundred employees, so it's very different from when I clerked in a law firm. There's no layer of hierarchy, in the sense that our president wanders around in shorts and we have lots of company events (we are known for our food events). Unlike my fellow lawyers, I have no secretary and there's none of the "he's the partner, she's the associate" stuff. Our company employs a lot of women, and has very liberal policies for time off, etc.—it's part of being owned by a larger corporation.

Chapter Two

The Right and Privilege to Be a Lawyer

We shall someday be heeded, and . . . everybody will think it was always so, just exactly as many young people think that all the privileges, all the freedom, all the enjoyments which woman now possesses always were hers. They have no idea of how every single inch of ground that she stands upon today has been gained by the hard work of some little handful of women of the past.[1]

Susan B. Anthony

Left Behind at the Start

Philadelphia, my hometown, is the birthplace of our nation. It was here that the Declaration of Independence was written and the Constitutional Convention convened, and here that the spirits of John Adams, Thomas Jefferson, George Washington, and Benjamin Franklin linger. Strolling past Independence Hall reminds us of a time when the foundations of our laws and liberties were debated. Philadelphia is home to one of the nation's first law schools, the University of Pennsylvania. Red-bricked and rooted in our nation's history, the city is home to the symbols of liberty: the Liberty Bell, Independence Hall, and Betsy Ross's house. Unfortunately, many were left behind in these auspicious beginnings. Slavery was accepted as an institution. Less severe, but also harmful, was the denial of equal rights to women. Rights and privileges equal to men would be denied them, even after the end of slavery in the next century. In fact, women's suffrage and recognition of the right to be treated equally under the Fourteenth Amendment would be postponed to the twentieth century. A woman's right and privilege to become a lawyer was denied by the U.S. Supreme Court in 1873, under the guise of the Fourteenth Amendment.

A Woman's Right and Privilege to Be a Lawyer—Denied

In the beginning, being a lawyer was not recognized as a woman's right and privilege as a citizen of these United States. For a long time, in many states, women were denied the right to attend law school or sit for a state bar exam.[2] In 1873, the U.S. Supreme Court, in *Bradwell v. Illinois*,[3] upheld the Illinois bar examiners' refusal to permit Myra Bradwell to sit for the Illinois bar exam and refused to hold that such a denial violated her right to equal protection under the Fourteenth Amendment to the U.S. Constitution.[4] The right to practice law, the Court held, was not the right and privilege of every citizen in the United States, and individual states could choose to exclude women from their bar associations on the basis of their sex. By denying women the right to practice law under the Fourteenth Amendment, the Supreme Court returned the issue to the individual states. The privilege became a matter of state law, subject to the whims of individual judges and state legislatures, some of whom harshly rejected the applications made before them.

Myra Colby Bradwell was born in Manchester, Vermont. With her husband, she moved to Chicago where she established and edited the *Chicago Legal News*. Her husband was a lawyer and a judge, and, in 1873, was elected to the state legislature. When Myra Bradwell was refused admission to the Illinois state bar, she challenged the action in the courts and ultimately lost on appeal to the U.S. Supreme Court. Eventually, in 1890, Myra Bradwell was admitted to the Illinois bar. Although suffering from cancer, she had the last word when she received her license to practice before the U.S. Supreme Court in 1892.

Myra was among a handful of "first" women in the law in the mid-nineteenth century. Arabella Mansfield was granted permission to practice law in Iowa in 1869, even though at the time, the Iowa Code specifically prohibited her admission. In her case, Judge Francis Springer, a man of good sense and sensibility, deigned to interpret male gender references in the statute as terms of convenience rather than exclusion. Ada H. Keply graduated from Union College of Law in Chicago in 1870. Belva Ann Lockwood was admitted to practice in 1879 and became responsible for lobbying Congress to pass the Lockwood Bill, which gave women lawyers the right to practice before federal courts. Phoebe Couzins was the first woman admitted to Washington University in St. Louis, Missouri, graduating in 1871. In 1870, Lemma Barkaloo became Missouri's first woman to pass the bar (without finishing law school). Marilla Ricker was New Hampshire's first woman lawyer, admitted in 1890. All were trailblazers, seeking a place in an all-male profession at a time when women did not possess the right to vote, to sit on juries, or to enter into contracts. Denied the right to vote until 1920, women continued to be denied the right to sit on juries in sixteen states as recently as 1947. (Alabama was the longest holdout; in 1966 it was compelled by judicial intervention to accept women on juries.)[5]

The Lawyers and Suffragettes

For women in the late nineteenth century, around the time of the Industrial Revolution, life was very difficult. This was a time when women still had very few rights—they were disenfranchised, and had no legal rights to own property in their own names or to enter contracts that could bind their husbands. They lived in a society that offered little or no opportunity to pursue intellectual or financial interests of their own. Women who needed to work to help support their families or themselves suffered in dismal conditions at factories, without the benefit of fair labor laws or decent working conditions. Opportunities for work were limited to acceptable fields for women, such as sewing, teaching, or caring for children. By becoming a lawyer, a woman had the opportunity to advocate for other women and to raise the station in life for all women. Having a career in the law meant having the opportunity for an independent life, free of the restrictions placed upon women. It also meant helping to empower a new generation that could advocate for women's equal rights, suffrage, and independent legal standing in the community.

Not surprisingly, the women's suffragette movement in the nineteenth century was inspired and led by many of these early advocates of women's rights. In 1848, in Seneca Falls, New York, the first feminists of this country met to advocate an end to slavery and to advance the rights of women. What resulted from that meeting was a strikingly familiar document, with significant alterations, entitled, "The Seneca Falls Declaration on Women's Rights":

> We hold these truths to be self-evident: that all men and women are created equal; that they are endowed by their Creator with certain inalienable rights; that among these are life, liberty, and the pursuit of happiness; that to secure these rights governments are instituted, deriving their just powers from the consent of the governed.

Women, the statement declared, are endowed with the same inalienable rights to life, liberty, and the pursuit of happiness promised to white men in the Declaration of Independence and inspired by the "Creator."

Imagine the day is July 4, 1876. Philadelphia is the site of the nation's one-hundredth birthday celebration. The women's movement has organized protests leading up to, and on the day of, July 4, when events culminate with the reading of the Declaration of Independence by the acting vice president of the United States. As he concludes his reading, Susan B. Anthony barges onto the platform and begins handing to the crowd copies of "Articles of Impeachment against the United States" and "Woman's Declaration of Rights."[6] Decrying the infringements upon women's legal rights as equal citizens with men, she attacks all arguments that attempt to justify unequal treatment on the paternalistic pretext of protecting women from the baser side of life and preserving women's special sphere as keepers of the home. Her arguments apply equally to women's rights to vote and choose a profession. On a platform across from Independence Hall, Ms. Anthony reads to the crowd from the Seneca Falls Declaration, enumerating the grievances of women in the nineteenth century. Among them are the following:

He has never permitted her to exercise her inalienable right to the elective franchise.

He has made her, if married, in the eye of the law, civilly dead.

He has taken from her all right in property, even to the wages she earns.

He has monopolized nearly all the profitable employments, and from those she is permitted to follow, she receives but a scanty remuneration.

He closes against her all the avenues to wealth and distinction which he considers most honorable to himself. As a teacher of theology, medicine, or law, she is not known.[7]

Women continued their organized efforts to secure an equal place in society and equal treatment under and by the laws of the nation. The Supreme Court's majority opinion in *Bradwell* mirrored other judicial opinions that denied women the right to vote, also on the basis of the Fourteenth Amendment. Voting, like the practice of law, they opined, was not one of the privileges and immunities protected by the Constitution. The suffragette movement and efforts to be admitted to the practice of law became intertwined.

In 1892, feminist leader Elizabeth Cady Stanton addressed the House Judiciary Committee in Washington, D.C., to advocate suffrage for women. Her mission was twofold. The right of women to

vote was, of course, paramount to her discourse. But equally important was expanding the natural assumptions about women that confined them to stereotypical lives and behaviors and restricted them by
law or by convention from becoming fully realized human beings.
The "sphere" of woman—the boundaries of her capabilities—is a subject that continues to be debated to this day, and was addressed by
Ms. Stanton in her comments:

> If God has assigned a sphere to man and one to woman, we claim the
> right ourselves to judge His design in reference to us. . . . We think that a
> man has quite enough to do to find out his own individual calling, with-
> out being taxed to find out also where every woman belongs. (Ward,
> Geoffrey, and Ken Burns, *Not For Ourselves Alone: The Story of Elizabeth
> Cady Stanton and Susan B. Anthony*, New York: Knopf, 1999, p. 34)

Feminist suffragette Lucy Stone echoed the following sentiments
in the year 1855.

> Too much has already been said and written about woman's sphere. . . .
> Leave women, then, to find their sphere. And do not tell us before we
> are born even, that our province is to cook dinners, darn stockings, and
> sew on buttons. (Gurko, Miriam, *The Ladies of Seneca Falls: The Birth of
> the Woman's Rights Movement*, New York: Macmillan Publishing Co.,
> Inc., 1974, p. 122)

Unfortunately, after suffrage was achieved, the enthusiasm and
support for feminist causes lost momentum. The number of women
in law remained remarkably low for nearly forty years. In fact,
women accounted for only 3 percent of all lawyers nationwide until
the resurgence of feminism in the 1960s.[8]

Equal Protection for Women under the Fourteenth Amendment

After passage of the Nineteenth Amendment in 1926, which granted
women the right to vote, federal and state statutes continued to cod-
ify sex-based distinctions that reinforced women's separate sphere

within society. Susan B. Anthony spoke of a time when state statutes permitted sex-based distinctions so that women's rights varied greatly from state to state:

> Women invested with the rights of citizens in one section—voters, jurors, office-holders—crossing an imaginary line, are subjects in the next. In some States, a married woman may hold property and transact business in her own name; in others, her earnings belong to her husband. In some States, a woman may testify against her husband, sue and be sued in courts; in others, she has no redress in case of damage to person, property, or character. In case of divorce on account of adultery in the husband, the innocent wife is held to possess no right to children or property, unless by special decree of the court.[9]

Even after suffrage and after women began entering the practice of law (assuming they found law schools that would admit them), states and the federal government continued to enact laws that singled out women for separate, and often paternalistic, treatment. Not until 1971, in the case of *Reed v. Reed*,[10] would the Supreme Court extend to women equality with men under the equal protection clause of the Fourteenth Amendment. Sally Reed had applied for appointment as administrator of her son's affairs following his tragic suicide that occurred while he was in his father's care and custody. A second application for appointment filed by the father was given preference by an Idaho court, which cited an Idaho statute that gave preference for males as estate administrators due to men's (allegedly) greater experience in financial affairs in comparison with women. Sally Reed's appeal reached the U.S. Supreme Court. Under Chief Justice Warren Burger, the Court declared the Idaho statute to be in violation of the equal protection clause of the Fourteenth Amendment of the U.S. Constitution. In *Reed*, the Court set forth the standard by which all other laws would be scrutinized. For all gender-based laws, "the classification must reasonable, not arbitrary, and must rest upon some ground of difference having a fair and substantial relation to the object of the legislation, so that all persons similarly circumstanced shall be treated alike."[11] The *Reed* case and several others brought later in the decade were the result of the inspired efforts of Ruth Bader Ginsburg, now a Supreme Court justice. The host of cases following *Reed* expanded women's rights under the equal protection clause of the Constitution, and systematically struck down similar laws that fostered gender distinctions.[12]

The Twentieth Century

Attending law school during any part of the twentieth century—indeed pursuing any career that was formerly dominated by males—meant more than just job training. It was an act of revolution. This revolution got underway in mid-century. For the small and select group of women entering law school in the 1940s, 1950s, and 1960s, the decision to apply meant challenging traditional societal and family expectations. By then, although women had gained admission to many, but not all, law schools, their numbers amounted to less than a handful, and society expected them to become teachers or psychologists. The traditional field of acceptable work for women of those decades was early-childhood education. Judge Dolores Sloviter of the Third Circuit was encouraged to enter teaching: "It was a nice stable job. People who had been through the Depression thought of teaching as a very attractive lifestyle for a young woman."[13] Philadelphia Court of Common Pleas Judge Lisa Richette recalls being told that she was "misguided" and that she "should be teaching very small children." From Taylor Williams, counsel to the Pennsylvania Supreme Court:

> My grandfather felt strongly that I should become a schoolteacher and marry a lawyer—that was the perfect combination. He never thought I would become a lawyer myself, which would have been something of an aberration, certainly in his generation, but even in mine, as women didn't begin to make inroads into professional schools in any number until the 1970s.

Women who attended law school in the 1940s and 1950s rode the apron strings of Rosie the Riveter out of the home and into the workforce. During World War II, Catherine Barone, Penn Law graduate of 1948, worked for the Securities and Exchange Commission, which was then located in Philadelphia. She explains:

> Because so many men had gone to war, women lawyers went back to work and worked for the Commission. These ladies were extremely lovely ladies and I admired them very much and was duly impressed. I basically think it was [out of] my respect for them that I decided to become an attorney.

In the post–Betty Friedan years, being a lawyer, for a woman, was a realistic option. It was also a chance to live earlier feminist dreams of equality in the sphere outside the home. Rather than feeling the pressure to become elementary school teachers, young women felt the pressure to "do better"—to become "professionals." In some way, women of the 1970s were still contending with the expectations of family and society, but this time those expectations were to propel them into the traditionally male professions, like law. The inner struggle that resulted from the clash of expectations to have families and be high-powered lawyers at the same time was uncharted ground. And though the law students of the 1970s and 1980s felt entitled to their place in the legal world, that predominately male world was not quite ready for them.

As young girls, many of us envisioned a traditional future of marrying our first boyfriend and having two or three children. After that, the future became fuzzy. Our first debates were whether it was better to have a boy first or girl first. All of this would be accomplished by the age of twenty-one, or twenty-five at the latest. The sixties revolution raised the consciousness of women and challenged the status quo. Women were encouraged to have careers, often by their mothers who, perhaps, were coming to the realization that they could have made more of their lives. A new generation of women gathered together—as their sister suffragettes had done in the previous century—to demand equal treatment and equal pay and to broaden their opportunities. This new generation would march into careers previously off limits and demand a place in the boardrooms and courtrooms. In 1966, the leading feminists of the day created the National Organization for Women (NOW), first to promote equality for women in the workforce and then equality for all women—and men—in all aspects of life. Some were freed by feminism to pursue their dreams, while others were swept up in its expectations.

I Wanted to Be a Lawyer Since Childhood

I am always impressed by people who knew at an early age what they wanted to be when they grew up. Judge Carolyn Engel Temin of the Philadelphia Court of Common Pleas tells of young women asking her if she had always wanted to be a judge while she was growing up. We laughed. In the 1950s, the notion of a woman becoming a judge was as foreign and unthinkable as becoming an astronaut. The possibility simply did not exist. Thanks to the trailblazing women of the nineteenth and twentieth centuries, women today grow up with thoughts of becoming lawyers and judges. I am heartened by the accounts of the following newly minted lawyers. Theile M. Branham of Columbia, South Carolina, graduated from law school at the University of South Carolina in 2000. She writes:

> I somehow always knew that I wanted to go to law school. My mother tells me that when I was in elementary school I decided I wanted to be a Supreme Court justice. I applied to law school my senior year of college. At that point, I thought I wanted the degree but did not want to practice. After my first year, I clerked for a plaintiffs' firm. I fell in love with the work. I saw that the law could really be used to level the playing field. As a lawyer, I could stand up and ask the big corporation or insurance industry questions on behalf of my client . . . AND they had to respond. That is why our justice system is so amazing. I am proud every time I go in court, that I get to be part of a system that allows the factory worker to call to task the CEO of Enron.

Moi Vienneau, of Hamilton, Ontario, graduated from the University of Windsor in Canada in 1992. She tells of her lifelong desire to become a lawyer, to bring justice to the world and take control of her destiny:

Believe it or not, I think I always wanted to go to law school. Not because I knew what it entailed or where it would lead me, but because I think early on I knew I wanted to be able to bring justice into the lives of others. I know that sounds hokey, but if I look at my "what do you want to be when you grow up" books, they all list "Lawyer," from as early as Grade 2. This desire to bring justice into the lives of others stems from the fact that my birth father left my mother with three kids when she was twenty-four, and I was one-and-a-half years old (my siblings were two-and-a-half and three-and-a-half). We were left to grow up in poverty. Now mind you, being left to fight for yourself, we also grew up in a very loving family, with a lot of humor. I always thought that I would bring my birth father to justice by making him pay back support all those years. As an ending to this story, I did not, as I realized that seeking justice for my mother would actually bring more injustice to a man who obviously lacked the understanding to know the extent of the effect of his actions. Growing up poor also made me think that I had to find something to allow me to do better. I had seen so many young women get pregnant or really do nothing of significance with their lives and I wanted to do better than all of them. I wanted to be able to support my family if they ever needed it.

A 1989 graduate of Stetson University College of Law, from Columbus, Ohio, offers her dreams from childhood:

I always wanted to go to law school and be a practicing attorney—since I was a little girl. I liked the idea of being able to help people, to change things, and to make a difference. I was also attracted by the intellectual requirements of the profession. Each day is different, and two clients rarely present the same problem or facts.

Law School—The Early Years

To throw obstacles in the way of a complete education is like putting out the eyes.[14]

From "The Solitude of Self," by Susan B. Anthony

We believe that it is as essential for every girl to be educated to her full potential of human ability as it is for every boy.

Excerpt from National Organization for Women (NOW) Statement of Purpose (1966)

Once women gained the legal right to practice law, it was not axiomatic that law schools would accept them. When they were eventually invited to matriculate, the initial reception was often quite chilly. In contrast, there are nearly 185 law schools in the United States today and, on average, nearly half the student body of those schools is female.[15] Women have come a long way from the days of Carrie Kilgore, who in 1870 fought for admission to the University of Pennsylvania Law School, years before her acceptance to membership in the Pennsylvania Bar Association was assured. As law schools were chartered, they very reluctantly and slowly began opening their doors to women. The first woman to graduate from Temple Law School was Anna Dickinson, member of the class of 1920.[16] Columbia did not admit its first woman student until 1927, a year after suffrage. Harvard would be one of the last holdouts, keeping its doors closed to women until 1950. Well into the twentieth century, women met with hostile and skeptical admissions officers who accused them of taking the place of more deserving and needy men, of husband hunting, or of wasting the resources of the school in training them for a profession they would soon leave for motherhood.

TAKING THE PLACE OF A MAN

By the 1940s and 1950s, women occupied only a handful of seats in the typical law school class. Their presence was not always welcomed. While some women reported that male colleagues were supportive or benign, others reported negative incidents relating to their gender, often from professors. For example, Professor Marina Angel remarks that her professor would address her as "Mr. Angel." U.S. Tax Court Judge Mary Ann Cohen experienced a new law school tradition known as "Ladies' Day," the day the law professors would call upon the "ladies" in class. There was one professor, she recalls, in whose class "every day was Ladies' Day." That meant all women in class got called upon every day to catch them unprepared. When Marina Angel became a Columbia student in 1965, Valentine's Day was Ladies' Day.

When Barbara Vetri sat for her prelaw exam in 1957, the proctor asked if she was in the right place. Being young, attractive, and blonde, Barbara stood out in her law school class. One teacher would call upon classmates by noting their relative proximity to her seat: "four seats to the left of the blonde" or "two rows behind the blonde." This practice tended to leave the seats around her vacant. But in other classes, Barbara learned that by asking intelligent questions (that others may have been too intimidated to ask) and offering correct answers to questions, she gained the respect and admiration of her male classmates and teachers.

There are numerous stories of women being chastised by peers, professors, or entrance examiners for taking the cherished place of a man in law school because they "certainly wouldn't need a degree after getting married." Similar sentiments were expressed to District Court Judge Norma Shapiro by some professors who opposed recommending her for a judicial clerkship after graduation. Being third in her class, Judge Shapiro was a most acceptable candidate for such a recommendation and, ultimately, over individual opposition, she did receive the clerkship.

Other teachers ignored the women in class. Still others singled out women to humiliate them with being unprepared. They taught in ways that exemplified insensitivity to women and willingness to make jokes at their expense. Philadelphia Common Pleas Court Judge Temin provided an example. On the first day of class, her property teacher singled her out with a hypothetical question to answer. The question required her to assume certain facts. "You are a young wife of an older husband," he began. "He dies leaving you all his property. His children object to you inheriting all their father's property. What do you do? Keep the property and fight in court, or take your one-third share of the estate as a surviving widow?" Judge Temin paused, taking in the situation and thinking about how ludicrous the question was. The teacher did not wait for a response (since apparently a serious answer was not what he sought), and provided his own punch line: "Take the one-third share because you are young. Take the money, move to Florida, and marry another rich man to take care of you." Echoes of laughter abounded.

By 1980, there was still a fair amount of sexism in law school but
at least no one was accusing women openly of taking the place of
more deserving men. Sexism was more likely to occur in other subtle
ways, such as by attacking women's character as unfeminine or
severe. When I began my studies in September of 1977, approximately
one-third of the students were women. The women's restroom was a
converted men's restroom and still hosted a wall of urinals left over
from other times. In 1972, the architects and planners of the new
Charles Klein Law Building, rebuilt after a fire, still hadn't anticipated
the need for a women's restroom near the classrooms. The percentage of women in each law school class at Temple, and elsewhere, has
increased in the past four years. The women's restroom at my alma
mater no longer has urinals. I take that as a good omen.

Conclusion

The women who graduated from law school in the 1970s and 1980s,
without consciously realizing it at the time, had an affinity with the
women of the nineteenth century. Both owed a great debt to the feminist movements of their generation, albeit one hundred years apart.
Both demanded equality of legal and social institutions, and both revolutionized the way women perceived their self-worth and self-esteem.
Because of the efforts of their forbearers, the women of the 1970s and
1980s had a true opportunity to enter the legal profession, to widen
the entry doors, and to permit their successors, the women of today, to
reap the rewards. By 1980, women accounted for 8.1 percent of the
legal profession nationwide; by 1986, their numbers leaped to
103,000, or 15 percent.[17] As of 2000, the number of women in the
legal profession increased to 275,000, or approximately 29.7 percent.[18]

The right to be a lawyer, to vote, or to pursue any vocation is justified by a woman's right to a complete existence in all spheres to the
extent of her ambitions, as is the case with a man. The need to pursue such ambitions is essential to a woman's independence and self-
reliance, as much today as it was in the day of Susan B. Anthony and

Elizabeth Cady Stanton. The opportunity to be a lawyer should never be taken for granted.

ENDNOTES

1. Quoted from Susan B. Anthony's speech, "The Solitude of Self," made before the House and Senate Judiciary Committee after she resigned from the National American Woman Suffrage Association. Ms. Anthony believed that each woman bore the "solitude and personal responsibility of her own individual life."

2. It was not until 1950 that Harvard Law School opened its doors to women.

3. Bradwell v. Illinois, 83 U.S. 130 (1873). 83 U.S. 130, 21 L. Ed. 442, 16 Wall. 130 (1873).

4. According to the Fourteenth Amendment of the U.S. Constitution, "[n]o State shall make or enforce any law which shall abridge the privileges or immunities of citizens of the United States; nor shall any State deprive any person of life, liberty, or property, without due process of law; nor deny to any person within its jurisdiction the equal protection of the laws."

5. White v. Crook, 251 F. Supp. 401 (M.D. Ala. 1966).

6. GARY B. NASH, FIRST CITY, PHILADELPHIA, AND THE FORGING OF HISTORICAL MEMORY 275 (University of Pennsylvania Press, Philadelphia, PA, 2002).

7. The Seneca Falls Declaration on Women's Rights (1848).

8. ABA COMM'N ON WOMEN IN THE PROFESSION, THE UNFINISHED AGENDA, WOMEN AND THE LEGAL PROFESSION 13 (2001) (prepared by Deborah L. Rhode). By 1926 there were only twenty-six women lawyers in Philadelphia, and by 1928, only twenty-eight. (Audrey C. Talley, *Walking with Destiny, Women Lawyers in Philadelphia*, 64 PHILA. LAW. 72 (2002).) Even by 1939, only 3.3 percent of Pennsylvania's lawyers—and 1.3 percent of Philadelphia's lawyers—were women. (VIRGINIA G. DRACHMAN, SISTERS IN LAW, WOMEN LAWYERS IN MODERN AMERICAN HISTORY 78 (1998).) It has been reported that from 1883 when Carrie Burnham Kilgore became Philadelphia's first woman lawyer through 1960, Philadelphia hosted a grand total of 300 women lawyers. (PHILA. BAR ASS'N COMM. ON WOMEN IN THE PROFESSION, CELEBRATING MORE THAN A CENTURY OF WOMEN LAWYERS IN PHILADELPHIA 1883–1997 (1997).)

9. The Seneca Falls Declaration for Women's Rights.

10. Reed v. Reed, 404 U.S. 71, 92 S.Ct. 251 (1971).

11. *Id.* at 404 U.S. 75, 92 S.Ct. 254 (citing Royster Guano Co. v. Virginia, 253 U.S. 412, 415 (1920)).

12. Justice Ruth Bader Ginsburg, *Remarks for the Celebration of 75 Years of Women's Enrollment at Columbia Law School*, 102 COLUM. L. REV. 1441 (2002); Justice Ruth Bader Ginsburg, *Remarks on Women's Progress in the Legal Profession in the United States*, 33 U. TULSA L.J. 13 (1997).

13. Interview with Judge Dolores Sloviter, conducted by The Oral Legal History Project of the University of Pennsylvania Law School (Apr. 2, 1999).

14. Quoted from Susan B. Anthony's speech, "The Solitude of Self," made before the House and Senate Judiciary Committee after she resigned from the National American Woman Suffrage Association. Ms. Anthony believed that each woman bore the "solitude and personal responsibility of her own individual life."

15. ABA News Release, *at* http://www.abanet.org/media/mar02/lawscholstats0302.html (Mar. 12, 2002).

	% women	*Year reported*
Harvard	45%	2002
Yale	48%	2001
Columbia	49%	class of 2006
Stanford	54%	2002
Temple	51%	2003
University of Pa.	51%	2003

(Source: Internet access for each school on Apr. 27, 2002)

Talley, supra note 8, at 80. Statistics are quoted from Catalyst, a nonprofit organization. In 2000, 50 percent of entering classes in "top tier" law schools were women.

16. Talley, *supra* note 8, at 74.

17. Nancy Blodgett, *I Don't Think That Ladies Should Be Lawyers*, A.B.A. J., THE LAW. MAG., Special Report on Gender Bias & Women in the Law, Dec. 1986, at 54.

18. ABA Comm'n on Women in the Profession, *at* http://www.abanet.org/women.snapshots.pdf (reported for the year 2001, based upon Department of Labor statistics for the year 2000).

"A DAY IN THE LIFE"
JAYNE, A LAWYER FROM WYOMING

I work for myself in a small law office, with one partner and one secretary. During regular times (not trial time), I come to work between 8:00 and 9:00 a.m. and leave at 5:00 p.m. I sometimes eat lunch at my desk, but often go out to lunch to either network or meet friends. I tutor Hispanic kids at the elementary school once a week for an hour or so. I attend board meetings for a couple of boards I am on. Other than that, I am at my desk or in court. I bill an average of five hours per day. The rest of my day is spent on the phone with potential clients, managing the office, meeting with my partner about our cases, and similar activities. Depending on my case schedule, my work involves writing complaints and briefs (for summary judgment, appeals, and motions), writing a lot of letters, talking on the phone or meeting in person with expert witnesses and other witnesses as well as clients, and talking on the phone with prosecutors for my criminal defense cases. I am also doing some volunteer work for the Innocence Project, which is a whole other kind of work!

My work is always interesting because I have a general practice and so I take all sorts of cases, with all sorts of different legal issues. I am always learning something new. I like my work for a number of reasons—but especially because it is intellectually challenging and because I feel like I am helping people. I do not like the part about worrying about money, overhead, "rainmaking," and collection. My situation is very flexible because I can take fewer cases if I want to and have more time for my personal life. I can take vacations when I want to, leave early, and answer only to myself. The drawback is I don't have a set salary and I don't have a pension or 401(k) with a large company. I probably would make more money if I worked for a large private firm. I would make less money if I worked for the government. But I love not having to answer to a "boss."

Living in Jackson Hole is really fun, especially for a single woman! The cost of living is high here and the income levels are low, except for the fabulously wealthy second-home owners. In the summers I change clothes at my office and mountain bike on phenomenal trails right from my office, or kayak on a famously beautiful river. In the winter, I backcountry ski in the mornings before coming into work and on every weekend, and sometimes ski at the resort.

I have a group of friends who are all professionals and small-business owners. Most of us don't have kids yet. When I arrived, there were six female lawyers in town and one hundred male lawyers. Seven years later, there are about twelve or fifteen female lawyers in town. I don't know if I am making a difference as a "woman lawyer." But I know that the guys (the male lawyers I deal with) are learning how to act with women lawyers, which is definitely different. I think there are some clients who really want a woman lawyer, so in that regard, I may be filling that need.

We have just one district court judge and one circuit court judge here. I mainly practice in district court. In January, the judge was actually voted out (a rare and controversial thing, to be sure). He had an unpredictable temper, and we were stuck with him. He and I did not normally agree on the law or the cases, and I was developing a serious losing streak with him. Now we have a woman judge, who moved here from Lander. She's been on the bench for about ten years and she is really great. Needless to say, my track record in court is improving. I don't think that is because the new judge is favoring me because I am a woman, but I think I had a hard time with the former judge because I am a woman. Judge Guthrie is one of three women judges in the state. There is one other district judge and one woman on the state supreme court.

One experience that stands out in my mind is a deposition in which the man I was deposing and his lawyer both lost their tempers and stood over me, in a physically threatening manner, yelling in my face and pointing fingers at my throat. I stood up and ended the deposition and ran into the bathroom to cry. I am sure my client knew I had cried. I don't think that sort of thing will ever happen again, because it is pretty strange. But if it did, I would probably stand firm in the room and have the wherewithal to create physical boundaries, stand up for myself and my client, and avoid crying until I got home. It seemed the men in this case were just acting in the same way they would with another guy they were angry with—physically aggressive. You can make all the assumptions you want about them, and you will probably be right. In any event, I have learned over the years to let other lawyers (men especially) know where I draw the line, and if they are rude to me I usually try to point it out by making it a joke. Today, for example, during mediation, a lawyer interrupted and mimicked me (yes, it's true) and after finishing my sentence, I asked him if I could mimic him. He said no. So I said, "I just wanted to be clear on the rules—you can mimic me and I can't mimic you." (All of this in a nice, sweet tone with a smile.) He apologized. I don't know if this kind of exchange is charged with gender-related tension or just plain rudeness. It's hard to say, really.

Chapter Three

Fair Treatment

He's fair. He treats us all the same—like dogs.

> Henry Jordan, Green Bay Packers right tackle, on
> Vince Lombardi, Hall of Fame football coach

All progress in social matters is gradual.[1]

Woman's Nature

My dear friend Dee was criticized by her employer for her pleasant demeanor and ready laugh. Her outgoing, easy persona conflicted with the toughness of spirit her employer felt was required of a lawyer. Her employer believed that toughness had to be worn at all times on the outside, like a navy blue suit. Employers, clients, and juries all have images of what it is to be a lawyer and, more often than not, that image is a stern man of a certain age in a three-piece suit. Many are still reluctant to assume that a woman will be tough enough to get results. They assume that, in former Supreme Court Justice Bradley's words, women lack "that decision and firmness which are presumed to predominate in the sterner sex."[2]

When women were excluded from the legal profession in 1873 by the U.S. Supreme Court or denied the right to vote, it seems the "real" reason was more than just a legal interpretation of the Fourteenth Amendment. For what seemed interminable years, men argued vehemently that women should never be permitted to vote, sign contracts, own property, or practice law on the intractable basis of their "nature." Local courts generated decrees that reinforced these popular prejudices. As one narrow-minded judge phrased it, "Womanhood is moulded for gentler and better things."[3] Practicing law was tantamount to "treason" and a threat to social order. The juxtaposition of a woman's "gentle" nature with the field of law entailed a vision of the legal profession as an arena of "all that is selfish and malicious, knavish and criminal, coarse and brutal, repulsive and obscene, in human life."[4] Justice Bradley clarified the view: Women could not—should not—be lawyers because the work was contrary to their "nature"; that is, they did not possess the "firmness" of character, perhaps the combativeness, that the job of lawyering, in his opinion, required.

The arguments about women's "nature" persisted for another hundred years (or more), keeping women from becoming lawyers and later limiting their fields of practice and opportunities within the profession. To this day, many of these prejudices about women's "nature" continue to manifest themselves in the opportunities offered to women lawyers.

In hindsight, the women of my law school class demystified the male practice of law for themselves and forged the way into positions of responsibility without forfeiting their personal styles. Taylor Williams provides this insight: "Men frightened women away from the profession over the centuries, but as we have come to find out, the practice of law isn't so complicated, and at least as many women as men are natural lawyers."

Not Tough Enough

It is hard to argue, as did Justice Bradley, that women lack the grit or stamina for hard work. In our talk, District Attorney Lynne Abraham pointed to the very tough, intelligent women leaders the world has known, such as Queen Elizabeth I, Cleopatra, Margaret Thatcher, and Golda Meier, to name a few. Throughout time, women have tended hearth and home single-handedly, while husbands went off to war or politics. They walked through the western prairies as early settlers and suffered hardships alongside men.[5]

Abigail Adams and other women like her ran the family farm and managed the household economy while their husbands spent years away in places like Philadelphia and Paris, creating our country and Constitution. The notion of women being only gentle and dependent falls far short of the truth. Women in the throes of the Industrial Revolution rejected the notion that their gentle natures barred them from male professions. In the words of one young milliner, "[I am] sure that no men would submit to the labour, which is imposed on the young dressmakers and milliners."[6] Many would even have trouble with painting all women as "too kind." Ask any mother of a middle-school-age daughter to describe just how mean girls can be to one another. If you have the opportunity, read the *New York Times Magazine* article entitled, "Mean Girls and the New Movement to Tame Them."[7]

That is not to say that women cannot be both tough *and* kind, or tough *and* feminine. The truth is always more than black and white. Women lawyers know that they can be both strong advocates and kind and caring souls. Furthermore, the accusations about women's character dangerously imply that certain qualities—like being kind, sympathetic, or emotional—are inconsistent with being a good lawyer. There is more to being an advocate than knowing the law. Being passionate about a position is often what is required. The challenge is having both in your arsenal, and knowing how and when to use each.

There are individuals—clients and lawyers—who test the limits of a woman's toughness by trying to bully her or make her cry. I was once called "girlie" in a pejorative way during the course of a contentious real estate closing. Another time, in the middle of a deposition, my opposing counsel called my partner to "tell on" me. He reported I was not being cooperative (and frankly, I wasn't going to let him walk all over my client). I cannot imagine him calling the firm of a man in the same situation. Others have told me similar stories of aggressive and rude conduct by opposing male counsel, also clearly designed to intimidate. Women should take heart and remember that the man who underestimates her toughness and acumen can be at a disadvantage, long before he ever realizes it.

Too Tough

No one can maintain that all women, by their nature, lack the toughness necessary for litigation or contract negotiations. One need only spend an hour or less with Philadelphia's district attorney, labor lawyer Deborah Willig, or others who contributed to this book to find incredibly competent and tough women litigators.

Being tough at what they do and being strong advocates for their clients often subjects women lawyers to personal, negative criticism abut their character, rather than their work. They are "too tough" or "too masculine." Notes one Los Angeles lawyer, "If you are aggressive then you are perceived as bitchy. A man who is aggressive is not perceived that way." Christine McCarthy Smith of Manchester, New Hampshire, chimes in, "I think we can be pegged as bitchy when we are just getting the job done." And from a Chicago lawyer:

> Women are taken less seriously everywhere. If they stand their ground they are considered bitches. That's just how it is. I stand my ground anyway. But many people from law school to the courtroom act as if this makes me somehow a bad person. It is a subtle sort of disapproval that you know is there.

Women know all too well that by exhibiting certain "male" traits, they are often put down, derided, and attacked. District Attorney Lynne Abraham confides that she is often the subject of criticism for difficult positions she takes that, were she a man, would be labeled "courageous."

A Woman's Touch

Women bring special qualities and life experiences to the practice of law that enhance their abilities to serve their clients and deal with their associates. For members of the judiciary, those qualities and experiences enhance the work of the court and, in the view of Pennsylvania Supreme Court Justice Sandra Schulz Newman, bring another perspective to decision making and a sensitivity that reflects more accurately who we are as a society.

My law school classmates offered their own experiences in bringing a woman's sensitivity and experience to the practice of law. As Taylor Williams explains, "My experience as a mother and teacher came in handy in dealing with [the lead partner's] childish tantrums. . . . Certainly explaining a case is very much like teaching." I find that settling disputes at home, among boards of directors, or between divorcing clients to be very similar. These are all "people" issues that arise at home and at work. Kathryn Carlson of Bucks County, Pennsylvania, holds similar views:

> I think that women have a lot to offer to the law. We tend to approach problems with less ego and more interest in resolution than in conflict. Obviously that is an overgeneralization, but has some truth. We should not try to follow the typical male role model of an attorney if it does not suit us. Different people have different styles of practicing law. Clients also have different needs and some cases call for different approaches. The skills of both genders improve the overall practice.

Can women practice law with an easy demeanor and a feminine flair? Most would answer in the affirmative. From Thiele Branham in South Carolina: "I think we can still be great lawyers without pretending to be men." And from one New York lawyer: "I do not think it is necessary to act like a man or to have no other interest than your job in order to be a good lawyer. But maybe that is what people expect." From another woman lawyer in Indiana:

> I suggest women be more prepared because they are more likely than men to be perceived as incompetent. Women can be assertive, but adopting stereotypically male mannerisms is usually not helpful. If a woman is going to take that tack, I suggest she look very femme to counteract what may be a negative reaction, especially from more traditional judges.

When choosing role models, women should be confident enough to adopt the best of their qualities, while retaining their own personal qualities that make them unique individuals. A style that reflects the person you are is the style that will bring the greatest success and satisfaction. There is much about this that is confusing. Qualities that may be interpreted as feminine may make a negative impression upon clients, judges, and juries. A woman who we might say is "tough as nails" often leaves a negative impression and is perceived as too masculine. Worrying about what others think can be a huge drain of energy. Understanding what is needed for the situation should be the focus. Sometimes a softer touch is better than stridency. Sometimes being tough about a position is better than being well liked. The woman lawyer should assess each situation and her approach to it in a way that best serves the interests of her client, and ignore the personal swipes so she can do her job.

It is said that "nineteenth-century women lawyers faced the gnawing problem of how to be at once a lady and a lawyer."[8] Philadelphia's women lawyers of experience—pre-1960 graduates— who responded to a Philadelphia Bar Association survey in 1997, unanimously stated that women lawyers should not capitalize upon their gender but neither should they sacrifice their femininity and special female qualities. Gender can be a disadvantage or an advantage by itself. I recall participating as a junior lawyer in a teamsters' labor negotiation on behalf of management. Shortly into the negotiations, the teamsters' negotiator looked at us and sputtered in frustration that he had difficulty "expressing" himself because of my presence and that we had put him at a disadvantage. In the words of Justice Sandra Schulz Newman, "Vive la difference!"

My husband (and law partner) offers his observations on my approach to being tough. He reminisced about our very first meeting—my initial job interview for an associate's position:

> I met Phyllis while she was teaching, practicing, and studying for her LLM in Taxation, somehow all at the same time. During her interview I asked her a question borne of what was then a common concern of us male bastions of the bar, that of her attitude toward law and her dealings with male lawyers. You see, we male lawyers had become used to dealing with women who seemed to have a chip on their shoulders, women who became defensive and took personally any questioning of the positions they took on behalf of a client. And so I asked, "How would you deal with a lawyer who disagreed with your position? Do you think it important to be tough? Is it better to respond softly? Or do you feel that a soft response would cause you to be taken lightly?" Her response was simple: "It depends—sometimes one works, and sometimes the other." And that was it. I was won over, just like that.

Speak UP!

The law is a social occupation that requires interaction with clients, peers, the judiciary, and government. A woman may have the "firmness" of character to practice law but fail to promote herself with equal strength, to the detriment of her career. For some, it may be necessary to brush up on appearances and demeanor in ways that may feel "unnatural." In short, women must learn to speak up about themselves—to be their own best advocates. As Judge Phyllis Beck of the Pennsylvania Superior Court puts it, "Sing your own praises; speak up about your accomplishments." Octogenarian Grace Kennedy mirrors this advice:

> Women are quiet about what they do. Women should push harder to have their abilities recognized. Men do boast, but women are quiet.

District Court Judge Norma Shapiro also urges women to speak out for themselves. Too often, she observes, women introduce themselves in soft-spoken voices. Women should speak confidently and clearly, in court and elsewhere, or run the risk that no one will be listening. From Judge Shapiro's vantage point on the federal bench, she offers the following advice:

> Be sure to stand straight when you are erect and sit straight when you are sedentary. A slump is not a sign of security. Most important of all, speak up, loudly and clearly. If you swallow your words, there are two distinct disadvantages: no one will understand you and no one will think you wish to be understood. If what you say is important, it's important enough to be heard. Don't worry about your voice being high pitched and feminine; worry about being heard at all.[9]

Men's Work versus Women's Work

Stereotypes about women's nature have been employed to steer women away from pursuing the more "masculine" practices of law, such as litigation or business, and to compel them to work behind desks as advisers in noncombative matters. Professor Marina Angel writes:

> Women may have been, and may still be, interested in certain fields, but, even if not interested, they traditionally were relegated to the fields of family law, trusts and estates, and research. If women entered teaching, these were the fields they taught, and if they practiced, these were areas of their practice.[10]

Many also assume that women do not have "a head for numbers." A recent report prepared for the ABA Commission on Women observes:

> First and most fundamentally, the characteristics traditionally associated with women are at odds with many characteristics traditionally associated with professional success, such as assertiveness, competitive-

ness, and business judgment. Some lawyers and clients still assume that women lack sufficient aptitude for complex financial transactions or sufficient combativeness for major litigation.[11]

From the vantage of former Philadelphia Bar Association Chancellor Jerome Bogutz, women continue to suffer from a presumption of incompetence in the field of major corporate transactions—not only from within their law firms, but especially from business clients who prefer male lawyers. Mr. Bogutz holds this view despite the fact that his own daughter specializes in major corporate transactions for a large Philadelphia firm. He adds that women face gender-based stereotypes from clients more often than others, particularly in the commercial transaction field of law: "In larger firms, clients in business often initially prefer male attorneys and can dictate who will handle their work. Smaller firms will also cater to the prejudices of their clients to retain their representation. Older men in business prefer male lawyers, and women will be at a disadvantage until given the opportunity to demonstrate their competence." Confirmation of this lingering bias came from a woman lawyer in Wyoming, who shared the following:

> Years ago, I spoke with an older attorney who came from a large firm in Philadelphia about working for him. He told me point-blank that his clients wanted an older man to give them advice.

Unfortunately, opportunities in business law are more difficult for women outside large law firms, where many large corporate clients gravitate, largely because women lack the network and contacts among businesses that are predominately male owned. While a "natural" fit for women lawyers might be women in business, census reports from 1992 reflect that of the 6.4 million women-owned businesses, *39 percent* had gross receipts of *less* than $10,000. The gross receipts of only *1 percent* exceeded $1 million.[12]

In the experience of Caroline Vincent, a Los Angeles lawyer, the preference for male lawyers carried over into her selection as a mediator and her international experience with Japanese clients:

As a young associate I was kept out of closings with Japanese clients because they were uncomfortable with women. As a mediator, I focus on areas such as employment and probate, where women and their ability to relate to the parties and deal with emotions is highly regarded—in large cases, women just usually aren't considered as much as men. As a practical matter, women are not given the same business development advantages unless they have business rainmaker champions introducing them and sharing with them and developing them.

Now that there is a choice, men and women seeking lawyers sometimes express preferences for male or female lawyers. There are anecdotes about women preferring women lawyers, particularly in divorces. Sometimes men prefer women lawyers if, for example, a lawyer must confront a female Internal Revenue Service agent and the agent might relate better to women. Men often look to women to represent them in divorce matters, hoping that a woman might overcome any judicial prejudice against men.

Women have always been stereotyped as being best at family law. The belief is that in comparison with men, women are more sympathetic and more interested in the concerns of women and children. These sentiments—over a hundred years old—were expressed by the prominent lawyer Clarence Darrow before a gathering of women lawyers in Chicago, in 1895:

> You can't be shining lights at the bar because you are too kind. You can never be corporation lawyers because you are not cold-blooded. You have not a high grade of intellect. You can never expect to get the fees men get. I doubt if you [can] ever make a living. Of course you can be divorce lawyers. That is a useful field. And there is another field you can have solely for your own. You can't make a living at it, but it's worthwhile and you'll have no competition. That is the free defense of criminals.

I recall an interview experience where I had been called back a number of times to meet with various partners who seemed enthusiastic and impressed by my corporate law experience and advancement toward an LLM in Taxation. At the final interview before all partners (all male), the very elder senior partner awoke, raised his head, and spoke these immortal words: "Divorce. Can you do divorce? We need someone to do divorce." Leslie Anne Miller relates her own experience in a firm where she was selected among the lawyers—the sole female—to return to law school for a class in family law so she could handle those cases for the firm. As a commercial litigator, she rejected this proposition outright and suggested the firm employ a family law practitioner who would devote the proper energy and devotion to this area of practice.

In fairness, Pennsylvania's divorce code was rewritten in 1980, presenting a vacuum of lawyers with expertise in this field. My classmate Kathryn Carlson became instrumental in developing local procedures and rules for instituting the new code in Bucks County. When the new office of "Divorce Master" was instituted in 1983, Kathryn served as the first one in Bucks County. Her authority extended to holding hearings and settling disputes over property division, known in Pennsylvania as equitable distribution, alimony, and support. Judge Dickman of the Montgomery County Court of Common Pleas commented that, in retrospect, the new code elevated divorce practice and made it more lucrative for lawyers practicing in this field. Times have changed, and "family law," as it is now referred to, is practiced by both men and women.

The Presumption of Competence

In 1974, Professor Diane Maleson was invited to become a law professor at Temple University by then dean, Peter Liacouras. At the time, she had two children, the younger being under the age of one. She related stories of students and colleagues undermining her and doubting her competence. One colleague professor, without informing or consulting with her, took it upon himself to inform her torts class that because she was new, and may not do such a good job of teaching or reviewing, *he* would review the semester work with them in advance of the class final. In that way, he consoled them, they would not suffer from her inexperience (read: lack of competence). In another incident, a (male) law student challenged a C+ grade by asking another (male) professor to review his exam. Fortunately, that professor refused. The student felt no inhibition in informing Professor Maleson that he had gone to another professor because he doubted her competence.

I suggested to Professor Maleson that today we would not hear such comments, although they might be felt. Years later, for her and for me, we are inclined to believe that women gain credibility with age and professional demeanor. Being young in the law profession seems to work negatively against women, more so than men.

Fifteen years ago, the *ABA Journal* interviewed a number of women lawyers who, almost unanimously, believed they were "presumed incompetent" by other lawyers, judges, and clients.[13] Catherine Barone suggests that changes in the acceptance of women and the new presumption of competence has come about in part because the young daughters of older male lawyers are becoming lawyers themselves, forcing a turnaround in attitudes:

> Years ago, many men did not believe women should be in the professions. However, I noted particularly after the Second World War the same men who admitted they did not like women in the professions changed drastically when their own daughters were raised and wanted to become professionals, particularly lawyers and doctors. These same men thought it was fine for their daughters—so I have seen a radical change in attitudes.

I have heard similar reports from other women. Judge Norma Shapiro speaks of that uncle who first told her ladies shouldn't be lawyers and how he has softened, now that his daughter has become a lawyer. However, the prevailing sentiment is still that women must work harder than their male counterparts to prove themselves at the outset.

Equal Treatment versus Special Treatment

As newcomers to the legal profession, women lawyers initially hoped for equality with men—equal opportunities for advancement within a firm, equal access to positions of power within the government and judiciary, equal pay, and equal sharing of interesting and lucrative assignments. Given the barriers placed in front of women at the outset, equal treatment became the rallying cry. But should women who choose to work as lawyers be content with equal treatment? Is "equal treatment" always fair? Some women may choose to work part-time (or less) to raise families, or take medical leaves for giving birth. This may entitle them to part-time status in their law firms, with part-time pay. A job may even be held open for a certain amount of time so a woman may return to work after giving birth, under the same rules that may apply to a man who has suffered a heart attack or taken a few weeks to be with his newborn. Some see these initiatives as equal treatment, some as fair treatment, and some as special treatment. Today, many women lawyers feel they are entitled to expect not only equal treatment, but perhaps *more than* equal treatment.

More than one hundred years ago, one of feminism's founders, Susan B. Anthony, wrote:

Make up your minds to take the "lean" with the "fat," and be early and late at the case, precisely as men are. I do not demand equal pay for any woman save those who do equal work in value. Scorn to be coddled by your employers; make them understand that you are in their service as workers, not as women. (Ward, Geoffrey, and Ken Burns, *Not For Ourselves Alone: The Story of Elizabeth Cady Stanton and Susan B. Anthony,* New York: Knopf, 1999, p. 114)

This is a sentiment I have heard over and over in my interviews with working professional women—a desire to render gender obsolete, and be given recognition as good lawyers, not as good women lawyers. The expectation is that each job will be filled on merit alone and great work will be rewarded without consideration of sex. And yet, there is a droning in the back of any working woman's mind that fair isn't always fair. Note the comments of Sylvia Hewlett in her recent book:

> The bottom line seems to be: Working mothers need more than equal treatment. Swimming in the mainstream and taking your chances doesn't produce equality of result if you're picking up 75 percent of home-related and child-related responsibilities.[14]

All things being equal, women's and men's lives are far from equal. In the race to keep careers in forward motion, women are dealt a handicap. As one California lawyer remarked, "A level playing field is good, but I'd settle for being on the same playing field." Like it or not, women, for the most part, remain the primary family care-takers for the young and the old, and supervisors of the home. Given those realities, equal treatment may have a hand in the dismal per-centages of women in positions of equity partner at larger law firms and in similar positions of power. Some may argue that part-time policies in larger institutions are cloaked as special treatment. But in truth, these policies are enormously unfair in practice. As most women find out, part-time work in a large law firm is a forty-hour workweek without benefits and without opportunity for career advancement. As a result, women's careers suffer setbacks in unequal proportion to their male counterparts.

In small firms or solo practices, equal treatment is less of an issue. As your own boss, you earn whatever you produce. There are no handouts or policies granting you maternity leave or even ensur-ing that your clients will be there tomorrow if you are not there for them today. In a smaller law firm, you make telephone calls to opposing counsel from the maternity ward when your water breaks early, as I did, to request continuances of hearings or confirm nego-tiations. There is no such thing as paid—or even unpaid—maternity leave.

In other settings, the employer's approach to a request for fam-ily leave is on a case-by-case basis. Judge Toby Dickman told me that at her former firm, an associate took several months of unpaid maternity leave and returned to work where, although not legally required, her employer held her job for her. For bonuses and profits calculated at year-end, the woman asked to have her months off excluded from the averaging of her work hours for the year. The partners declined. They had held her job open, but could not in a small firm overlook her lack of productivity for those months and compensate her by ignoring them. Clearly it was fair—maybe even "special"—treatment for the firm to hold this woman's position for her. Equal treatment dictated a different allocation of compensation, even if this woman considered it unfair treatment.

The city of Philadelphia has an unofficial, unwritten maternity leave policy that, by all accounts and consensus, gives a woman six months of unpaid maternity leave with her job back at that time. On the other hand, there is no such policy at the city's district attorney's office. District Attorney Lynne Abraham explains that the cases go on day after day and she requires lawyers on the job to pick up the work. For anyone departing for a period of time, a job will not be held but will be filled as soon as possible by someone new to take up the burden. There is no guarantee of reentry. Is this equal treatment or unfair treatment? The policy itself is gender-neutral, but may affect more women than men for an unequal result.

Laurel, currently working as a federal judicial law clerk in Tampa, Florida, writes:

> I think the basic answer is equal treatment. However, I think we're still clawing up the hill right now, and could use some help on the way.

And yet, would the woman lawyer in Judge Dickman's former firm agree? If employers would allow women the flexibility they need to work through certain periods in their lives when family demands more of them, there are certain to be long-term rewards for both. Firms would benefit by retaining employees with training and expertise. Of course, employees would benefit from continued employment and continuity of client relationships. As a public official with limited funding and unlimited work to face, District Attorney Abraham may well have a special situation to deal with, but that does not necessarily carry over to the private sector, or to most corporate and governmental offices.

Upon accepting her firm's award for the Promotion of Women to Leadership Positions, from the Pennsylvania Bar Association, Deborah Willig enunciated her and the firm's strong advocacy of equality and flexibility in the workplace, a position she views as "common sense":

> In every walk of life, you can *find* reasons to discriminate. Most often, it's bad business. Our firm's ancillary benefit is that by adopting what were at the time innovative approaches, we, and therefore our clients, reap the rewards.

Deborah's firm accommodates its lawyers' needs for flexibility without compromising opportunities for advancement; obviously the business of her firm is not suffering, or the firm would not follow a flexible program. The policies are gender neutral, and far more "fair" to women than other policies that afford part-time or flex-time work while requiring career suicide.

Tokenism

There was a time when the appointment of a woman to a position of importance meant the slamming of doors for all other women. Judge Carolyn Engel Temin spoke of feeling this way when she was hired by the public defender's office as the only woman among an office full of men. The U.S. Tax Court operated this way for decades. There was one place set aside for a woman judge and, upon her retirement, another woman would fill that vacancy. There was never more than one woman on the court until 1985, when Carolyn Miller Parr joined Judge Mary Ann Cohen on the bench. Today there are three women judges out of a full complement of nineteen regular judges.

Women's participation as legal advocates and judges in the field of tax law has for many years been the product of tokenism. The Board of Tax Appeals was established by Congress in 1924 under Article II of the U.S. Constitution, and later reconstituted under

Article I as the U.S. Tax Court, with jurisdiction to resolve disputed taxpayer assessments by the Internal Revenue Service. The U.S. Tax Court is a federal court centrally located in Washington, D.C., although its judges travel throughout the country to major cities where cases are presented for trial. The court is composed of nineteen judges appointed by the president of the United States for fifteen-year terms. The docket is handled by these judges, as well as by senior judges on recall and special trial judges.

Nine women have served as U.S. Tax Court judges as of this writing. The first, Annabel Matthews, took office on February 18, 1930, and retired when her term expired six years later on June 1, 1936. Marion Harron then held the "woman's spot" on the bench when appointed on July 29, 1936, by Franklin Delano Roosevelt. Judge Harron retired in 1960 and served on recall through December 1970. She was followed by Irene Scott, who was appointed to the bench in 1960 and served until her retirement in 1982. Judge Scott also served the court on recall subsequent to her retirement. Cynthia Hall overlapped Judge Scott on the bench with her appointment in 1972. However, she was elevated to the U.S. Court of Appeals in California in 1981. In 1980, Edna Parker, formerly a special trial judge, was appointed to serve on the Tax Court, where she remained until her retirement in 1995. Judge Parker also continued to serve the court on recall after her retirement.

Although more women have been appointed to the bench since Judge Scott's retirement in 1982, the court's female representation has remained in the minority. Judge Mary Ann Cohen joined the bench in 1982 and served as Chief Judge from June 1, 1996, until May 31, 2000. Judge Cohen was joined on the bench by Carolyn Miller Parr in 1985 (who was replaced by Diane L. Kroupa in 2003), Carolyn Chiechi in 1992, and L. Paige Marvel in 1998. Four women now sit as judges on the U. S. Tax Court, out of a total of seventeen, with two remaining vacancies.

Today, the presence of women in positions of authority more often opens—rather than shuts—the door for others. Deborah Willig's election to Philadelphia Bar Association Chancellor broke the ice for others to follow. Since her tenure, two others, Doreen Davis and Audrey Talley, have served the bar as chancellor. With more appointments, the presence of a woman as chancellor or district attorney or judge becomes more acceptable and less newsworthy. These positions come within the grasp of other women who wish to follow. Rather than slamming the door shut, the door is opened wider.

I do not mean to imply by this reciting of success stories that discrimination against women has been eradicated in all parts of our nation. The situation for women lawyers varies drastically from cities to small county courthouses, where the prevalence of women judges and women lawyers dissipates. From Atlanta, Georgia, one woman lawyer reports:

> Despite the number of women attending law school in the past ten to twenty years, I am still often the only woman among men in a group. There are still relatively few women trial lawyers where I practice, although this is improving.

Moving farther south, or into rural areas, women lawyers will frequently find themselves without the company of other women lawyers. For many, the prospect of being the token woman is still very real and the education curve for the public still at its earliest rise. From Utah, Mary Gordon shares the following thoughts about representing her profession as a woman:

> What I tell new attorneys and women law students is that while overt discrimination is less and less common, it still happens and any woman who enters this profession believing there isn't work still to be done in this area is either in denial or grossly underinformed about American society. And even if one never experiences overt discrimination, we have to realize that part of how others we deal with view us will always include our gender. For instance, for a lot of clients and/or opposing counsel, dealing with me may be the first time they've ever dealt with a woman lawyer. I feel the burden of being a representative of my gender and profession in that regard and always try to handle myself particularly well and professionally because of it. The women of

preceding generations worked way too hard to give me the opportunities I enjoy for me to wallow in complacency.

There are still areas in the country where women lawyers have yet to become less of a rarity. In these areas, women may feel they have become tokens within the profession. A better description would be trailblazers who are opening the doors for others to enter. Economics will be the ultimate end of tokenism. As women become experts in their fields and attract business, men will clamor for their alliances and women will have the choice of joining the firms that provide them with the best opportunities, both in their practices and in their lives.

Have All the Battles Been Won?

Women lawyers in the first half of the twentieth century were the advance troops for women lawyers today, fighting for admission to law school and for employment as lawyers. Each law school class had less than a handful of women, and employers did not greet them with open arms upon graduation.

Looking at the statistics, it might seem that for women lawyers, the battles have been won. Today our law schools are graduating classes that are 40 to 50 percent women. Two Supreme Court justices, as well as many circuit court and district court judges, are women. A woman has held the highest law enforcement position in the country. In many law firms, there is a substantial female presence. Can women lawyers finally exhale and assume that gender is no longer going to hold them back in their professional lives?

In 1997, the Philadelphia Bar Association Committee on Women in the Profession sponsored a gathering of Philadelphia's women lawyers who graduated from law school before 1960, some as early as 1930. The meeting was entitled, "A Reception in Honor of Trailblazing Senior Women Attorneys." Thanks largely to the efforts of Audrey Talley, a future Philadelphia Bar Association Chancellor, these "trailblazing" women contributed their thoughts on paper, in response to questions about their experiences as law students and lawyers. Their experiences are typical for women lawyers of their day.

All reported that the number of women in their law school class was less than a handful, in contrast to a class of about one hundred men. Their experiences in school varied. For some, the environment was collegial, respectful, and exhilarating. More than one reported feeling like "one of the boys." For others—the majority, actually—the law school experience was an endurance of slights by teachers who refused to call upon them to participate in class, slights by fellow students who refused to invite them to join study groups, and outright antagonism by fellow students who accused them of taking the place of more worthy men who needed jobs to support their families. Some experienced unwanted sexual harassment and groping in the library stacks. But, for the most part, the majority of women reported experiencing their most difficult times *after* law school.

In Philadelphia, before 1960, a graduating lawyer was required to work under the tutelage of a "preceptor"—a senior lawyer who was supposed to train the new graduate in ethical behavior and the nuts-and-bolts of a law practice. The inability to find preceptors prevented more than one "trailblazing" woman from taking the bar examination or pursuing a career in the law. In the 1940s and 1950s, most lawyers in Philadelphia were male, and most, though not all, were unwilling to train women, as they believed women were likely to marry and quit working and therefore any investment in their training was a waste of time; they also believed giving women positions deprived more deserving and needy men of work. Though the preceptor requirement has since been abolished, the women respondents also remind us that at that time in our country, young men were returning from war and, in most industries, including the law, women were stepping aside to make way for the returning GIs.

Many women lawyers of those years reported that their initial work was secretarial. They found they could be hired—indeed gain "preceptorships"—by becoming typists and taking shorthand. The Honorable Juanita Kidd Stout (class of 1948) of the Philadelphia

Court of Common Pleas reports that she was advised by a professor to conceal her typing and shorthand skills or risk being hired as a secretary. Seventeen of these notable three hundred women became judges.[15] Success, either modest or great, came only with perseverance and hard work. In addition to being offered only secretarial work, several of these women started as librarians in either the University of Pennsylvania's Biddle Law library, or the libraries of large law firms. One reports that her firm did not expect her to stay because, as a woman, she would get married and quit, and so the office managers refused to put her name on her office door like her male counterparts. Another relates that she was instructed to never put her name on a letter or memo because clients would not accept a woman doing their legal work. Many found work as partners with their husbands.

But whether they started as typists or librarians, or in firms with their husbands, these trailblazing women were generally positive about their work and, in time, if they continued working, enjoyed great satisfaction in being lawyers and judges. As an example of the great spirit and grit of these women, I found remarkable the life story of the Honorable Rita E. Prescott, class of 1949 of the Temple University School of Law. Judge Prescott served her six-month preceptorship as a "secretary/law clerk to a sole practitioner." Through her friendships, she became connected with a Philadelphia judge who invited her to work with him in his office—also as a secretary. Judge Prescott seized upon this job as another opportunity, rather than a setback. She found she could combine her secretarial work with working as a law clerk to the judge, thereby continuing to advance her career. In time, she was able to shed her secretarial duties and hold down just one job as law clerk. Through hard work and determination, Rita Prescott became the first female law clerk of Delaware County, Pennsylvania, and the first woman court administrator. In 1975, she won election to the Delaware County Court of Common Pleas. By her willingness to take on whatever work was available, and being alert for opportunities, the Honorable Rita Prescott was able to succeed admirably as a woman in her profession. She claims she was always "lucky in a man's world." But she ends with this bit of advice: "[A]s a judge said to me in reply: Luck may be defined as being in the right place at the right time with all the appropriate skills called for."

Upon graduating from the University of Pennsylvania Law School in 1948, Catherine Barone, like so many others, found it difficult to get work. She graduated from a class of ninety-nine, as one of five women. Unfortunately, finding a preceptor and work would prove daunting. Like many other women graduates of her day, finding work often meant agreeing to do secretarial tasks like answering phones or typing, or working for next to nothing, just to acquire "experience." Although her first desire was to become a trial lawyer, the firms that may have considered her for her shorthand skills clearly were not about to hire her as a trial lawyer. She says of those times:

> There were no women. They weren't used to women. . . . But I didn't really care. If they didn't like me, I was still going to be a good lawyer. I was a very confident, self-assured lawyer.[16]

Catherine was fortunate to secure an appointment as law clerk to then Pennsylvania Supreme Court Chief Justice Maxey. Subsequently, with his support, she obtained a position in the legal department of the Pennsylvania Railroad. Catherine Barone ended the last century as a sole practitioner. Her love of the law is enduring.

Women lawyers today are no longer hired as secretaries or librarians. They are no longer given the cold shoulder by prospective employers. But the battles have not all been won—they have changed. Sexual harassment, stereotyping, and discrimination still exist to deny women equal pay, equal work, and safe working environments. More often than we care to recognize, women are excluded from the inner power circles within their firms and legal communities by the practice of all-male lunches and all-male socializing. Women have yet to lock on to a solution that allows them opportunities to advance their careers, or at least keep them on hold, while other matters like families demand their time and attention. These are the new battles of gender.

Secretarial Strife

Women lawyers often find their arrival in firms to be unwelcome to the secretarial staff, who are still predominately female. Interactions between seasoned legal secretaries and young female lawyers can be particularly stressful. In the way a short-order cook in a restaurant can foul up a waiter's orders, a legal secretary can make or break a new lawyer. One woman in Naples, Florida, offers this tale from her first job:

> The secretaries decided they were not going to do my work. Two of them refused to pick up items in my "outbox." They were reprimanded but my work was never handled properly.

Soon after law school, I experienced friction with my boss's secretary, who was about my age. She undermined my work, and my social life, by intentionally losing my messages. Accomplished legal secretaries sometimes take the position that they know more than novice lawyers and should not be pushed around or taken for granted. And they are right. Many have years of practical experience with pleadings, cover sheets, filing rules, and such, and resent a "know it all" attitude from a recent law school graduate who may have never actually prepared a complaint. A secretary and lawyer can avoid friction by being sensitive to their relationship, acknowledging their mutual dependencies, and recognizing the specialized knowledge of the other. By being less of a boss and more of a colleague, and adopting the right attitude and approach, a lawyer can have a legal secretary who is her virtual right arm. A good secretary can teach you tricks it would take years to learn on your own.

Exclusion from the Inner Circle

Lawyers interact with one another on a daily basis to exchange ideas, refer clients, and share legal strategies. Partners and associates within a firm interact in ways that benefit clients, as well as individual lawyers who strive for upward mobility. Lawyers in solo practices and smaller firms do the same type of interacting among their friends and classmates, which generally leads to cross-firm referrals and more business for all in their areas of practice. This interaction is vital to any successful legal career.

Entering the legal network was, and still is, critical to a woman's successful legal career. That is why the exclusion of women lawyers from all-male social institutions and play functions has such a negative effect upon their careers. Initially, the exclusion of women from the male network was part institutionalized behavior of the times, and part obliviousness of male lawyers. In 1964, Third Circuit Judge Dolores Sloviter became the first woman partner at the law firm of Dilworth, Paxson, Kalish, and Green. The men at the firm frequently lunched at a popular local establishment, in a private room for men only:

> Stouffer's restaurants at that time had a men's dining room in the back, which would serve men who were dining much more quickly and I wasn't allowed to go in there. Unless, every once in a while, we would put on a little fuss, and they would let us in. I remember that it was a disincentive to the men in my firm to invite me along with the group to have lunch, from time to time. (Interview with Judge Dolores Sloviter, conducted by The Oral Legal History Project of the University of Pennsylvania Law School, Apr. 2, 1999)

Years later, after her appointment to the Third Circuit, Judge Sloviter was invited to a reception at Philadelphia's historically Republican private club, the Union League. At that time, the Union League refused to admit women as members and only allowed them to dine in the basement dining hall. Judge Sloviter's official refusal to attend a formal function at an institution that would not have her as a member made headlines in the local papers.

How disappointed I was to hear from women around the country with similar stories of exclusion still going on today. From Sacramento, California, one woman wrote about the following incident:

> Once, I drove past the local bar and saw the managing partner's car as well as several other male associates' cars in the parking lot. So I called the bar, ordered a shot and a beer, and had it sent over to the managing

partner with my compliments. The next day, I was told that what he does on his time is his business. So now, I only say something when he takes the male associates out at 4:00 p.m. DURING BUSINESS HOURS.

Philadelphia's Union League now admits women as members but, as these stories indicate, it is apparent that all-male clubs still exist and senior male law partners still dine there, to the exclusion of their women partners and associates. From Lyle in Atlanta, Georgia:

> I interviewed at a firm [that] held their partners' meetings at a club that was a men's-only facility. I inquired how it was their one female partner was able to participate, and did they include her. They responded that she was able to attend the business portion of their meetings, but could not stay for dinner. Needless to say, I didn't take that job.

From Los Angeles, Caroline Vincent remarks:

> In 1980, I was recruited to work for a large law firm under an EEOC consent decree to hire more women. The attorney interviewing me took me to a male-only membership club for lunch! The moral of the story: They just don't get it.

Men often socialize and network at the softball field, on the golf course, and while playing cards. These forms of play often leave women out of the inner circle of friends and associates. Laurel from Tampa, Florida, shares her experiences with male socializing:

> They'd have poker night or other activities when male associates were invited, but not female. Since there were no female partners, exclusion from poker and golf meant exclusion from socializing with the partners. We are often excluded from the "inner circle" because so often that circle meets informally. Whether it is on the golf course, at poker night, or elsewhere, we are often not a part of the gathering. Unfortunately, senior partners and judges are still disproportionately men, and it is more difficult for us to gain access to them.

Nichole Berklas in Los Angeles offers:

> There is clearly an old-boys network in the firm, the male partners interact socially with the male partners but not with the women, and

we have few if any women partners, so the connection to partners is much more tenuous for women. There is really not much to do; I don't golf and don't care to spend my evening drinking. It is difficult as a woman to gain the same level of confidence and enter into the "inner sanctum" of both clients and senior attorneys unless you are interested in engaging in traditionally male activities, and it is nearly impossible to do those if you, as is often the case with women, are the primary caregiver for children or family.

Many women are able to credit men in their lives with having paved the way for their successes. Fortunately, not all male lawyers insist upon dining in male-only clubs or excluding women from the inner sanctum in social activities like golf, football pools, poker, or the gym. To a degree, women can become proactive by engineering the location of dining functions. Not every woman can play catch-up on the golf course, although I am sure many are just as good at the game as men. It's just that women do not have the hours it takes to get through nine holes if they are also driving carpools. Women can retaliate by creating their own networks and their own social functions, but until women wield the power of the male inner sanctum, this is a second-best remedy. If enough women come to occupy positions of authority in their firms, commandeer significant client bases, and hold positions of power in government and the judiciary, then women's networks can rival men's.

Confronting Sexism

The off-color remark, the inappropriate gesture, and the all-male business lunch, I'm afraid to report, are alive and well. Our women in law school today relate the subtle but ever-present denigration of them for outspokenness. I was called a bitch the other day by a client (not mine, fortunately) in a divorce negotiation, because I filed legal motions to produce documentation.

Some acts of sexism are the result of hostility toward women, and some are simply old habits. My classmate Paula M. Szortyka had one such story:

> When I first started working in the district attorney's office, I was the only woman attorney on the staff. There were seven other assistant district attorneys, all male. There were seven judges, also all male. Whenever in-court hearings were concluded, it was the habit of the presiding judge to say, "Gentlemen, court is adjourned." I would keep standing there as everyone else filed out and I would say, "What about me, your honor?" The judges finally got used to dispensing with the gentlemen-only ritual.

In the decades preceding my law school class, lawyers like Judge Dolores Sloviter were confronting sexism on a grander scale. Sexism in the 1950s and 1960s meant more than off-putting remarks—it could very well curtail careers. Many believe it is best to venture forth with good humor into acts of consciousness-raising. Christina Lewis counsels, "Be very thick-skinned and focus on your clients rather than your treatment in the firm." My classmate Taylor Williams shares this experience:

> When I first started there weren't many women in my field. I would attend many meetings where I was the only woman. Keeping a good sense of humor when the men would make wise remarks always seemed to diffuse the situation.
>
> I have experienced sexism in another way that I think is unique, and it occurs because I work with my husband. Lawyers or salespersons sometimes call my husband to complain about my behavior if they think I am being too unreasonable. This one always makes me laugh. I take it as a sign that I have done something right. My husband gets a kick out of these calls and, of course, backs me up completely.

We all have stories—from the past and the present—about ongoing sexist remarks, inappropriate behavior, and subtle discrimination. I appreciate the words of Judge Shapiro offering her perspective on the subject:

> As a woman who began practice in 1956, it would be nonsense to announce that I never suffered acts of discrimination or sexual harassment. But I can say that I coped satisfactorily by never assuming that the mistreatment resulted from the fact that I was a woman or, indeed, because of anything I said or did. Discrimination and anti-female prejudice I considered a defect of the discriminator and a sign of insecurity—not mine, but his. It was a sign that he feared me and had something to learn. In other words, I used it to support my own sense of security. Such an attitude seems to work; at least it did for me.
>
> Humor, indeed good humor, helps. Macho-ism rarely survives when it is not taken seriously. Just take yourself seriously.[17]

Gender Matters

Actual discrimination and sexual harassment still occur in the workplace, some of which may be addressed through the legal process. Title VII of the Civil Rights Act of 1964[18] offers women lawyers a weapon in the arsenal against sexual discrimination. The act provides in part:

> It shall be an unlawful employment practice for an employer
> (1) to fail or refuse to hire or to discharge any individual, or otherwise to discriminate against any individual with respect to his compensation, terms, conditions, or privileges of employment, because of such individual's race, color, religion, sex or national origin.[19]

The term "because of sex" includes conduct that is related to a woman's "pregnancy, childbirth or related medical conditions."[20] In workplaces of fifteen or more employees, Title VII affords women some protection from sexual discrimination.[21]

In 1984, the U.S. Supreme Court extended Title VII's protection of women to associates in large law firms who are denied access to partnership on the basis of their gender.[22] In *Hishon v. King & Spalding*, the Supreme Court found that a promise of partnership to a new associate may be within the "terms, conditions, or privileges of employment" that are protected by Title VII. The general remedies to women under the act and the 1991 amendments[23] include injunctions, reinstatement or front pay, back pay, lost benefits, attorneys' fees, and compensatory and punitive damages. Later, in 1992, the Third Circuit Court of Appeals held, in the case of *Ezold v. Wolf, Block, Schorr and Solis-Cohen*,[24] that a Philadelphia law firm's denial of partnership to a woman associate was not discriminatory, even though the standards for partnership were subjective. The opinion detailed every evaluation given by every partner in the firm in deciding whether the woman was denied promotion on the basis of her gender or her mediocre legal skills. The revelations are difficult to read and the experience for the litigants, as I recall, was particularly embarrassing. Given this precedent, women have reason to believe Title VII is a paper tiger in their struggle against unspoken gender bias in the workplace. Even worse, once a woman is made partner in her firm, Title VII no longer affords her any protection.[25] As a "partner," a woman lawyer is no longer an "employee" for purposes of Title VII, even if her firm is a P.C. (personal corporation) and her status is defined as something other than partner for tax purposes.[26] The qualities of management and control, rather than mere title, determine status.

Title VII also lends its blanket of protection to women subject to sexual harassment at work. In *Meritor Savings Bank v. Vinson*, the U.S. Supreme Court set the foundation for all future case law by stating—unequivocally—that sexual harassment is sexual discrimination.[27] A legally sufficient number of sexual remarks or acts can create a hostile work environment, for which there may be a legal remedy. Unfortunately, our courts require more than a "stray remark" or series of "stray remarks" over time to conclude that sexual harassment has occurred. In *Ezold*, six remarks over five years were not enough to define a hostile work environment, in the opinion of the Third Circuit Court of Appeals.

Many—probably most—acts of harassment go unaddressed in court or in the workplace. Women need to report all such incidents to create a record of pervasive and regular conduct that is required to bring a successful Title VII action.[28] Reporting also can help put an end to the offensive behavior. But a woman lawyer needs to know that not every incident can be or will be resolved by a higher authority. One woman with whom I spoke was harassed by a kissing judge in his chambers, begging the question of where to go to report such conduct. One day, just out of law school, I was the first to arrive at my place of work. I was in the library when a lawyer sharing office space entered, shut the door behind him, and said, "I could rape you right now and no one would know." I laughed him off and made for the door, and I knew there was no way to get legal satisfaction for what was clearly sexual harassment, if not criminal behavior. Christina Lewis of Austin, Texas, describes how her working conditions suffered after a lawyer for whom she worked was found to have had an affair with a coworker. Under pressure from his furious wife, the lawyer fired his girlfriend, assigned all of Christina's good cases to a male lawyer, and avoided all contact with Christina and other female lawyers in the workplace. Acts of discrimination and harassment persist. They are hard to prove and largely go unremedied.

Today, it is unlikely that a woman interviewee will be asked about her intentions to get married or her plans after she has children, although it is probably assumed that both will happen. Certainly a woman would not have to promise not to have any more children, as happened to Philadelphia Common Pleas Court Judge Temin. Interviewers are not likely to overstep the bounds of proper questioning overtly, but concerns will remain, particularly in small firms where a senior partner may invest two or three years training a new lawyer. But what if a new male hire leaves for a better job with better pay? You can be certain that no lifetime commitment was ever sought at his interview. From her vantage of more than fifty years practicing law, Grace Kennedy offers her view that women lawyers today still face "unspoken biases."

There is optimism that a woman can walk through any door and not be denied a position of employment on account of her sex. Certainly, a woman who commands her own lucrative practice can write her own ticket. Judge Temin commented in our conversation that women today have more alternatives than when she was starting her career in the 1950s. They should feel encouraged that although they may not get the judgeships or partnerships they want, they can put all their efforts into any aspiration and gender will not be the factor holding them back. Nevertheless, though it is generally agreed that gender alone is becoming less of a roadblock to seeking any job, women must make choices and, in that respect, gender is still very much a factor in how they ultimately practice law. A woman can be or do whatever she wants professionally, but if she wants to have a husband and children, she cannot devote the kind of time and energy required to climb the traditional ladder of success in a traditional manner. Nontraditional pathways will be required, whether in her profession, or in her commitments as a wife and mother.

Professor Marina Angel admonishes women law school graduates to bear in mind the impact of gender upon their career choices. Many, she asserts, "won't find that out until they are out in the world six or seven years. At that time they will feel that their difficulties are individual problems of theirs." Hopefully this book will disabuse them of that notion, for the truth is, we are all in this together. Matters of gender persist beyond our legal community. The presence of gender bias among lawyers is most certainly reflective of attitudes of the community at large. This may vary given the geographic area where we practice and live, and the prevalence of women lawyers in the community. Even though two women sit as U.S. Supreme Court justices, the collective consciousness of our society still requires uplifting. Acceptance of women in positions of authority, the sharing of domestic responsibilities, and simple human respect for one another will go a long way toward minimizing the unwarranted acts of discrimination and sexual harassment that persist.

Feminists and Queen Bees

Women who attended law school in the 1950s preceded the women's movement led by Betty Friedan and Gloria Steinem in the 1960s. Their impetus for entering a predominately male career world was more a statement of personal revolution. No wonder many senior women confided that in the early years, they did not consider themselves "feminists." Only later were their achievements placed into context within the women's movement.

At first, these women believed that by doing their jobs well, they would open opportunities for women to be accepted in the field. Eventually, many senior women lawyers came to understand and embrace their potential for smoothing the way for other women entering the profession. They came to accept that they had unwittingly become role models for a new generation of women. For many, awareness led to activism.

I have also observed women of power who do not see women's advocacy as something that deserves their time and attention. These women believe they are competing in a male profession on men's terms and doing just fine. Because they are successful, discrimination is nonexistent for them, and they feel their efforts on behalf of women at large are not needed. These women distance themselves from the advocacy "clique" in the way middle-school girls divide into separate cliques based upon clothes, behavior, or friends. The divisions exist with a passion and intensity I was surprised to encounter. One woman lawyer in Sacramento, California, shared a similar experience:

We have a women lawyers association here, but I have been reluctant to join because some of the women at the social events are very "catty" or aloof.

Some divisions among women are attributed to the "queen bee" syndrome: the queen bee is the woman at the top of the ladder who has "made it" in the male world, and is antagonistic toward other women so she can preserve her uniqueness. Women working their way through the ranks are cautioned to be wary of those who seek to undermine their advancement. One Florida lawyer reports:

When I started practicing in Naples, the women attorneys I met were very unsupportive. It was as if they were thinking, "I had to do it on my own, so you do, too."

Queen bees are not award winners. The most scathing description of a queen bee I found was suggested by early feminist Germaine Greer:

We know that [some] women do not champion their own sex once they are in positions of power, that when they are employers they do not employ their own sex, even when there is no other basis for discrimination. After all, they get on better with men because all their lives they have manipulated the susceptibilities, the guilt and hidden desires of men.[29]

Not all women who fail to advocate women's causes are queen bees. Queen bees are rejectionists—rejecting friendly associations with other women and rejecting any sense of debt to the trailblazing women before them. From Chicago, another woman lawyer offers:

I have, of course, seen things I have liked in other female attorney friends. But basically the very successful women in my field of law seem more interested in excluding than mentoring others.

How unfortunate that when fighting for equality and fair treatment, women are often fighting a civil war from within. Petty jealousies and sabotage from other women provide another set of roadblocks to careers. If women are to improve the environment in the legal community so their careers and personal lives can flourish, then women must be supportive of each other as professionals and people. That means they must network, mentor, and live up to the highest expectations of ethical conduct, as well as treat each other with civility.

Conclusion

If fair treatment is to be the goal of women lawyers, it will require acceptance of two basic axioms. The first is the tenant that law is a business as well as a profession, and lawyers and law firms will always consider the economics of their practices as the cornerstone of their policies. If you produce, you will be accepted, needed, and treated fairly, or you will leave the firm and go elsewhere and the firm will be the loser. If it pays economically, the firm will maintain flexible work policies. Special treatment is always given to those who produce. Consider the rainmaker who spends days and hours on the golf course or engaged in civic and charitable endeavors and hears no complaints about a lack of billable hours. When equal treatment and flexible policies make good business sense, they will be employed. Our efforts must make good business sense for the firm, or we will earn less than our counterparts who make such efforts.

The second axiomatic principal for success in achieving fair treatment is that women must encourage and support each other. The queen bee cannot be the future. We must provide mentoring for our younger colleagues and become their unofficial "preceptors." As a young lawyer, I was told of a preceptor who admonished a new lawyer to remain civil and professional to opposing counsel. "Remember," he said, "that the other lawyer is representing his client, as you are representing yours. Your differences are not personal between the two of you, and you will go on to other cases where the two of you may be on the same side."

Recently I was involved in an effort to settle a marital dispute. When I objected to a last-minute additional demand, I was rewarded by a letter from another woman lawyer admonishing me and telling me, "I was disappointed in the tone of your letter." This kind of personal attack, with a copy of the letter sent to her client, is not only unnecessary, but represents the antithesis of the kind of mutual support and professionalism that will enhance our status in the profession and lead to equality. If we do not support and encourage each other, whom may we expect to do so?

ENDNOTES

1. *In re* Petition of Leach, 21 L.R.A. 701, 134 Ind. 665, 34 N.E. 641 (Ind. June 14, 1893) (citing *In re* Mary Hall, 50 Conn. 131 (1882).

2. Bradwell v. Illinois, 83 U.S. 130 (1873) ("[T]he civil law, as well as nature herself, has always recognized a wide difference in the respective spheres and destinies of man and woman. Man is, or should be, woman's protector and defender. The natural and proper timidity and delicacy which belongs to the female sex evidently unfits it for many of the occupations of civil life. The constitution of the family organization, which is founded in the divine ordinance, as well as in the nature of things, indicates the domestic sphere as that which properly belongs to the domain and functions of womanhood. The harmony, not to say identity, of interests and views which belong, or should belong to the family institution is repugnant to the idea of a woman adopting a distinct and independent career from that of her husband. So firmly fixed was this sentiment in the founders of the common law that it became a maxim of that system of jurisprudence that a woman had no legal existence separate from her husband, who was regarded as her head and representative in the social state; and, notwithstanding some recent modifications of this civil status, many of the special rules of law flowing from and dependent upon this cardinal principle still exist in full force in most States. One of these is, that a married woman is incapable, without her husband's consent, of making contracts which shall be binding on her or him. This very incapacity was one circumstance which the Supreme Court of Illinois deemed important in rendering a married woman incompetent fully to perform the duties and trusts that belong to the office of an attorney and counselor.").

3. *In re* Goodell, 292 Wis. 232, 245 (1875) (motion to admit Lavinia Goodell to bar).

4. *Id.*

5. For a fascinating account of one woman's experience, written in 1873, see Mary Abell's letter to her mother in Victorian Women, A Documentary Account of Women's Lives in Nineteenth Century England, France and the United States 312 (Erna Olafson Hellerstein et al. eds., Stanford Univ. Press 1981).

6. *Id.* at 324 (quote from dressmaker in London in 1840; she describes her working conditions: "The common hours at this establishment in the spring season are from 8 A.M. till 1 or 2 the next morning; often till 4 or 5. If they work till 4 or 5, they get up to work at 8 A.M. as usual. It very frequently happens that for 3 or 4 days in the week the hours are from 8 A.M. till 1, 2, 4, and 5 the next morning. It is almost invariably the case that the work is carried on all night, on the night before court days. On Saturday night it is usual to work till 3, 4, and 5 on Sunday morning. If the young persons fall asleep at work they are aroused by the overlooker. When witness an apprentice, has sometimes laid down on the rug and slept a few minutes, till she was called. In the intervals of the busy season the hours are from 8 A.M. till 10 P.M. . . . No particular times are allowed for meals, it is expected they should be taken as quickly as possible; [o]n an average, in the season, a quarter of an hour or less is all that is allowed for dinner. . . . All the workwomen, in the season about 50, work in one large room. In the season, with the sun in the day, and the lamps at night, this place is extremely hot and oppressive. Several young persons have fainted at their work. The sight is frequently affected.").

7. Margaret Talbot, *Mean Girls and the New Movement to Tame Them*, N.Y. Times Mag., Feb. 24, 2002, at 24.

8. Virginia G. Drachman, Sisters in Law, Women Lawyers in Modern American History 78 (1998).

9. Norma Shapiro, *Bench with a Point of View: How to Create Confidence in the Courtroom, in* The Woman Advocate 215, 217 (Jean Maclean Snyder & Andra Barmash Greene eds., ABA 1996).

10. Marina Angel, *Women in Legal Education: What It's Like to Be Part of a Perpetual First Wave or the Case of the Disappearing Women*, 61 Temp. L. Rev. 799, 808–09 (1988).

11. ABA COMM'N ON WOMEN IN THE PROFESSION, THE UNFINISHED AGENDA, WOMEN AND THE LEGAL PROFESSION 15 (2001) (prepared by Deborah L. Rhode). Reprinted with permission.

12. LaVerne Vines Collins, Chief, Public Information Office, U.S. Census Bureau, U.S. Department of Commerce (Feb. 28, 1997) (citing from "Census Facts for Women's History Month").

13. Nancy Blodgett, *I Don't Think That Ladies Should Be Lawyers*, A.B.A. J., THE LAW. MAG., Special Report on Gender Bias & Women in the Law, Dec. 1986, at 49.

14. SYLVIA ANN HEWLETT, CREATING A LIFE, PROFESSIONAL WOMEN AND THE QUEST FOR CHILDREN 149 (2002).

15. The Hon. Caroline "Carrie" Burnham Kilgore, Hon. Genevieve Blatt, Hon. Hazel Hemphill Brown, Hon. Wanda P. Chocallo, Hon. Lois G. Forer, Hon. Patricia A. Green, Hon. Doris May Harris, Hon. Judith J. Jamison, Hon. Phyllis A. Kravitch, Hon. Harriet M. Mims, Hon. Merna Marshall Reiter, Hon. Lisa A. Richette, Hon. Norma L. Shapiro, Hon. Dolores K. Sloviter, Hon. Juanita Kidd Stout, Hon. Carolyn Engel Temin, and Hon. Evelyn M. Trommer.

16. Robert Nigro, *Guideposts for New Generations*, 61 THE PHILA. LAW. 68 (1998).

17. Shapiro, *supra* note 9, at 218–19.

18. 42 U.S.C. § 2000e *et seq.* (1964).

19. *Id.* § 2000e-2(a)(1).

20. *Id.* § 2000e(k).

21. *Id.* § 2000e(b).

22. Hishon v. King & Spalding, 467 U.S. 69 (1984).

23. 42 U.S.C. § 1981a(a)(1) (1977).

24. Ezold v. Wolf, Block, Schorr and Solis-Cohen, 983 F.2d 509 (3d Cir. 1993).

25. Burke v. Friedman, 556 F.2d 867 (7th Cir. 1977); Hishon v. King & Spalding, 467 U.S. 69 (1984) (concurring opinion of Justice Powell).

26. EEOC v. Dowd & Dowd, Ltd., 736 F.2d 1177 (7th Cir. 1984).

27. Meritor Savings Bank v. Vinson et al., 477 U.S. 57 (1986).

28. A woman needs to demonstrate the following: (1) intentional discrimination because of sex, (2) pervasive and regular misconduct, (3) detrimental effect upon the woman plaintiff, (4) that the conduct would have a detrimental effect upon another reasonable person, and (5) respondeat

superior—that is, an employer who knew or should have known of the ongoing misconduct. Andrews v. City of Philadelphia, 895 F.2d 1469 (3d Cir. 1990) (totality of circumstances review); Lilly v. Roadway Exp., 6 Fed. App. 358, 2001 WL 312321 (7th Cir. 2001).

29. Germaine Greer, The Female Eunuch 313 (1970).

"A DAY IN THE LIFE"
LINDA, A BANKRUPTCY AND DIVORCE LAWYER FROM OMAHA, NEBRASKA

My day varies depending on any court appearances I might have, but my mornings are usually spent with paperwork—writing letters, motions, pleadings, bankruptcy filings, billing, and so on. I then spend some time returning any missed telephone calls and follow up with any necessary paperwork. In the afternoons, I see clients and run any necessary personal and business-related errands. In the evening I finish up anything that I wasn't able to complete during the day or prepare for any hearings coming up.

I spend a good deal of time working in front of a computer—doing research, writing letters, and generating documents. As a sole practitioner, I don't get a lot of interaction with other lawyers.

The best thing about being a sole practitioner is that I am able to pick and choose my cases. The worst thing is that I don't get a lot of interaction with other lawyers and have to deal with every emergency that arises.

This is a career that I think women can be flexible with in order to start a family, but primarily because I work for myself. I don't think I would have enough flexibility in a traditional law firm environment.

There are the challenges in acquiring business and being your own boss. Selling myself isn't my favorite activity and every social occasion is really a chance to sell myself, so I can't just sit and watch. I have to interact and be friendly.

Chapter Four

Career Choices

Develop your own talents to prepare yourself for a life of public service and do not depend upon men for life-sustaining gifts.[1]

Judge Lisa Richette

Women become lawyers for a variety of reasons: intellectual challenge, desire to help others, a sense of empowerment, financial rewards, and civic mindedness, to name just a few. Career paths in the law are many and varied. Graduating from law school and passing the bar exam does not imply only one type of future. It is only a beginning. Women can work on their own, in small firms, or in firms that have hundreds of lawyers. They can work in-house for a corporation or for government. They can practice in a variety of fields, such as criminal law, civil rights, taxation, real estate, estate planning, or family law, or in small firms in some combination of fields of law. The list goes on and on. They can become trial lawyers, spending much of their time in court. Or they can become law professors, teaching and writing in an academic atmosphere. They can clerk for judges or become judges. They can establish businesses of their own, performing services like alternative dispute resolution for litigants, or indeed any business at all. Or they can work in related fields, such as financial advising or pension planning. They can abandon the law entirely and engage in business, privately or in large companies. They can work from home or from the office or both. The possibilities are limited only by the imagination and determination of the individual.

Large Firms

Life in a large firm is in many ways like working for a large corporation, but worse. The firm is not selling cars or toasters; it is selling the lawyer's stock-in-trade—time. As a result, there is an overwhelming push for each lawyer to work as many hours as possible and to bill as many hours as possible. Lawyers in large firms are usually expected to bill 2,000 or more hours per year; when you consider that a lawyer must spend some time each day on nonbillable matters, such as administrative tasks or continuing legal education, a large-firm lawyer can expect to spend 50 to 60 hours a week at the office, or more. A 40-hour workweek is considered part-time. Late nights and weekends in the office are the norm. The lawyer accounts for each hour of each day, usually in ten-minute increments.

In a large firm, each lawyer eventually works in a selected department in one type of law practice. If you are in the tax department, you work only on tax issues. You may even be limited to one type of tax issue, such as domestic corporate mergers, partnership taxation, or real estate taxation. Unlike a lawyer in a smaller firm, you have little variety in the type of work you are expected to do, though the cases and clients change. If you enjoy being a specialist in one certain issue or type of transaction, then a large firm is best for you. But if the thought of analyzing shopping-center real estate agreements day in and day out drives you to distraction, then a large firm should not be your environment of choice.

On the other hand, a brief large-firm experience has its advantages. One Los Angeles lawyer writes:

> Large firms teach you a lot about practice. They have a broad clientele, which gives you the opportunity to see a lot of variety in the law and

obtain a lot of experience. They have a lot of support staff, which allows you to see how to manage your time and become a good biller.

In a large firm, for those who can handle the long hours, the financial rewards can be great, with the income of partners supplemented by the toils of associates. But long hours are not the only downside. One large-firm veteran observes:

> They may care for you and your family, but only so long as it doesn't affect their bottom line. Once your visibility changes (that is, your door is closed while you are pumping your breast milk three times or more per day, or you have doctor visits once a month for the first year for each child), it doesn't matter how you are performing because it makes partners nervous not to see their bees being busy. I figure that my child is young only once but, God willing, I'll have many years left to be a full-time lawyer. The law firm doesn't think this way.

Early in my career I participated in a multimillion-dollar closing on the sale of a privately held media business that took place in the offices of a large New York law firm. Midnight rolled around. The young lawyers had not yet left for the day. The cafeteria bustled and the second shift of secretaries was hard at work. It is no surprise that many lawyers burn out and depart after just a few years.

Solo or Small Firms (Being Your Own Boss)

Women who move from large firms into solo practice or into small firms are part of a recognized trend. A National Association for Law Placement study concluded that "less than 4 percent of lawyers leaving firms did so to pursue full-time family or community responsibilities. Rather, they move to more accommodating workplaces."[2] Inflexible schedules also are "a primary cause of early attrition and glass ceilings for women in law firms."[3]

Like me, a number of women lawyers have opted for solo or small firms to make their lives work, and statistics reflect a growing trend in this direction. For example, in 1920, 32 percent of women practicing law were in private individual practice, 41 percent in 1939, and 43 percent in 1949.⁴ In preparing this book, I received many comments like this one from a woman in Columbus, Ohio:

> I was a partner with a twenty-member firm and quit two years ago to open my own firm to regain control of my schedule.

For me, private practice in a small firm affords the greatest control and flexibility over my schedule. Other than court dates, I can generally arrange my week to accommodate any school play, class trip, or doctor's appointment for my son or myself. That is not to say I have never needed to rely upon a network of friends and family to back me up from time to time.

The women in my class and in generations before us have had varied approaches to balancing work and domestic spheres. Many have chosen to go out on their own or enter small firms. Fellow 1980 graduate Carmen Matos has chosen this road after having first been employed with the U.S. Department of Housing and Urban Development. As a trial lawyer with the U.S. Equal Employment Opportunity Commission for fourteen years, Carmen's busy schedule included travel from Pennsylvania to West Virginia, New Jersey, and Delaware. In 1995, Carmen left the government and two years later became a sole practitioner. She explains:

> I really enjoy being a sole practitioner since it gives me flexibility in time. This allows me to be involved more with my family. It also allows me more involvement in client selection and in the cases I work on. . . . In hindsight, I wish I would have gone into private practice sooner. Private practice has given me flexibility in terms of being with my family. I think women need to be aware of this as a real option—law school should include courses on how to set up your own practice. I think women should be aware that it is possible to balance both a legal career and a home.

After a six-month position as a clerk to a Philadelphia Court of Common Pleas judge, Jacqueline M. Roberts became a sole practitioner in Philadelphia and has remained self-employed all these years. She began her own title insurance agency in 1983, and was the first licensed minority title agent in the Commonwealth of Pennsylvania. She says of her experiences:

> Being a single parent since the age of eighteen, there were times when I thought I would not make it through another day. However, I am strong and persistent and I'm still here. I knew that I had to be self-employed when I interned in the D.A.'s office during the second summer of law school and had to write three memos to obtain permission to leave once by 3:30 p.m. to pick up my child's report card. I thought there had to be a better way. Private practice allowed me to arrange my afternoons so that I could be a parent. I would pick her up after school and return to work. I would continue my duties and she would do her homework.

Barbara Vetri, a graduate of the Temple University Law School class of 1960, found her most flexible work arrangement was with another lawyer/mother. Barbara was able to maintain a schedule that permitted her to work from 9:00 to 5:00 and take off evenings and weekends. She and her partner covered for each other in and out of work, depending upon what was needed. If she had to be in court with a client, her partner could take her child to the doctor. Barbara turned down offers of partnership with male lawyers in small firms over the course of her career because she had found the perfect professional situation—one that afforded her the flexibility to devote time to her family, free of pressure or disapproval from an outside employer. Barbara firmly believed that only another woman would be accepting of her desire to be part of her children's lives.

Patricia Hirsch Frankel was admitted to the Pennsylvania bar in 1958, having been an undergraduate student at Bryn Mawr College and law school graduate of the class of 1957 of the University of Pennsylvania. Her graduating class of ninety-nine people included just three or four women. Patricia Hirsch Frankel is a resident of the town of Reading, Pennsylvania, about an hour's drive north of Philadelphia, at the foot of the Poconos. She married before law school and confesses, "I never became a 'high-powered' lawyer, nor did I ever make a lot of money. I opted to focus more on family than career and remained a sole practitioner in order to do that." As she sums up her experiences, "I have had (thank God) a wonderful life."

Kathryn Carlson began law school when she was thirty-one, on a part-time basis so she could balance school with being a mother of two preschool children. Given the demands of both, it is an incredible achievement. Later, being part of a small firm afforded her the flexibility to work and be a mother. She writes:

> Working for the county and being in a small firm helped me to balance career and home life. As a county employee, I had steady and reasonable hours. When working in a small two-person firm, I had the flexibility to be at home when necessary. I was also able to work from home at times. Nevertheless, it was not easy to balance a family and a full-time career. You make sacrifices in both but you also receive great rewards in personal satisfaction. One thing that helped me was having my children before starting law school. I did not have to interrupt my career when they were born. By the time I started working full-time, both of my children were in school all day. I have seen numerous young mothers struggle with being away from their preschool children to practice law.

Being in private practice means being master of your own ship. When I spoke with Deborah Willig, first woman Philadelphia Bar Association Chancellor and partner in the labor law firm of Willig, Williams & Davidson, she brightened as the subject of the anticipated arrival of her life partner's baby arose. As a leading partner of her law firm, Deborah can set her schedule, to the extent work permits, to accommodate her new domestic sphere. She already maintains a flexible schedule, albeit full-time, by working later at night and arriving later in the morning.

Another Los Angeles lawyer left her large firm after the birth of a child to take back control of her schedule. She writes:

> Three and a half years ago, I had a baby. I thought I would want to go back to work. When people asked while I was pregnant if I was going to

continue working, I was insulted that people would assume I wouldn't continue to work. After my daughter was born, my entire perspective changed. I didn't want to go back to work. I was working in a firm an hour from home. After three months of working after maternity leave, I left and went into solo practice from my home office so I could be with my daughter when I wanted to, not when my firm let me leave. (My daughter is with relatives for about fifteen hours a week). I have learned that you cannot have the absolute best of both worlds, but I feel I have come close. The nature of my practice allows me to work on my computer at night and schedule a lot of daytime hours with my daughter. I feel as though my life is "24/7" for both work and family but my quality of life is very good! My practice is going strong and I believe my daughter has benefited from being home with her mom almost all of the time. It is very hard to do both. I am glad for my law degree because it let me be my own boss.

Short of finding the most understanding employer, being one's own boss is, for many women, the best of all worlds.

Demanding Fields: Labor, Mergers and Acquisitions, and Litigation

Not all fields offer the flexibility that comes with being one's own boss. Deborah Willig is a high-profile labor negotiator in Philadelphia. Even though she is a founding partner in her firm, with a great deal of independence in establishing her daily schedule, full-blown labor negotiations can usurp all other preoccupations. At times, labor negotiations carry on for weeks, around the clock, with barely enough time to rush home for fresh clothes.

A trial lawyer has almost no flexibility or control over the day. If a case has been prepared for trial, in many jurisdictions, the lawyers receive only twenty-four hours' notice to appear in court and begin selecting a jury. The paperwork accumulated for litigation—motions, pleadings, discovery documents, exhibits, and expert reports—can fill a room and must be organized and ready for trial when the court calls. There are time constraints for filing pleadings, time constraints for answering, and severe consequences involving malpractice if deadlines are missed. Litigation is an all-encompassing line of work. You cannot step back and say you need to be at a class play or have a freezer delivered instead of appearing in court. If a case is to be tried on Monday, your weekend will be spent getting prepared and not biking in the park.

Susan Schulman, a Philadelphia trial lawyer, has worked as a plaintiff's lawyer specializing in medical malpractice and products liability. She relates:

> Being a trial lawyer puts incredibly difficult demands on your time and ability to deal with anything other than work. It is not an area that meshes well with raising a family. Working independently allows for more time, less stress, and greater flexibility. However, it is less secure and less financially productive.

There can be great satisfaction in being a plaintiff's trial lawyer and the financial rewards can be tantalizing. For some, the benefits outweigh the enormous time demands and stress that are part of a trial lawyer's life. Defense work rarely provides the same financial rewards, except in a large firm.

Not unlike the intensity of litigation or a labor contract dispute, mergers-and-acquisitions practice offers little or no flexibility while everyone is in the midst of completing a deal. Buying and selling companies, whether privately owned or publicly held, is a fast-paced and intense occupation that generates an enormous volume of documents connected to financing and disclosure, in preparation for an agreed-upon "closing date" that can rarely be postponed. At least that closing date is usually scheduled well in advance. While deals are being struck, no one goes home for the night for a personal appointment.

Nontraditional Field—Tax Law

Some fields of law have always been perceived as best suited for women. For example, fields involving the representation of women and children, like family law, have been considered naturally suited to women lawyers. Today, many accomplished women lawyers can be found in more nontraditional areas, such as tax and finance, where they are often in the minority. The field of tax law has traditionally been an all-male, blue-suit bastion, but times are changing. I was attracted to the field of tax law for its clarity and intellectual challenges. Professor Alice Abreu has written about her interest in specializing in tax law:

> I became a tax lawyer because I found tax challenging and fascinating as a law student when I took my first tax course. I love the intellectual challenge and the rigor of it, but I am also drawn by the deeper meaning of taxation, for in a tax system a society reveals its values.[5]

A tax practice affects all other fields, including family law, where there is a transfer of assets or accumulation of wealth. I have found that my tax practice is far from dry and practical—on the contrary, it invokes more than its fair share of human drama.

Counsel to the Court

Serving as counsel to the court is unlike the daily practice of law in many respects. The "client" is the judiciary and the issues are matters of law and legal interpretation. The office is with the court and compensation is salaried. The job offers some level of stability. Most state supreme courts have counsel positions, as does the U.S. Tax Court.

Taylor Williams currently works as counsel to the Pennsylvania Supreme Court. Her experiences leading to her present position include a clerkship with a Philadelphia Common Pleas Court judge and several years as a litigation associate with a midsized Philadelphia firm. In her position as counsel to the court, Taylor primarily litigates cases on behalf of Pennsylvania's justices, judges, and the judicial system. Taylor considers her work "fun" as, in her words, she gets to "wrestle with constitutional and federalism issues, argue frequently before the Third Circuit [Court of Appeals], and help develop some distinct doctrines related to the judiciary and judiciary decisions." The job is not entirely legal research; as Taylor explains, there is ample opportunity to appear in appellate court to argue before the federal bench.

A job that differs somewhat from counsel to the court is that of law clerk, a position often filled by recent law school graduates. A clerkship usually has a one- or two-year term, and offers a wonderful opportunity to learn the ropes before entering private practice or moving to a government position. It involves intensive research and writing drafts of opinions for review and issuance by the judge. Some law clerks use the position as a stepping-stone to a position of counsel to the court, and some derive such enjoyment from their work and the general flexibility granted by most judges that they stay permanently. Of course, much depends upon the court itself, and there is a significant difference in clerking for the U.S. Supreme Court and, for example, a lower trial court.

Government Practice

Many women seek government positions for the guaranteed income, generous insurance benefits, paid vacation, and sick leave. Because of the enormous difficulties in maintaining a private practice—generating clients and all the other things involved in being in business—and because of the enormous time pressures of working for a large firm, many women consider government to be a good alternative. Government service can offer interesting work, job security, and good benefits. Nevertheless, women should be cautioned that government work, particularly in our underfunded and understaffed cities, can also be enormously demanding.

Describing the opportunities in government employment is like describing the classifications for all living things. To begin, there is the division of federal, state, and local governments. Washington D.C. is a magnet for people, young and old, who come to work for the federal government in the legislature, the judiciary, the White House, or the numerous federal agencies that oversee all aspects of our lives. In addition to our politicians holding elected office, there are myriads of support staff, many with legal degrees, whose work involves drafting laws and regulations, overseeing the congressional library, and advising our lawmakers and the president. Federal workers employed throughout the country do the work of federal agencies, most notably the local offices of the Internal Revenue Service and the Environmental Protection Agency. Wherever there is a federal district court, there will be an office of federal prosecutors who represent the federal government in prosecuting individuals who violate federal laws.

Our state governments likewise have numerous opportunities for employment. Pennsylvania's Leslie Anne Miller, the first woman to serve as president of the Pennsylvania Bar Association, was appointed general counsel to newly elected Governor Rendell. She oversees the work of nearly five hundred Pennsylvania government lawyers. Each agency or department within the Commonwealth of Pennsylvania is staffed with its own chief counsel. The departments of revenue, education, retirement benefits, and labor and industry, for example, all require the services of lawyers. Not only does Leslie oversee the work of each department, she advises the governor on legal issues affecting the Commonwealth of Pennsylvania, sometimes appearing in court on its behalf or addressing the passage of new legislation. Those who work in state agencies may find themselves outside the office and in front of a judge on legal matters when the state's interests are at stake, such as in collecting revenue or advocating the interests of minors, beneficiaries of trusts, or nonprofit institutions.

Finally, our cities and local governments hold many opportunities for lawyers. In larger cities, like my own Philadelphia, the government is represented by a large staff of city solicitors who work in even greater subdivisions of specialties ranging from housing, labor, contracts, revenue collection, equal employment, insurance, and so on. City solicitors represent the city when other lawyers sue on account of personal injuries from a sidewalk slip-and-fall. Criminals are prosecuted by the city's office of the district attorney. In our cities and local communities, there are opportunities for lawyers on zoning boards, school boards, and revenue departments.

Many new lawyers work for the government initially to gain experience in particular areas before entering private practice. Washington tax lawyer Jane Bergner began her law career working for the government. The formal benefits, generous maternity leave policy, and relative job security offered by a federal government job were enormously attractive to her as a young mother. Jane also found that by working for the government, she had some flexibility in her schedule and could still "leave work for the kids" when struggling to manage her share of car-pool duty.

There is a general perception that the hours are more predictable and manageable in government employment. This is not always so, particularly for legal staff. Cheryl Kritz, Chief Deputy City Solicitor for the Philadelphia Commercial Law Unit, Corporate & Tax Group, works long hours and weekends. Government offers her employment security, challenging work, authority, and leadership within the city solicitor's office, as well as the opportunity to be at the center of the action where she meets frequently with the mayor and city council. There is rarely a lull in the action. But . . . in a city that never sleeps (not New York—Philadelphia!) Cheryl finds that her workload easily spills over into weekends, vacations, and late nights. Her work is often unpredictable and we frequently must reschedule lunch around an emergency gathering of political forces that requires her presence. When her family takes to the mountains for ski weekends, Cheryl takes work. When the rest of the city has the day off for a government holiday, Cheryl is at the office catching up on work. The city is notoriously understaffed and those who work there never coast.

The District Attorney

Many young women work for their local governments in the district attorney departments, prosecuting those arrested for breaking criminal laws. This is an enormously demanding occupation and, in Philadelphia, it is commanded by District Attorney Lynne Abraham. A district attorney is a trial lawyer, and the job is as demanding as any trial work that exists. There are witnesses to interview, cases to prepare, victims to ready for trial, and an overwhelming caseload. As with any trial lawyer, the day's schedule is dictated by the will of the judge who decides when a case is tried and when to break for the day.

A day in the life of a district attorney in Philadelphia starts in court and ends late in the evening back at the office, doing paper work, preparing for trials the next day, locating and talking to witnesses, and returning every telephone call that came in that day—a requirement of D.A. Abraham. The district attorney appears at trial, motions, and arraignments, seeing a prosecution through the steps of due process. It is a difficult job for a woman with young children and offers very little flexibility whatsoever. This enormously necessary work promises a life with the intensity of a trial lawyer, the overworked (and relatively underpaid) schedule of a government employee, and the stress of engaging in life, death, and liberty issues on a daily basis. At times—depending upon the case, the victim, or the perpetrator—newspaper or television reporters scrutinize the D.A.'s work almost as poignantly as the length of her skirt or the style of her hair.

In-House Counsel

Some large corporations engage lawyers to work for them "in-house" as corporate employees. Midlevel associates in larger firms may find themselves approached by their corporate clients to jump ship and work in-house. These jobs are as varied in nature as their employers. Often, in-house lawyers advise management on issues pertaining to employment, discrimination, employee benefits, leases, service contracts, and general operational matters. Other times, in-house counsel are engaged to deal with outside firms in connection with mergers, acquisitions, environmental issues, defense of lawsuits, or union activities. According to Catalyst, "Women in Law, Making the Case, Executive Summary" (2001) page 2; and ABA Commission on Women in the Profession, "A Current Glance of Women in the Law" (2002), women account for only 13.7 percent of general counsel of Fortune 500 companies. Only 10 percent of all women lawyers work in private industry or associations. The imprint of the woman lawyer on major private industry is slow in the making.

Adelina Gerace Martorelli is currently employed with Nationwide Trust Company in Newark, Delaware, as a trust officer. She "works with clients, their attorneys, and investment advisors to help plan their estates and financial plans." Adelina graduated from college with a business degree and quickly decided in law school that she would seek a career applying business law. She has worked for various profit and nonprofit corporations, often where she was the only woman present at meetings. But for Adelina, a mother as well as a lawyer, "at night and on weekends . . . family is key." Working in-house for Nationwide affords her that time away from the job.

One Chicago-based lawyer appreciates the flexibility afforded by working as in-house counsel to a large national corporation. She still must bill 1,800 hours per year and travel once a month, but her Monday-to-Friday schedule is tailored to allow her to arrive at 7:00 in the morning, leave by 5:30 on Monday, Wednesday, and Thursday and by 12:30 on Tuesday, and remain home the entire day on Friday. In contrast, if she had continued working in a large firm on a "partnership track," she would have been required to work nights and weekends to bill 2,200 hours per year.

The Judiciary

A career in the judiciary can be immensely rewarding, and the office solves many problems for women. What to wear? Black robes! What name to be called by? "Your honor" or "Judge." The office brings respect and the government pay scale ensures parity with men. The hours are controllable to some extent, and scheduling around major family events can be arranged in advance. But once a trial starts, the flexibility of a judge's schedule disappears. The courtroom drama commands the energies of judge, jury, lawyers, and witnesses for however long the trial takes. It can be days or weeks before a case is completed. During the course of the trial, lawyers may raise objections to questions asked by the opposing lawyer and a judge must rule immediately from the bench on whether a question is proper or an answer allowed. In a jury trial, the judge instructs the jury on how to debate the facts and law when reaching a verdict.

Outside the courtroom, judges are called upon to rule on written motions regarding all sorts of issues, such as the admissibility of evidence, the scope of allowable testimony, the limits of discovery, and the sufficiency of the pleadings prepared by the lawyers. At some levels, the judge must write an opinion detailing the basis for the decision rendered in a case. When there is disagreement about how a trial judge ruled upon an issue or objection, an appeal can be made to a higher court. Appellate judges listen to lawyers' arguments and read briefs arguing legal issues before they write opinions of their own on whether lower-court rulings should stand or be overturned. Most judges and justices relish the opportunity to write. In some cases, a full day on the bench hearing legal arguments is followed by long evenings of writing and rewriting an opinion that can withstand the scrutiny of any subsequent appellate review.

Just as there are many layers to government work, the judiciary has many subdivisions in which to find careers. Federal and state courts have trial levels and appellate levels where the nature of the work varies from finding facts to interpreting the law or establishing legal precedent. There are additional federal courts that overlay this simple description. The U.S. Tax Court, a federal trial court based in Washington, D.C., tries cases in most major cities around the country, with the expressed purpose of trying tax disputes. Courts of claims, bankruptcy courts, and courts of patents and customs are all specialized federal trial courts.

Perhaps more accessible are the numerous local lower courts that touch our lives on a very real and everyday basis; these courts provide interesting opportunities for employment. Small-claims courts, sometimes known as municipal courts, are sprinkled throughout local townships and typically address claims of $20,000 or less. These courts rarely render written opinions, and though their decisions can be appealed to trial courts, their rulings are usually accepted. Hearing officers, sometimes called masters, do the bulk of the work in family courts, dispensing justice on matters of child custody, support, division of property, and legal grounds for divorce. Intake officers known as "trustees" interview Chapter 7 applicants under the federal bankruptcy code and make quick determinations of eligibility in routine interview sessions. Social security masters/hearing officers use informal hearings to determine eligibility for benefits. Privately, there are numerous opportunities to serve as arbitrators or mediators in dispute resolution, an alternative that many choose instead of going to court. (But do not count on becoming Judge Judy.)

The opportunities are many, yet women remain a minority in the judiciary—as of this writing, they comprise two of nine U.S. Supreme Court justices, 19.2 percent of U.S. district court judges, 20.1 percent of U.S. circuit court judges, and 26.3 percent of justices on state courts of last resort.[6] Statistics in local courts can be much lower. In some federal district courts and local state county courts, there is a complete absence of women on the bench. I believe the increased number of women in the legal profession will, in time, result in increased numbers of women in the judiciary.

For women, a judgeship can offer stability not found in private practice, with opportunities to create flexibility in the daily schedule, as it is the judge who sets the trial schedule. However, mounting a campaign for judgeship can be a roadblock, given the enormous time and expense required for the election process in the state judiciary system or the political process in the federal system.

My classmate Toby Dickman successfully ran for the Montgomery County Court of Common Pleas in Pennsylvania. She is a great resource for any woman wanting to follow in her footsteps. Montgomery County is, or was at the time, predominately Republican, and so the future Judge Dickman joined that party when she began her quest for the judgeship. Campaigning is an enormously time-consuming endeavor. Candidates spend most nights of the week and weekend speaking, meeting, and socializing with groups like rotary clubs and professional associations, all of which takes considerable time away from hearth and home. Judge Dickman did so, which in her situation meant time away from her husband, also a lawyer, and young daughter.

Pennsylvania Supreme Court Justice Sandra Newman also experienced a lengthy campaign for election, which took her far from home, her husband, and children. Justice Newman visited every county in Pennsylvania to secure her election. Once elected, a judgeship can bring stability to a woman's life, but getting elected requires enormous sacrifices.

I asked Eastern District Senior Court Judge Norma Shapiro this question: If I picked up any court opinion, could I tell whether it was written by a woman or a man? Her answer was no. Women's and men's decisions are equivalent, addressing issues of fact and law. But we agreed that a woman's presence on the bench preserves the notion of equal representation and opportunity to be heard, and that a diverse judiciary reflects our diverse population and engenders greater respect for the system. Some, like Justice Sandra Newman, believe that women bring special qualities to the judiciary. They are typically sensitive and good listeners, and possess good communication skills; above all, they bring to the human drama another perspective grounded in a woman's life experience.

Law School Professor

Although some may view the life of a law professor as an ideal position for women with young children, that view can be deceptive. Like any teaching position, most of the work is done outside the classroom in preparation for the lesson that day. Professor Laura Little, a former Supreme Court law clerk and now professor at Temple University's Beasley Law School, reports that a lot of the work is not obvious or visible to the outside observer. Though she often has the ability to rearrange her schedule to attend "major life events," she is constrained by the class preparation, research, and writing that fill the days and hours around classroom time. To retain their status, law professors must publish scholarly works with some frequency. During the summer months you can find them squirreled away in their offices, trying not to answer telephone calls, and writing, writing, writing.

Women seeking law school positions are hampered by any reluctance to relocate their families to go where the jobs are, and by becoming sidetracked with family concerns that prevent them from putting in the effort required to obtain these positions.[7] Temple University Law School Professor Diane Maleson told me about a number of offers she received from out-of-state law schools for deanship positions that she turned down to avoid uprooting her children and her husband. Professor Maleson started teaching at Temple Law School in 1977, with two children under the age of five. After some trial and error, and at the cost of nearly her entire paycheck, she was able to find a woman to help with watching the children. Even with full-time help, Professor Maleson was home by 4:00 or 5:00 in the afternoon and, with rare exceptions for a night class, was home for the rest of the evening with her family. Professor Maleson described her schedule for ten years: wake up at 6:30 a.m. with the children, head to work by 8:30, arrive home by 4:00, prepare dinner, spend time with family, and work from 10:00 p.m. until midnight. It can be done.

In the 1950s and 1960s, the presence of women as law school faculty members was even more rare than the presence of women as law students. Of 1,239 faculty positions nationally in 1950, 5 were held by women. In 1960, only 11 of 1,645 law faculty were women. The women who attended law school in those years rarely, if ever, had a woman law professor. Most law schools hired their first women law professors in the 1970s. Columbia hired its first woman law professor, Ruth Bader Ginsburg, in 1972. In 1974, women held only 5 of 157 law school dean positions. Statistics compiled by the American Bar Association and the Association of American Law Schools reflect that by 2001, there were significant increases since midcentury, with women holding approximately 31 percent of all full-time law school faculty positions and 28 percent of all part-time faculty positions.[8]

Examining these statistics more closely regarding tenure reveals that women make up approximately 28 percent of all tenured faculty. More women are found as legal research/writing instructors or adjunct professors. Neither position offers the prospect of tenure. Rather than hiring professors on a tenure basis, universities are increasingly hiring them "under contract." The implication of hiring "under contract" is a subject of great debate. Professor Maleson has noticed that universities across the board, in all schools, are being forced by severe economic constraints to hire contract professors. The short-term contract arrangement permits flexibility in hiring and firing. But Professor Marina Angel sees the loss of tenure positions as disproportionately harmful to women. In her view, based upon an analysis of five Philadelphia-area schools, these positions are disproportionately offered to women.[9] Women law professors are often the first women lawyers law students meet. They have a tremendous impact upon the image law students will have of women in the profession, and can be important role models to the young women taking their classes. Though their increased presence in law schools is a welcome trend, women professors should have opportunities to achieve tenured status rather than filling the ranks of the lower-tiered writing and research faculty. That itself sends to male and female students a negative message about women's opportunities.

Alternative Careers

I have only begun to describe the variety of ways a law degree can be put to good use. Another example is shown by Wendy Girardin, a Florida lawyer who parlayed her legal experience and passion for espionage into a private business as a professional investigator. Wendy is an expert assistant to other lawyers in asset location, business valuation, and case settlement analysis. Michele Lellouch is a software specialist in Jacksonville, Florida. She maintains and updates retirement plan software in an office that is the antithesis of a stodgy law firm and where jeans and shorts are the normal attire. Cherie Fuchs, a 1980 graduate of Temple University Law School, is a member of the Judge Advocate General, holding the distinguished position of colonel in the U.S. Army Reserves. Greta Van Susteren is a television legal commentator who the public came to know through her on-the-air contributions during the O.J. Simpson trial. Lisa Scottoline is the best-selling author of a series of mystery novels featuring the partners of an all-woman law firm in Philadelphia. Hillary Clinton became a U.S. senator, and Congresswoman Geraldine Ferraro ran for vice president of the United States. The possibilities are endless. A legal degree is the key that unlocks the door to them all.

Business

A lot of men have used law school as a prelude to entering business. There is no reason why women cannot do the same. My law school classmate Susan Holmes is currently designing and making jewelry for her own business called ACCESSORIES BY SUSAN. She has never practiced law, and believes she entered law school "for all the wrong reasons." She writes that as a graduate of Stoneybrook College in 1976, the message for young women "was to break into a man's world." That meant shunning teaching or psychology—"girls' jobs"— and "go for something tougher." In business for a short while, Susan and her family moved from New York City to the suburbs where, contrary to her original fears, she did not go "to suburb hell" or turn into "Donna Reed or June Cleaver." Susan is the mother of two teenagers and, by her account, does not bake cookies or bread or drive a minivan. Her business in Chappaqua, New York, is thriving.

Karen W. McDonie, also a classmate of mine, lives in Texas, where she and her husband raise cattle, Irish Draught, and Irish Sporthorses. She writes, "I spend a great deal of time outdoors with a fair amount of physical labor and very little time behind a desk! The transition from law was sometimes confusing and the learning curve steep, but I don't miss the practice of law. My education and training has been invaluable—analytical skills, issue identification, and marketing are tools I draw on daily." Before moving to Texas in 1996, Karen was a corporate lawyer with Rohm and Haas, a job that entailed extensive travel to European subsidiaries and work in the marketing and purchasing departments. She served as corporate secretary for a number of years.

Jane Broderson, a 1983 law graduate of Cornell and mother of five boys (ages one to fifteen), has created several businesses, combining her practical skills as a lawyer with her creative muse "to think outside the box." Out of law school, Jane created an adoption agency that grew to employ a staff of twelve with statewide prestige. Her philosophy was proactive, encouraging couples to be involved in the adoption process. Her legal skills were called upon when it came to the nuts-and-bolts of the adoptions. Jane sold her business and took time out for full-time motherhood, but then started a new business as an executive recruiter. When business waned, she began a third enterprise. Having experienced the mind-numbing boredom of a typical continuing legal education (CLE) session, Jane began a successful CLE operation in a comfortable setting with music and dynamic speakers. Her operation proved not only financially successful, but also enormously beneficial in expanding her network of lawyers in the community. Having sold most of her ownership in this last enterprise, Jane now applies her talents from 9:00 to 3:00 at a nationally based staffing agency, devoting much of her energies to sales and marketing. Being in business for herself is something Jane has always enjoyed. Her experience working at a large firm for two years further convinced Jane that this was her niche. One New Year's Eve, a Friday night, Jane was called by one of her senior partners and assigned a project that had been overlooked and was due after the weekend. A large firm "owns you," she offers. In business, Jane can be creative, independent, and her own boss.

New Opportunities

Senior women lawyers remarked to me that they have observed new opportunities for women in fields of law that were once so difficult to enter. Senior Philadelphia Court of Common Pleas Judge Lisa Richette observes that today, women are trial lawyers in important cases and have those cases routinely assigned to them. In contrast, when she was an assistant district attorney, she was "relegated" to family court. I am mindful of the fact that many of these women were offered positions as librarians, stenographers, and telephone answerers when they began. Senior lawyer Catherine Barone remembers:

> There just is no comparison, in my opinion, about the opportunities today as compared with when I graduated. So many firms wanted to hire the woman graduates as secretaries and not lawyers. It was tough getting a job. Some dear friends of mine worked for almost nothing to get experience and then went on their own. I was just lucky because I could take shorthand well and type well. Upon graduation, I secured an appointment as law clerk to then Pennsylvania Supreme Court Justice Maxey. He only kept his clerks for about one year and then got them jobs. He secured me a position with the Legal Department of the Pennsylvania Railroad.

Eyebrows are no longer raised when women lawyers are present. Labor negotiators like Doreen Davis and Deborah Willig note that at times they may be the only women at the negotiating table, which might take some labor leaders aback. But not for long. More women are gaining acceptance in traditionally male fields, such as securities transactions, labor negotiations, tax, judgeships, and business trans-actions—even though women remain in the minority. Professor Alice Abreu concurs: "We should bring our insights and our diversity to different areas of the law—including tax and business areas—where we continue to be seriously under-represented."[10]

When I attended my first ABA Tax Section meeting in Washing-ton D.C. in 1981, I was one of a handful of women members. Today the female presence is much greater, but still the section remains predominantly male; the breakdown of membership has remained constant since December 2001, at 79 percent men and 21 percent women. Pamela Olson recently became the first woman chair of the section. The tax field seems to remain one of those male-dominated specialties, perhaps for the same reason that business law proves so difficult for women to enter: the lack of mentors and professional relationships that help build practices and financial success.

In other respects, the practice of law has changed for men and for women over the years. Taylor Williams observes:

> Certainly the last generation of lawyers saw the influx of lawyer adver-tising and the change from trial lawyer (who simply tried cases) to liti-gator (who engages in endless discovery and motion practice). But the law, like everything else, evolves. Of necessity, we have many more lawyers now than there were in 1980, new specialties, new kinds of suits being brought, new statutes to apply. With the exploding case-loads that courts must deal with, certainly the law has changed. And, so long as the change is from the good old boys (white) club we graduated into, to a profession, which includes women and minorities, the profes-sion has changed for the better.
>
> In fact, many of the changes are positive ones: alternative dispute resolution is certainly an example. Studies show that the influx of women into the law has brought new and different problem-solving skills into the profession. New practice specialties are developing and available to the practitioner.

Most often decried is the change that has brought about a decline in civility among lawyers, leading to the adoption of new written ethics standards that, in truth, have had little impact upon ongoing misbehavior.

Recommending the Practice of Law to Women

Success and satisfaction are attained by developing your own skills to serve others.[11]

District Court Judge Norma Shapiro

The women who shared their experiences in this book offered their endorsement of a law career for young women as they begin their work lives. A law degree opens the door to infinite possibilities and careers, and, for that reason alone, many women find that a law degree is just the beginning. Taylor Williams, counsel to the Pennsylvania Supreme Court, writes:

> I know former lawyers who have abandoned the law, who tell me they hated the law and they hated other lawyers. I believe, however, that those nay-sayers just didn't find their legal job fit. There are a vast number of law and law-related jobs; if one law job isn't fulfilling, certainly another might be. It's not a perfect profession, but I see lawyers as persons with the potential to lead in any area. Our justice system is the best one the world has yet come up with, and it is a great thing to be a part of that machinery—and to work to make it better. I am proud to be a lawyer, and would recommend it as a profession. The more good people we recruit to the law, the stronger our profession will become.

Finding the "right fit" requires a sense of priorities about life. Paula M. Szortyka, an assistant district attorney in Bucks County, Pennsylvania, offers the following:

> Whether a career in the law is a good choice for the young women of today depends on just what that young woman wants out of her career. I believe that it's a very good choice even if one is a young mother.

Unless the young woman wants to make a lot of money in a certain length of time, she can pretty much tailor her hours as she chooses in order to balance motherhood and career. I see young mothers doing just that and having a very interesting and satisfying life experience. On the other hand, if one wants to get to the top in a high-powered law firm, then the hours are long and I see those women who practically give up any personal life. So it's up to the individual.

One self-employed family law lawyer offers similar advice about finding a "legal fit" that is just right, and she gives some hints about her personal leanings:

Although it is hard to know how your life will play out, think about the things you want out of life and plan how you will achieve those goals in the context of being a lawyer. Will you work for yourself or be a government lawyer? Do you want to make partner and be a big-shot lawyer? That's okay, but understand that your family and family life will take a back seat to your life. If you are a blue-collar single mom and you have no choice but to work, that's one thing. But, in my opinion, spending 100K and doing all the hard work to become a lawyer, you should be able to have some control in your work and family life. What is the point of having kids if you are going to have a nanny raise them while you are in your office from 7:00 a.m. to 6:00 p.m. each day?

Nancy, a lawyer for the state trial judges in Florida, with seventeen years of experience, offers her perspective:

There are many options for a person with a legal education. I think the worst option for a balanced life is the law firm, billable-hours path. There are many ways to use legal writing, legal research, public speaking, public performance, legal analysis, and other skills one might attain from a legal education and legal positions. Young women must define their goals and keep refining them. This allows a person to choose law-related jobs that lead to those goals. I would recommend the legal field to a young woman who is language-oriented and enjoys people, history, and a touch of gossip.

One of the advantages of a legal career is the opportunity to shift from one employment situation to another. A judgeship is usually the culmination of work as an associate, and then as partner in a law firm. Women lawyers need not feel "stuck" in a bad employment situation. Alexis, working in a large law firm doing trusts and estates work, advises:

> Don't feel that your only option is to conform to the norm/ideal of working for a big law firm or corporation. Make your own way.

Women recommend the practice of law to other women for very much the same reasons they felt motivated to become lawyers: the opportunity to effectuate change, find interesting work, and become financially secure. Adelina Gerace Martorelli offers:

> Yes, I would recommend a law career for women today and I think that it can be for women of any age. I just recently met a woman in her fifties who had been a nurse. She went to law school in her late thirties and now has her own law firm that handles hospital issues. She felt that she had enough experience and knowledge in health issues to make a difference in the health industry. She wants to effect change, and in becoming a lawyer, she can.

Kathryn Carlson hesitates to recommend the field of law to younger women, because of the constant conflict in her practice of family law that just may not be suitable for everyone. And yet she concludes:

> On the other hand, the work is always challenging and interesting. I seldom have a dull day or one in which I feel I have not accomplished something. How many people can say that?

The growing lack of civility among lawyers—male and female—is sharply noted by many lawyers and is one of the biggest drawbacks to endorsing a legal career wholeheartedly. Kathryn Carlson, a trial lawyer in Bucks County, notes:

> Since 1980, the number of lawyers has increased and the competition for business is greater. Along with that comes less collegiality among

lawyers and greater anonymity. Both foster a more negative atmosphere and less civility between lawyers. The issue of civility has been a hot topic lately and rightly so.

Trial lawyer Susan Schulman shares the following, after twenty-three years of practicing law:

> The level of sophistication has increased in trial practice, which makes each case more challenging. However, there is less camaraderie among opponents, and maintaining pleasant adversarial postures is harder to do. When each point is litigated to its death, the lawyers either burn out quickly or become entrenched in opposition. It seemed easier to conduct good working relationships with opposing counsel than it is now.

Friction among lawyers is just an extra drag on the work that needs to be done. Lawyers who seek an advantage by misbehaving do a disservice to the profession. You know who they are: lawyers who "redraft" agreements on their own PCs and sneak in changes, lawyers who alter documents without providing marked-up drafts for opposing counsel to review, and lawyers who serve pleadings after 5:00 p.m. or by fax at night. This is simply not acceptable. Taylor Williams offers some words of optimism:

> I have heard many a complaint about how uncivil the practice has become. (Is this really new—don't the *Perry Mason* reruns always pit Perry against the down-and-dirty uncivil prosecutor?) The bar association has recently promulgated rules of civility. Perhaps they will have an impact. On this point, however, I have generally found that if I am civil to my opponent, he/she is civil with me.

The second biggest drawback to recommending a law career to other women is the stress and time demands involved. My classmate Josy Ingersoll provides her own "reverse role model" experience. The practice of law is "stressful and time consuming," she says. "Recognizing this, my daughter became a speech pathologist and my son a Ph.D. biologist. Both say they would not want to work the hours I do, and want more flexibility to spend more time with their families than I could!"

The women who participated in the 1997 Recognition of Trail-blazing Senior Women Attorneys sponsored by the Philadelphia Bar Association were asked to give their advice to the next generation of women entering law school. The advice includes both extremes, from "Don't!" and "Do not practice!" to more-encouraging words like "Stick to it." The "don'ts" emphasize the conflicts and time demands of law careers. In general, the advice seems to be this: Women should be prepared to work hard, perhaps harder than men. They should always do their best and always be prepared. They should be willing to start at the bottom and do any type of work, all the while networking and becoming active in extracurricular and bar association activities.[12] Others practicing today offer their own brand of advice:

> Work hard when you work and get away from it totally on a regular basis. Don't work for assholes; you don't have to. Admit your mistakes and learn without being defensive. Be true to yourself; if you don't give a rat's ass about baseball, don't pretend you do. Don't be afraid to be compassionate, to be female. It's a strength, not a weakness. If you're working with people who think it's a weakness, leave them. Find a great mate.

Karen McDonie, now raising horses in Texas, commented that "far too many people enter law school without really understanding what the practice of law is like." In recommending the practice of law to women, I hope we have offered more than platitudes about how "interesting" or "fulfilling" the law can be. Hopefully by now, our readers have a real sense of options, opportunities, and compromises they need to make. I also hope that in deciding to join the legal profession, women will take a tip from those like Alice Nelson, who suggests this: "Stay true to yourself and your values; try not to let pressures divert you. I would also encourage all women to participate in women bar associations and support groups. The support of other women has played a significant role in my life." We *can* make a difference. On a final note, Moi Vienneau from Ontario offers her own recommendation on the practice of law, which includes a plea for unity among women lawyers:

> I think practicing law can be great for anyone. I think that I would recommend that they go into the practice of law with their eyes open. I did not. I did not have someone I could speak with to ask certain questions. I think that would have been extremely helpful. I would not recommend practicing law as a sole practitioner, to a recent graduate. It's too hard, and you have to be extremely dedicated and prepared to give up a lot. I would love to see more women in law—more women who share in the philosophy that you hold your hand out to someone and pull them up the ladder, rather than leaving your sole imprint on their head.

We should not recommend law careers to other women with our words alone. Be a supporter or mentor to another woman. Teach her, if you will, civility and professionalism, to improve the practice of law for all of us. Give her the skills and opportunities needed to remain in the profession, so women maintain a voice in our society. By doing so, we help ourselves and enhance our own lives. There may be no other profession where women can define their own lives and achieve such personal satisfaction, achievement, security, and self-worth.

The law is a profession, not just another job. Our clients rightfully expect us to be their advocates and advisers on matters concerning their livelihoods and families. It is incumbent upon us to honor that trust, and our profession, by being the best we can be. Being a professional means many things. It means going to work each day dressed appropriately. It means being prepared and knowledgeable about the work we are doing. To Karen Richardson, it means this: "Know the law you are practicing. Be polite to bench officers and court staff. Be a tough adversary." Being a professional means showing respect to those who serve in our courts and aid us in our work at the office. Being a professional means serving the needs of our community and demonstrating civility to each other in our practice of the law. I heartily recommend a career in the legal profession to intelligent, socially conscious women everywhere.

Conclusion

A law career commands full-time attention, regardless of the hours one originally intends to work. In most types of practice, and more so in litigation, there are elements of work that are not within a lawyer's control. Court dates, levy notices, client demands, and responsive motions and pleadings all require immediate attention and cannot be postponed. I recall being in bankruptcy court one afternoon when the judge said, "Take ten minutes and call your families. I'm going to have you try this case right here and now." As the author of *Balanced Lives* reflects, a law career is fraught with "unpredictable and uncontrollable timing."[13] Moreover, "[m]ost lawyers in private practice now bill close to 2,000 hours a year or more."[14] That means 60 hours of work each week. This sentiment is echoed by the ABA Commission on Women in the Profession: "Unpredictable deadlines, uneven workloads, or frequent travel pose further difficulties for those with substantial family obligations."[15] Luckily, there are many arenas from which to choose when practicing law, with a variety of specialties from which to create a satisfying professional and personal life. But consider also that the hours and responsibilities are not directed only by firms or bosses. Much depends upon the inner drive that motivates the lawyer—the drive of competition to succeed and achieve. It is not an empty phrase that the "law is a jealous mistress."

ENDNOTES

1. Girl Scouts of Greater Philadelphia (Mar. 12, 1990).

2. ABA COMM'N ON WOMEN IN THE PROFESSION, BALANCED LIVES, CHANGING THE CULTURE OF LEGAL PRACTICE 20 (2001) (prepared by Deborah L. Rhode). Reprinted with permission.

3. *Id.* at 12.

4. Virginia G. Drachman, Sisters in Law, Women Lawyers in Modern American History 259 (1998).

5. Alice Abreu, *Lessons from LatCrit: Insiders and Outsiders, All at the Same Time,* 53 U. Miami L. Rev. 787, 802 (1999).

6. ABA Comm'n on Women in the Profession, A Current Glance of Women in the Law (2002).

7. Joan Williams, Unbending Gender, Why Family and Work Conflict and What to Do About It 250 (2000).

8. Ass'n of Am. Law Schools, *Statistical Report on Law School Faculty and Candidates for Law Faculty Positions 2000-2001, at* http://www.aals.org/statistics/index.html (Nov. 9, 2002) (prepared by Richard A. White, AALS Research Associate/Data Analyst); Marina Angel, "Our Faculty: Gender and Race," Aug. 26, 2003, Temple University Beasley School of Law.

9. Marina Angel, *Women in Legal Education: What It's Like to Be Part of a Perpetual First Wave or the Case of the Disappearing Women,* 61 Temp. L. Rev. 799, 827 (1988).

10. Abreu, *supra* note 5, at 810.

11. The Honorable Norma Shapiro, Address before Girl Scouts of Greater Philadelphia (Mar. 12, 1990).

12. Phila. Bar Ass'n Comm. on Women in the Profession, Celebrating More Than a Century of Women Lawyers in Philadelphia 1883-1997 31 (1997) (quoting F.S. Davidow).

13. ABA Comm'n on Women in the Profession, *supra* note 2, at 14.

14. *Id.* at 11.

15. ABA Comm'n on Women in the Profession, The Unfinished Agenda, Women and the Legal Profession 17 (2001) (prepared by Deborah L. Rhode). Reprinted with permission.

"A DAY IN THE LIFE"
JANE BRODERSON, LAWYER AND MOTHER OF FIVE

My day starts at 5:30 when the first alarm rings. I wake to feed the baby, now one, reset the alarm for 6:15, and head out for the gym. My companion rises with the 6:15 alarm to ready my two older boys, now fifteen, for high school. Home from the gym, I see the two older ones to the school bus, wake my twins, now twelve, and ready them for school. My daily routine includes walking the half mile to middle school with my boys while pushing the youngest in the stroller. I'm home before 8:30 and prepare for my day at the office.

My current job at a national staffing agency runs from 9:00 until 3:00 in the afternoon. By this time, my sitter has arrived. By having her drive me to work, I have the chance to breastfeed my little one in the car. At lunch, she arrives with the baby at my place of work so that I can breastfeed again. I am home by the time my middle-school twins walk home from school. Evenings are devoted to homework, dinner, and all the things the house and home require.

Chapter Five

Supporters, Mentors, and Role Models

To my mother In Spirit-Life, Whose Form Memory Cannot Trace; to the Women of Pennsylvania, and All Women who desire to be free; and also, All the men, possessed of sufficient noble manhood to bear equality, I dedicate my first effort in Court.

Carrie S. Burnham Kilgore
Philadelphia, April 4, 1873

Throughout life, each of us is presented with challenges that threaten to destroy our dreams. If we are very fortunate, we can experience the loving arms and encouraging words of supporters who help us meet our challenges and make our dreams reality. A supporter is someone who believes in you and in your dream, and is there to lend a hand. Sometimes supporters come through with financial assistance; sometimes with emotional or moral support. Supporters can share our responsibilities so we can turn our energies to pressing emergencies at work or at home. Supporters champion our lives. Speaking of her family and former boyfriend, Moi Vienneau of Hamilton, Ontario, Canada, defines what it meant to her to have supporters:

They did nothing overt, just always believed that I could do whatever I wanted to do. Not one of them ever questioned my ability, be it too lofty or otherwise.

Some supporters are our mentors, offering their expertise to help us become better lawyers. The dictionary defines a mentor as "somebody, usually older and more experienced, who provides advice and support to, and watches over and fosters the progress of, a younger, less experienced person."[1] No one doubts the value of a mentor in shaping a legal career. The law is a profession of traditions, rules, and peer networks. A mentor can ease the transition from law school to practice by sharing practical experience and by introducing the new lawyer to the legal community. In the past, women relied solely upon men as their mentors, and many men in the legal community served as worthy mentors. Today, because enough women have been practicing law long enough to be "older and more experienced," young women entering the law can rely upon women, as well as men, as their mentors.

To Become a Lawyer

A young woman's dream to become a lawyer is helped along when someone shares her enthusiasm. Many of the women with whom I spoke were encouraged by their parents to become lawyers, or simply to reach for their dreams. Some say their mother was the supportive parent who nourished their ambitions. In an article written by Doreen Davis's husband, Robert Simmons, he explains how Doreen—the second woman Philadelphia Bar Association Chancellor—was "encouraged" to attend law school by her mother, "even though her father opposed them." Others had different experiences. They named fathers or uncles who cheered the way while their mothers tried to steer them into marriage or more traditional women's fields of work. Unfortunately, some women experienced a complete absence of family support. In fact, due to divergent cultural expectations, some families overtly try to discourage any youthful ambitions. One young woman, born in 1967 and now living on Long Island City, New York, overcame the lack of family support. She is a 1996 graduate of the Benjamin N. Cardozo Law School, and the hurt from the lack of support is felt through her words. In spite of the general feeling today that the law is an acceptable career for women, it is not worth forgetting that in some families and in some cultures, women's independent ambitions are not embraced:

> My father said that only men should be lawyers. My mother said it would be too expensive. Everyone else thought it would never happen. Throughout law school and during my first internship I had great financial difficulties. I paid for my first year of law school with an installment loan and did not know how I would pay for the other two. I was not eligible for federal loans. I did not have the means to buy or borrow a computer and was competing with very wealthy students. I worked the entire time I was in law school, although I was told I should not. I had no choice but to work. The stress I was under must have mistakenly indicated to others that I was not serious about school or the internship and thus not worthy of their time. Or perhaps they just thought they should not waste their time on a Spanish woman.

This young woman overcame the lack of family support in part because of the encouragement she received as a young student from her teachers:

> There isn't one person that I ever saw as someone I would want to model my life after. However, the nuns that ran the all-girl Catholic school I attended in South America had a great influence on me, in so far as they believed men and women were capable of holding the same types of jobs, meaning that they were intellectually equal.

Our spouses and children can be great supporters, as I know mine are. Even by doing little things to contribute to the running of the house, or reading yet another draft of this book, they are my supporters and champions.

More Than a Few Good Men

Husbands, fathers, brothers, male friends, and even understanding judges stood behind—and next to—the pioneer women lawyers. They continue to do so today. In an article recently published by Stanford law professor Barbara Allen Babcock, she concludes after an exposition about many (if not most) early women lawyers:

> Generally, male progressive lawyers took up women's cause, and even practiced law with them. Our study so far shows that early women lawyers who succeeded without male aid were as rare as early women lawyers who were anti-feminists.[2]

In the mid-nineteenth century, Carrie Burnham Kilgore, Philadelphia's first female lawyer, was married to a lawyer who was uniquely supportive. Young lawyers of her day in Philadelphia trained under the tutelage of senior practicing lawyers, known as "preceptors." Carrie "read the law" in the office of her future husband and then entered law school at the University of Pennsylvania while she still had two young children. Her husband stood by her side from the very first day of class. Ada Kepley, an 1870 graduate of the Union College of Law in Chicago, was also married to a lawyer, as was Margaret Wilcox, who attended law school at the University of Michigan with her husband. Myra Bradwell's case before the U.S. Supreme Court was argued by a male lawyer, as was the case of every other woman who presented her appeal to practice law.

Along the way, many women were fortunate to find mentors or supporters who helped by providing scarce jobs or preceptorships and training, especially when it was difficult to gain general acceptance among most men in the field. For every doubter, there was a Richardson Dilworth to hire future Judge Lisa Richette, and a George W. Maxey to extend a Pennsylvania Supreme Court internship to Catherine Barone. Charisse Lillie, Philadelphia's first woman and first African-American city solicitor, offers the names of Judge Clifford Scott Green and Judge A. Leon Higginbotham, Jr. of the federal bench as being her mentors. And the list goes on.

My classmate Toby Dickman holds firmly that being a mother and a judge would be impossible were it not for her husband, also a lawyer, who shares the duties of raising their daughter, and who has strongly supported her throughout her career and campaign for the judgeship. Throughout her school years and career, Justice Sandra Schulz Newman credits her husband with being her right arm and cheerleader. She describes him as "father of the millennium," giving baths to the children when she was in night school and being continually supportive of her aspirations, which led her to become a justice of the Pennsylvania Supreme Court.

Support can come in unconventional ways. Naomi Norwood, now a business litigator, offers a backhanded compliment to her uncle:

> My uncle was a small-town trial lawyer and I thought his life was pretty neat. He inspired more than supported me, although in that era just the fact that he didn't discourage me as a woman was a form of support.

I give credit to the supportive men in my life, beginning with my father, brothers, uncles, and grandfathers. These are the men who always believed in me, empowered me with an education, and approved of my ambitions outside "the domestic sphere." When I bought my first car, my dad insisted I negotiate the contract. He gave me resources for my history term papers, taught me how to listen, and demonstrated the value of hard work. I am a daughter sandwiched between two brothers, and I have no memories of being told I could not play or climb like my brothers. My husband is one of those special men who, as my partner in life and in law, has mentored me and encouraged me to be my best. Professionally he has been my guide and teacher, seeing the lawyer I could be, well before I could see it. At home, he shares the domestic sphere so I have time to mother and to lawyer. My son Charles, all of thirteen now, sits with me as I write this book. He offers encouragement and editing suggestions. His pride in his mom is all I need.

And so, for every detractor like the long-departed Supreme Court Justice Bradley, there was a supporter like Philadelphia's Judge Thayer, opening the door for women to the legal profession. For every unnamed lawyer who discouraged women from applying to law school, there was Dean Peter Liacouras of Temple Law School, who hired women as full-time professors, encouraged women to matriculate, and introduced a part-time program to facilitate their schedules. For every discouraging interviewer who asked inappropriate questions, there were those like Lee Abbott, who hired Judge Mary Ann Cohen and treated her as an equal in the firm. For every woman who has been discouraged by some law school admissions officer, hiring partner, husband, or father, there has been a man who encouraged a woman's career, mentored her, became her partner, or assured her that he was most proud to be her father, husband, uncle, or partner. With the increased presence of women in the law, and in positions of leadership, there will also be women of experience to encourage and mentor younger women looking for their first jobs or struggling through their first cases—and fewer men to discourage them.

With Thanks to Our Mothers

The first working woman many of us know is "Mom." Children are often oblivious to the juggling acts performed by mothers as they work, keep the house going, provide decent dinners, and clean the clothes. As much as a woman lawyer needs a role model to reinforce her own professional aspirations, she needs a role model on how to live a balanced life. As young girls grow into young women, they look to their mothers for inspiration and guidance in "doing it all." Naomi Norwood from Los Angeles offers this tribute to her mother:

> My mother was my emotional and financial support. She was the valedictorian of her high school class, went to M.I.T. on a scholarship at seventeen, and worked as a scientist my whole life until her recent retirement. With that role model, I grew up thinking I could and would do anything I wanted to do. I started out in physics, which she supported wholeheartedly. When I changed to political science and later went to law school, she supported me completely—even though I'd left her field. She always just wanted me to be happy and interested. Her humility

would not permit her to admit it, but she's very proud of her daughter, the lawyer. My mother was my mentor from time to time on how to be a professional woman and wife and mother without going crazy. Mostly, she listened and commiserated and reminded me of things she survived that I hadn't really focused on at the time, being a typically self-absorbed kid who had no idea how extraordinary my mother was.

Rebecca Swan, also of Los Angeles, names her most important role model:

My mother. She was a fabulous mother in that she was always there for us as children, but she also worked as a teacher in our school. When I start to feel overwhelmed by my life as a lawyer and a mother, I call her for moral support.

My mother was the oldest of three children. At nineteen, she married my father and left school to start her own family. My two brothers and I arrived shortly thereafter and my mother returned to school to finish her degree. As an artist and elementary art teacher, my mother kept a frantic schedule with three young children. My dad worked three jobs. I recall this image: after arriving home from work around 4:30 in the afternoon, my mother was stabbing at a block of frozen spinach over a steaming pot of boiling water to get dinner on the table by 5:00 so my dad could be out the door to his second job by 5:30. This was before the invention of the microwave oven. We kids came home from school for lunch, which must have been a nightmare for any working mother. We had neighbors and help and family to smooth the edges. Her gift to me and to my brothers has been to make each of us feel special in this world. She opened my eyes to what could be, and never wavered in her complete faith in me. She has read every page of this book, many times in many versions, and has propped me up when I doubted my own efforts. I have shared her clothes, her recipes, and her style. For me, the most important gift from my mom is her sense of balance—not by what she has told me, but by how she has lived. More than anything else, and sometimes at the sacrifice of all else, family has been and remains the most important value in her life and, because of her, in mine. She is my constant supporter.

Women Lawyers as Role Models

Some of the more recent graduates of law school have the good fortune to observe women lawyers or judges as respected competent professionals and as women who balance work and family. Women who find other women to be mentors and role models often find that the roles overlap. One 1989 graduate from Georgetown University Law School recalls a woman lawyer after whom she was able to model herself:

> Early in my career, the office managing partner at my firm was a woman. I admired her because of her accomplishments. She managed the office, maintained her clients, took care of a family, and found time to guide and teach other women attorneys.

Nancy, a 1986 graduate from Stetson University College of Law, observed more distant examples of women lawyer role models:

> Role models have been scarce. As a college student, I revered Sandra Day O'Connor because I thought her job was the pinnacle. As I have gained experience and perspective, I have observed two of the female judges in our area who are the mothers of four children, as I am.

Women entering law school more than twenty-five years ago often relied only upon men as role models or mentors, due to the simple fact that there were not enough women lawyers to fill those roles. Women pursuing law careers often did so without ever having met a woman lawyer.

Grace Kennedy, a lawyer now in her eighties, who attended Fordham Law School in 1937, summed up the positive changes she has observed all these years. Things have changed "totally," she exclaims:

> In my day, women were encouraged to get married and have a family. They were advised to acquire hobbies so that when you washed dishes you would have something to think about. There weren't very many women doing anything. There were no "models" to follow. Nobody [female] ran for office. Now, women have come to be "accepted" in the profession.

A young woman's first personal interaction with a woman lawyer often occurs in law school. Women who attended law school before 1970 shared similar stories about the lack of women professors at law school. "There were no women professors at Columbia in 1965," says Professor Marina Angel. "There was one woman graduate student teaching a small legal writing section." In 1972, Ruth Bader Ginsburg would become a tenured faculty member but, for Professor Angel, that was too late. She met a woman lawyer for the first time in 1969, in Washington, D.C., where, on a job quest, she met Barbara Babcock, then head of the public defender's office in D.C.

There were no women law professors at the University of Pennsylvania when Judge Sloviter attended, and she was the sole woman in her law firm for many years. The experience was the same for many women, like Judge Carolyn Engle Temin and Judge Norma L. Shapiro (who became a legal writing professor upon graduating from the University of Pennsylvania Law School). In those years, reflects District Attorney Lynne Abraham, also a 1965 law school graduate, role models were chosen from among the great male lawyers in history, like Clarence Darrow, because there were so few women lawyers to emulate.

Ten years later, Deborah Willig graduated from Temple University School of Law, and times had begun to change. Deborah was able to include among her role models and mentors women like Judge Lisa Richette, with whom she did an internship, and Miriam Gafni, a flamboyant and steely lawyer who many Philadelphians may remember for her hats and her appearances on television as a parent advocate before the Philadelphia school board in the years of Mark Shed.

Many of today's senior women lawyers, like Professor Maleson, are at first surprised to learn they had become role models for younger women. Professor Maleson, who joined the faculty at Temple Law School in 1974, recalls women looking up to her as a role model for her "togetherness" and professionalism, yet she had never seen herself as a role model. Though outwardly her life seemed in order, she was the mother of two very young children. That meant a high level of chaos at home, early mornings, and children up at night, all of which, to her, belied the image of a proper legal role model. Professor Maleson was unwittingly a role model for me. I had never met or seen a woman lawyer before I had Professor Maleson for torts. I think now that much of my time in her class was spent in fascination at how there could be, in the same person, someone attractive and outspokenly brilliant. For women who have been practicing law for some years, it is important to bear in mind that other women lawyers are watching how you work and how you live your life. You may also be surprised to learn that, unbeknownst to you, another woman has chosen you for her role model.

Today, we have women in positions of power, something unheard of twenty-five years ago. We have women on the U.S. Supreme Court and at every other level of our federal and state judiciaries, a woman has run for vice president of the United States, and another has held the office of U.S. Attorney General. In Philadelphia, a woman serves as our district attorney, three women have been Philadelphia Bar Association Chancellor (one of whom is African-American), a woman is president of the Pennsylvania Bar Association, an African-American woman is city solicitor, and women are equity partners in large law firms and named partners of their own firms. When women fill these positions, they open careers to which younger women may aspire. The women who fill these positions become role models to the next generation.

A role model is, according to Encarta® World English Dictionary (North American Edition, © 2004), "somebody who is regarded as somebody to look up to and often as an example to emulate." Role models afford us the opportunity to see how it is to practice law in a certain setting, such as government or private practice. Role models can open our eyes to what it means to practice within a certain field of law. The presence of women lawyers as role models is critical. Women lawyers offer other women the opportunity to observe the unique and myriad ways in which they can combine work and their personal lives to achieve personal happiness. They can also offer strategies for coping with sexual harassment, unequal pay, attire, demeanor, and professionalism. Women lawyers should be mindful that even if they are not actively mentoring other individuals, they are teaching by example. Young women lawyers are watching and learning.

I found an unexpected twist when discussing role models and mentors with former Chancellor Doreen Davis, now an equity partner at the law firm of Morgan Lewis. In her mentoring of younger lawyers, she finds that no one wants to be like her. Younger women, and men, observe her long hours, travel schedule, and enormous pressures at work and decide *not* to emulate her. Doreen feels like a "reverse" role model for younger lawyers seeking a more balanced lifestyle.

Conclusion

No man, or woman, is an island, and no one should feel that she or he can go it alone. The women with whom I have spoken all agreed that the support of someone in their lives has been critical to their professional success and, I think I may add, to their personal self-esteem. Someone along the way believed in their dreams and encouraged them. It may have been parents or one parent. It may have been an uncle or a teacher. Look for, and listen to, that person who believes in you and your dream.

No one doubts the importance of finding a mentor. If possible, find one. If there are none, seek a role model. Twenty-five years ago, mentors were usually men, simply because there were so few women lawyers to serve in those roles. Look for mentors and role models around you, and in the history books, as did District Attorney Lynne Abraham and District Court Judge Norma Shapiro. Also, although there are more women in positions to become role models, do not ignore the best that men have to offer. And last, from Judge Beck, "if you are unable to find a mentor, look around and emulate the best."

Participation in women's bar associations and other groups can be immensely rewarding. The ABA Law Practice Management Section Women Rainmakers group offers mentoring, networking, and educational opportunities to members at both the national and local levels. (See the form at the back of this book for more information.)

Everyone needs to find people who will be supportive in ways that contribute to happiness and success. Some supporters are within our own families and are present from the time we are young. They support our dreams and encourage our ambitions. Teachers, friends, and other associates can inspire us and be our supporters as we grow into young adults. Their influence can be even stronger when there are no supporters within our own families. Professionally, our supporters, mentors, and role models play key roles in helping us become the best lawyers we can be. Listen to the supporters around you and learn from their words and by their examples. Look around for other lawyers you respect, and absorb their methods. Try to attend meetings with clients and other lawyers, read the work of other lawyers, attend open court proceedings and, if possible, find someone who will be your mentor. Some law schools have mentoring programs to match students with practicing lawyers. Some law firms have mentoring policies that match new associates with more senior lawyers. Take advantage of these programs and cultivate the friendships that can result. My advice, particularly to young women preparing to become lawyers, is to do your best, surround yourself with good people who will support your efforts, and steer clear of detractors. To those who have the years and the experience, take the time to offer some friendly advice to the young people around you. Take the time to talk with the younger men and women who have yet to enter college and are wondering what it means to be a lawyer.

ENDNOTES

1. ENCARTA® WORLD ENGLISH DICTIONARY (NORTH AMERICAN EDITION, © 2004), *available at* http://encarta.msn.com/dictionary (Microsoft Corporation, All rights reserved; developed for Microsoft by Bloomsbury Publishing Plc.).

2. Barbara Allen Babcock, *A Real Revolution*, 49 U. KAN. L. REV. 719, 727 (2001).

"A Day in the Life"
Cheryl Kritz, Chief Deputy City Solicitor, Commercial Law Unit, City of Philadelphia Law Department

My day starts the night before by making lunch for my daughter to take to school and setting the timer for the morning coffee. After getting up by 6:30 in the morning, I let out the dog, skim the newspaper, have coffee, and am out of the shower by 7:00. After waking my daughter and husband, I hurry to get dressed for work. One of us waits with our daughter outside for the school bus that arrives by 7:35. As soon as the bus leaves, I hop in the car and drive to my office in the city. My day consists of answering phone calls, responding to regular mail and dozens of e-mails, and attending meetings, sometimes with the mayor or other city officials or my staff. In a given day I may be drafting or reviewing a particular contract for the city or in the midst of negotiations. On occasion, I drive to the administrative office of the city's prison system where I am involved in the negotiation and implementation of the city's contract for inmate health services. On most days, I can be home by 6:30 (except for days that I drive carpool or Wednesday nights when I work late), where my husband, also a lawyer, prepares dinner (except for Monday nights, when my in-laws come over and prepare spaghetti for us). After dinner, my husband generally retires to his home office to continue working (except for when it is his turn to help our daughter with homework). After making my daughter's lunch for the next day, I may continue working or confirm/arrange after-school coverage for the next day or read the newspaper.

Chapter Six

A Glass Ceiling

Oh, Kitty! How nice it would be if we could only get through into
Looking Glass House! I'm sure it's got, oh! Such beautiful things in it!
Let's pretend there's a way of getting through into it, somehow, Kitty.
Let's pretend the glass has got all soft-like gauze, so that we can get
through. Why, it's turning into a sort of mist now, I declare! It'll be
easy enough to get through . . . ! And certainly the glass was
beginning to melt away, just like a bright silvery mist.

"Looking Glass House"
Through the Looking Glass, by Lewis Carroll

Male and female law school graduates may enter the working world
on equal footing, but ultimately their paths diverge, with women
lawyers generally earning 73 percent of men's median weekly
salaries.[1] Nearly half of all law school graduating classes are women,
yet women comprise merely 15 percent of all law partners and 13
percent of general counsels at Fortune 500 companies.[2] The glass
ceiling for women lawyers is very real, considering the highest-paying
positions are in large firms or corporations and the majority of those
positions are filled by men.

What Do Lawyers Earn?

To no one's surprise, the highest starting salaries for new lawyers are at the largest law firms. The 2002 annual starting salary at the law firm of Ballard Spahr Andrews & Ingersoll ranges from $111,000 in Washington, D.C., to $95,000 in Denver and Salt Lake City.[3] The prominent Washington, D.C., law firm of Akin Gump Strauss Haver & Feld LLP, is currently offering its first-year associates $125,000.[4]

These salaries put this rarefied group of lawyers at the highest tier of professional earnings nationwide. The U.S. Department of Labor, Bureau of Labor Statistics, reports that in 2002, the median salary for lawyers six months after graduation was $60,000. The lowest median salaries were in positions of public-interest law ($34,000), academics, judicial clerkships, and government ($40,300). The median salary of all lawyers in 2002 was $90,290. Only 10 percent of all lawyers were earning more than $145,600 annually. The class of 2002 experienced slight gains, with overall median salaries of $42,000 for judicial clerkships and government, and $36,000 for public service. In private practice, the median salary rose to $90,000, although the number of lawyers in private practice earning between $35,000 and $55,000 was nearly equal to those earning more than $75,000.[5]

The disparity between the public sector and large law firm private sector is more like a canyon than a gap. A district attorney in Manhattan, New York, earned $48,000 in 2001. For the same year, a U.S. attorney in New York's eastern district earned $63,173, while a lawyer in the New York Civil Liberties Union earned $35,000.[6] On the other hand, first-year law graduates who went to work in the Big Apple for Skadden, Arps, Slate, Meagher & Flom, LLP, in 2001 earned a salary of $140,000 and a bonus ranging from $5,000 to $30,000. Others hired at New York's prestigious firms at $125,000 were eligible for bonuses ranging from $20,000 to $60,000.[7]

Lawyers in large firms fare much better than their counterparts in smaller firms. In 2003, the National Association for Law Placement, in a survey based upon its 2002–03 directory of legal employers, reported that the national median salary of first-year associates in a law firm of 2 to 25 was $59,500, and $113,000 for firms of 500 or more. For all firms, the first-year median salary was $93,190.[8]

After years of legal practice, the opportunity to become a judge or justice on the federal bench may present itself. Federal judicial salaries, as posted for January 2003 by the Administrative Office of the U.S. Courts, are at $198,600 for the chief justice of the U.S. Supreme Court, $190,100 for all associate justices, $164,000 for courts of appeals judges, and $154,700 for all judges of the district courts, tax court, court of federal claims, and court of international trade. Bankruptcy court judges and full-time magistrates are posted at $142,300. Though highest in prestige, these positions do not compare well economically with those in large law firms.

Near the top of the income ladder are the equity partners of the largest law firms. The income of an equity partner is largely tied to the firm's profits, with only about half paid on a fixed basis. In contrast, nonequity partners have less participation in the operation of the firm and do not share in the firm's profits. In 2001, the New York law firm of Wachtell, Lipton, Rosen & Katz reported seventy-two equity partners, with the highest average annual income at $3,285,000. The very top of the income ladder belongs to in-house corporate counsel. In 2000, in-house counsel for Cablevision Systems, Inc., is reported to have earned combined cash and equity compensation of $19,483,500. Many others were reportedly earning between $1 million and $3 million for that year.[9]

The disparity in earnings among lawyers is a function of several things. Private practitioners, particularly those in larger firms, will usually (but not always) have higher incomes than those who work in government, public service, or even the judiciary. Within a large firm, equity partners clearly outshine the rest, but may themselves be out-earned by private in-house corporate counsel for the world's larger corporations. There are stars in the legal profession and lawyers at small boutique firms who rival the compensation of large-firm equity partners. Length of service, seniority, and, most important, the ability to bring business to the firm are the greatest earnings-determining factors in any private practice. These are often the very factors that undermine women's economic parity with men.

Starting the Same and Ending Apart

Although men and women may start on equal footing, a nationwide gender gap ensues, with women earning anywhere from 70 to 77 percent of their male counterparts' salaries.[10] In some locales, even greater disparities are reported. In Wisconsin, for example, the results of a 2001 survey conducted by the bar association concluded that women's net income was 48 percent less than men's in private practice.[11] The disparities are not limited to private practice. A recent study of the U.S. Department of Justice (DOJ), brought to light by the Freedom of Information Act, concluded that male DOJ lawyers earned an average of $79,600, while women earned an average of $76,100, even when factoring out seniority and pay grade.[12]

An internal audit prepared for the state of Washington's law firms similarly found that the majority of lawyers (77 percent) across the state who received the top 25 percent of compensation were male. Twice as many women as men were in the bottom 25 percent range of compensation. In 1990, the Philadelphia Bar Association membership survey reported the average income of all male lawyers in Philadelphia at $119,300, and the average income of all women lawyers at $61,200, *less than half.*[13] Women lawyers in Philadelphia have marginally improved their compensation scheme overall, but the disparities are still great and the studies show women lose significant ground to men over time.

The Philadelphia Bar Association membership survey for the year 2000 reflects an ongoing and significant disparity in earnings for women and men. Though women were hired at salaries comparable with men, they did not sustain the same career momentum. Under age thirty-five, men and women began at nearly the same salaries—on average, men earned $77,000, while women earned $70,000. Not one woman in that age category earned more than $150,000, compared with 6.2 percent of men who did. Between the ages of thirty-six and fifty, the earnings gap between men and women widened to $31,000. For women older than fifty-one, the earnings gap was increased to $66,000, with women in that age category earning $4,000 less than men under age thirty-five.[14] Are these statistics evidence of discrimination or proof of a real glass ceiling, or are other factors at work?

The reason or reasons for the gap are always more complex than the question itself, and sometimes we are left to speculate. And there are always individual exceptions to the general trend. The answer is best found by starting with another question: Where are women lawyers employed? The ABA's Commission on Women has gathered information to help locate the women.[15] Within the judiciary, women are 19 percent of all U.S. district court judges, 20 percent of circuit court judges, and 26 percent of judges from all state courts of last resort. Women are represented within 28 percent of the federal judicial department, 21 percent of local governments, 32 percent of other government agencies, and 34 percent of other state and local judicial departments. Women comprise 41.9 percent of all legal-aid lawyers and public defenders. In the law schools, women are 5.9 percent of tenured faculty, but 46 percent of associate professors and 48 percent of assistant professors. They are 10.9 percent of all law school deans, but 69.4 percent of assistant deans without professor title. Seventy-one percent of all female lawyers are in private practice, as compared with 75 percent of all male lawyers. Clearly, not all law careers are equal or equally compensated. Though women are underrepresented in many of these areas in proportion to their overall representation in the bar (30 percent), the disparities in some law careers, like law school professorships, are more outstanding than others. But, before comparing apples and oranges, it is important to look further into these numbers to see what accounts for the disparities in income. Women's underrepresentation in tenured professorships and deanships directly contributes to the disparities in income between men and women. The DOJ's internal audit revealed that 38 percent of its employees were female; however, men are 50 percent more likely than women to hold higher-paying, senior executive service jobs. Outside private practice, women still have years to go before they can gain enough to bring them up to par with men economically.

The real source of the income gap, I believe, is found by examining the earnings of men and women in private practice, where most lawyers work. In private practice, a lawyer's income is a subjective matter. How a law firm divides the pie is left to individual and creative methods, usually dictated by senior partners or rainmakers—the firm's revenue sources. Disputes about compensation are legendary, and are often the impetus for whole departments picking up in the middle of the night and moving to other firms or out on their own. One element of subjectivity can be gender, often manifested in acts of nuance—such as diminished responsibility or low-revenue assignments for women—rather than overt acts of discrimination. Of course, assignment and responsibility levels factor into compensation levels. Law firms are voluntary associations where personal relationships are still important. The "climate" of a workplace can do much to encourage women's careers or extinguish them.

Earnings of the self-employed are always based upon personal effort. As with men, earnings for women in private practice depend upon the ability to bring in business. The disparities in male/female earnings call into question women's ability to acquire legal work and become rainmakers for their firms. But this alone may not explain the wide disparities.

Nationally, women account for only 16.81 percent of all law firm partners, but 43.02 percent of all lower-paid associates.[16] In some cities, the percentages for partnership are higher, such as 18.24 percent for Los Angeles, 21.43 percent for San Francisco, and 19.72 percent for Miami.[17] In 2003, in the nine most profitable law firms in the country, the presence of women equity partners (those highest compensated) ranged from 6.9 percent to 20 percent.[18] The gender disparities in income are explained, in part, by women's underrepresentation in the highest-paying positions law has to offer.

Statistics can be misleading. The Pennsylvania Bar Association's Ninth Annual Report Card for 2003, prepared by the Committee for Women in the Profession, indicates that 29 percent of all lawyers in the hundred largest law firms in the state are women, a fair number overall. A closer examination, however, reveals that women are concentrated in lower-tiered positions of part-time and associate status in those firms. According to the Ninth Annual Report Card (2003) of the Pennsylvania Bar Association, women are 15 percent of all managing partners and equity partners, 17 percent of all partners generally, 42 percent of associates, and 78 percent of all part-time workers. Though the original statistics gave the illusion that women were being fairly represented in large firms, women are not represented in positions of power or economic wealth in numbers equal to their proportion of all lawyers.

Women "fail" to make it to the top in their firms because they feel it necessary to make an either/or choice. About the time women reach their thirties, they are confronted with the inevitable deadlines related to starting families. Rather than devoting full energies into career advancement, many women pull back. In greater numbers than men, women leave large law firms, often for other work in smaller firms or to become self-employed.

Women who demote themselves to nonpartner tracking almost always do so at the expense of compensation. A survey shows that in the state of Washington, two-thirds of the nonpartnership positions in law firms were offered to women.[19] The survey also found that a woman who works in a firm is more likely than a man to leave before having had the opportunity to become a partner. One hundred percent of those working at part-time positions who left their law firms were women. While an equal number of male and female associates departed their firms for other work, 92 percent of the women left for reasons related to family. Among the women equity partners leaving for other work, 75 percent left for family-related causes. These statistics bear out the conclusions of the national Catalyst Survey of 2000, which reports that "the top barrier to women's advancement is commitment to personal and family responsibilities." A desire to have a family and devote time to raising children becomes an impediment to further advancement in the firm. In the state of Washington, a majority of the departing women associates—nearly 75 percent—left either for the public sector or private practice.

The circumstances that cause women to reject these positions will not change. Whether law firms change to promote women who have taken time out or cut back for a time will make all the difference. Until then, the result is a "glass ceiling," not necessarily imposed by overt discrimination, but by circumstances that create a class society nonetheless. Is there a "glass ceiling"? Most certainly. How many women can land the largest of corporate clients? How many are counsel for the Fortune 500? The numbers are low and are likely to remain so until women manage these Fortune 500 companies. Large firms that reward hours worked over efficiency run counter to women trying to finish projects to have time for personal demands. Some large firms have a philosophy exemplified in this example: if one paragraph in a lease is sufficient, three pages are better.

Women have hit the "occupational" glass ceiling. In time, as more women move up the ranks, develop networks for business, and become their own "rainmakers," the statistics may change. But this will not happen until the "climate" of the office is conducive to women leading full lives.

"Women Are Doing Terribly"

In spite of gains in the sheer number of women emerging from law schools, all is not well in the community. When I first spoke with Professor Marina Angel, she expressed the sentiment emphatically: "Women are doing terribly." A high attrition rate for women lawyers from larger firms has been recognized as the symptom of a system that does not serve women well. In 2002, the Philadelphia Bar Association Board of Governors, Association of Governance, adopted a resolution entitled, "Statement of Goals of Philadelphia Law Firms and Legal Departments for the Retention and Promotion of Women." Let me say at the outset that the mere existence of a statement from the bar association expressing cognizance of women's unique hazards in the profession is to be applauded. The statement is also to be applauded for reflecting an institutional, supportive posture toward women in the profession, which was unheard of twenty years ago. However, the body of the statement is disheartening, because it reveals that the advancement of women in the legal field has not been improved by their numbers:

> Even though women have entered the legal profession in increasing numbers over the past two decades, women lawyers continue to be underrepresented at the higher levels of the profession. It is difficult to account for all of the discrepancy between the number of men and women entering the profession and those achieving full participation in the profession. To the extent that women encounter obstacles based upon stereotypes and gender-based considerations, correction is essential, not only because it is professionally responsible, but also because discrimination is illegal. As leaders of the Philadelphia legal community, the signatories can and will use their best efforts to ensure that the attitudes and practices at law firms and legal departments promote the full representation and participation of women at all ranks of the profession. (Philadelphia Bar Association Board of Governors, Association of Governance, "Statement of Goals of Philadelphia Law Firms and Legal Departments for the Retention and Promotion of Women," 2002)

Equal Pay Act

In today's world, gender and ethnicity are not going to be factors in setting salaries for new associates. Many large firms post their starting salaries and they are not going to deviate when they hire. After the initial hire, compensation is generally a function of billable hours and business generation. However, subjective factors may also come into the mix, and that is when the possibility of gender discrimination manifests itself.

The Equal Pay Act of 1963 is an addition to the Fair Labor Standards Act of 1938, as amended.[20] The Act prohibits employers from discriminating between men and women by paying different wages for work that "requires equal skill, effort, and responsibility," and is "performed under similar working conditions." The exceptions carved out of the general rule are wage tiers based upon seniority, merit, production, or some factor "other than sex." Lawful factors may include education, experience, or prior salary. If an employer establishes one of these affirmative defenses, a woman may then attempt to demonstrate that the purported nondiscriminatory justification is merely a "pretext" for discrimination. Women lawyers may have come under the umbrella protection of the Equal Pay Act, but the burden of proof remains a barrier to protection.

Comparing the work of legal associates is difficult, but not impossible. To be successful in presenting a claim under the Equal Pay Act, a woman must demonstrate that her work is "substantially equal" to that of her male coworker who is being given greater financial rewards. The jobs must share "a common core of tasks," measured by factors such as similarity of quality and quantity of production, education, relevant prior work experience, conduct, and skill.[21]

Courts have examined a multiplicity of factors, down to the very details of work assignments, when determining whether a man and woman are performing work that is "substantially equal." For example, they have distinguished between litigation work that is "fact specific," thereby requiring less legal analysis, and litigation work that is more legally complex. They may consider the level of importance the work has to the firm, the expectation of billable hours, the level of stress and pressure, the need for training, and the difference between supervisory work, transactional work, and litigation.[22] Within a firm, women may be "equal" in title, but not compensated equally if their work is considered less stressful, less technical, or less important to the firm. Not all partners are equal in the eyes of the firm, but that is true whether they are men or women.

Conclusion

Women who want to work the billable hours that a large firm demands and who can bring in the high-paying corporate clients can achieve on the same economic scale as a man. However, the statistics indicate that women are much more likely to trade off economic rewards for lifestyle choices that include children, family, and control over their lives. For example, the State of Washington statistics showing that 92 percent of women associates and 75 percent of women partners left their firms for family reasons indicate that women, rather than men, are making these personal decisions. The disparities that begin to arise are partly a reflection of women's inability to bring in larger clients to generate fees, in both large and small firms. Developing a network of peers and clients takes a considerable amount of time and energy, both inside and outside the office—something a woman with a family has in short supply.

Women lawyers helping other women lawyers, from positions of authority or by simply referring business to each other, will bring about changes for the better. Particularly in smaller firms where women are choosing to practice, women can create their own power networks. Deborah Willig, Philadelphia's first woman chancellor of the bar, urges women to help each other. Maybe, she says, having more women in the field will effect change, but only if women promote one another. As for change occurring in large law firms "in our legal lifetime," Deborah is pessimistic, given who is at the top, how unconducive those environments are for most women, and how long it will take for women to rise to leadership positions with those firms. All these factors are related to gender, and yet many women embrace their choices, trading off the top tiers of economic success for flexibility and independence.

ENDNOTES

1. ABA COMM'N ON WOMEN IN THE PROFESSION, A CURRENT GLANCE OF WOMEN IN THE LAW (2002) (2001 statistics; women in general population earn about 76 percent of what men earn, according to 2001 statistics released by U.S. Census Bureau for Bureau of Labor Statistics, Current Population Survey, 2002).

2. Catalyst Survey 2000, "Women in Law, Making the Case, Executive Summary" (page 2), (based upon statistics provided by National Directory of Legal Employers, NALP 2000, a 2000 Catalyst Census of Women Corporate Officers and Top Earners.)

3. Ballardspahr Andrews & Ingersoll, LLP (2002), *available at* http://www.ballardspahr.com (Baltimore—$102,000, Denver—$95,000, Philadelphia—$107,000, Salt Lake City—$95,000, Voorhees, N.J.—$102,000, Washington, D.C.—$111,000).

4. Akin Gump Strauss Hauer Feld LLP, *available at* http://www.akingump.com.

5. "Employment for New Law Graduates Down Slightly, but Remains Relatively Strong" (July 24, 2003), *available at* http://www.nalp.org/press/jido2.htm; Bureau of Labor Statistics, U.S. Dept. of Labor, *Occupational Outlook Handbook, 2004-05 Edition, Lawyers, available at* http://www.bls.gov/oco/ocos053.htm.

6. "New York Government, Non-Profit First-Year Salary 2000, 2001" (Dec. 5, 2003), *available at* http://www.law.com/special/professionals/nylj/2002/salary_survey/ny_govt_non_profit_1st_year_salary.html.

7. "New York 2000, 2001 Year-End Bonus Sampler" (Dec. 5, 2003), *available at* http://www.law.com/special/professional/nylj/2002/salar . . . / ny_2000_2001_year_end_bonus.html; "New York 2000, 2001 First-Year Salary" (Dec. 5, 2003), *available at* http://www.law.com/special/professionals/nylj/2002/salary_survey/ny_2000_2001_1st_year_salary.html.

8. "Entry-Level Associate Salaries Again Remain Stable in Large Firms" (August 8, 2003); CONGRESSIONAL RESEARCH SERVICE, *The Library of Congress, Salaries of Federal Officials: A Fact Sheet*, prepared by Sharon S. Gressle (Jan-

uary 24, 2004), *available at* http://www.senate.gov/reference/resources /pdf/98-53.pdf; *New York Lawyers Chart: Equity Partner Compensation at Highest 25 New York Firms* (Jan. 27, 2003), *available at* http://www .nylawyer.com/news/03/01/0127036.html.

9. Annual Survey, *2000 Top In-House Legal Officers Compensation, Cash & Equity Compensation, Tri-State Region,* N.Y. L.J., Feb. 2002; Annual Surveys published each year in various sources, i.e., Corporate Counsel, American Lawyer Media.

10. *See, e.g.,* AFL-CIO, *The Pay Gap by Occupation* (2004), *available at* http://www.aflcio.org/yourjobeconomy/women/equalpay/ThePayGapBy Occupation.cfm (AFL-CIO statistics show full-time salaried median weekly earnings of $1,610 for male lawyers and $1,237 for female lawyers, a wage gap of $373/week or 76 percent); *see also A Snapshot of Women in the Law in the Year 2000* (2000), *available at* http://www.abanet.org/women/snap shots.pdf (citing statistics gathered by Paycheck Check-Up 2000, WomenCONNECT.com (1999), *at* www.womenconnect.com/linkTo/PC2000 .htm) (ABA statistics show median salary of $1,610/week for male lawyers and $1,237/week for female lawyers, a difference of 77 percent; year 2000 earnings reported by ABA show annual median salary of $69,680 for men and $50,648 for women, a difference of 73 percent).

11. State Bar of Wisconsin, *The Economics of Law Practice in Wisconsin: 2001 Survey Reports,* 74 WIS. LAW. 6, 28 (2001).

12. Vanessa Blum, *An Inside Look at DOJ Lawyer Diversity,* LEGAL TIMES (Oct. 28, 2003), *available at* http://www.law.com/jsp/article.jsp?id= 1067014203039 (reviewing internal review conducted by KPMG Consulting—now Bearing Point—& Taylor Cox Associates).

13. PHILA. BAR ASS'N, PHILADELPHIA BAR ASSOCIATION MEMBERSHIP SURVEY 1990, EXECUTIVE SUMMARY 2 (1990); FINAL REPORT, 2001 Self-Audit for Gender and Racial Equity, A Survey of Washington Law Firms Conducted for the Glass Ceiling Task Force by Northwest Research Group, Inc. (2001), p. 24.

14. Melissa Sepos, *Survey: Philadelphia Lawyers Fewer in Number,* PHILA. BUS. J. (Oct. 9, 2000), *available at* http://philadelphia.bizjournals.com /philadelphia/stories/2000/10/09/focus5.html.

15. ABA COMM'N ON WOMEN IN THE PROFESSION, *supra* note 1 (2001 statistics).

16. Women and Attorneys of Color, 2003 Summary Chart (2003),

available at http://www.nalp.org/nalresearch/mw03sum.htm (based upon analysis of 2003-04 NALP Directory of Legal Employers).

17. *Id.*

18. Measuring the Power (Dec. 2, 2003), *available at* http://www.law.com/special/professionals/amlaw/2003/measuring_power.shtml (American Lawyer Media's Law.com).

19. FINAL REPORT, 2001 Self-Audit for Gender and Racial Equity, A Survey of Washington Law Firms Conducted for The Glass Ceiling Task Force by Northwest Research Group, Inc (2001).

20. 29 U.S.C. § 206(d) (1963).

21. 29 C.F.R. § 1620.13 (1999).

22. *See, e.g.,* Dubowsky v. Stern, Lavinthal, Norgaard & Daly, 922 F. Supp. 985 (D.N.J. 1996), 77 Fair Empl. Prac. Cas. (BNA) 1059 (1996).

"A DAY IN THE LIFE"
TEXAS LAWYER MARY ALICE McLARTY

My day today began with a 7:30 breakfast at a Washington, D.C., hotel. Then throughout the day, I visited with six congressmen and one congresswoman. I attended a press conference of the Texas Democratic Congressional Delegation at noon and I flew home on a private jet that belongs to a friend of mine. And no—this was not a typical day, although lobbying is a big part of my life this year.

Tomorrow, I will preside over the Dallas Trial Lawyers Luncheon and then meet with a client. Hopefully, at 4:00 p.m., I will meet with my decorator at my new house and pick out some colors. Then I will fly to Austin tomorrow night so that I can be there the next morning when the debate begins in the Texas Senate on the medical mal-practice/tort reform bill. The rights of the citizens of Texas and the United States are in jeopardy as we speak. The insurance compa-nies and big-corporation special-interest groups have literally taken over the United States Congress and the government of Texas.

A typical day begins around 8:00 a.m. with coffee and the *Dallas Morning News*. Then I cook breakfast for my husband and myself and arrive at my desk at my home office around 9:30. If I have a hearing or am in trial, I have to be at the courthouse in downtown Dallas by 8:30–9:00. Most days begin as I said before. I may have a client appointment at my office (three to five minutes from home) around 11:00 a.m. or in the afternoon. But most weeks, I only go to my office three or four times a week. My paralegal or secretary often brings my important mail to me in the afternoon, if I am not going to the office. I often work until 7:00 or 8:00 p.m. I typically work every day that I am not traveling. On the weekends, I play tennis, but still work four to seven hours a day.

We have a dedicated line with a T-1 between the office and the house. We can all access the same documents, case management system, calendars, etc., from either location. I can also access my hard drive when I travel with my laptop. My phone system is run through the T-1 also. We do not have a phone service. My staff can transfer a call to me at home as if I were in my office. My husband also runs his Internet business out of our home and is the reason I have such an efficiently run office. He also designed and maintains my Web site.

My life is incredibly interesting, stressful, rewarding, and fulfilling. I have three grown children and seven grandchildren, who are all beautiful and intelligent. My thirty-five-year-old son is presently in Baghdad and I worry and pray for him constantly.

I really care about all of my clients, although I am closer to some than to others. I have never been afraid to care about my clients or to get involved with them personally. The only thing I dislike about my career is the occasional rotten defense attorney or thoroughly disagreeable judge. Sometimes a client is cranky, but often for a good reason. The deadlines are quite stressful for everyone in our office, as in any law office.

Chapter Seven

Appearances Are Everything

The attention of my audience was fixed upon my clothes instead of my words.

Susan B. Anthony,
explaining her objection to wearing "bloomers"[1]

It has been expressed to me time after time, in interview after interview for this book, that the gender battles have *not* all been fought and won. Many skirmishes have gone underground and become more subtle, and it would be wrong to assume there are no remaining issues that present roadblocks to women's professional aspirations. For the woman lawyer, her outward appearance is just such an issue.

As recently as twenty-five years ago, a woman found in the office or courtroom was not presumed to be the lawyer, but rather, the secretary, so clothes served a dual purpose: setting the woman lawyer apart from support staff, and demanding that she be taken seriously as a lawyer. The public is now accustomed to seeing women behind the desk, yet women still have every reason to present the *appearance* of being serious players. This is because gender is *still* an issue and because, as with any lawyer, one's professional image will always be an issue.

I believe that what is at stake is our credibility. As stated in the report of the ABA Commission on Women in the Profession, "[w]omen do not receive the same presumption of competence as their male counterparts."[2] This truth is often manifested in attire; perhaps that is why men have the luxury of "dressing down," which women do not share.

A Professional Appearance

Before a lawyer opens her mouth, an impression is created simply by the way she looks. Is she stern and fearsome? Is she approachable? Is she serious? Hair, makeup, jewelry, hemlines, and pantsuits broadcast a message about her the moment she enters a courtroom, boardroom, or office. A lawyer wants to convey confidence, seriousness of purpose, an aura of "success," and preparedness. The image one hopes to project may be undermined by a fashion faux pas. Outward appearances still contribute much to a positive lawyerly image.

In general terms, all the debates about specific fashion choices come down to the need to appear "professional." In law school, we were taught to "talk like a lawyer" and "think like a lawyer." The need to "look like a lawyer" is just as important to our work. U.S. District Court Judge Norma Shapiro offers the following pearls of wisdom:

> I have never learned how you "look like a lawyer," but until recently, no sex stereotype suggested any young woman fit the mold. Sign carrying is not in vogue but briefcases are: they help. So do glasses; they suggest seriousness. Simplicity, not imitation of "masculine" severity, sets the proper tone. The able advocate will want to call attention to the message, not make a fashion statement. Clothes should fit and complement the person. Be conservative, not avant-garde; jewelry will be pleasing if neither obviously expensive nor clearly distracting. Studies have shown, rightly or wrongly, that appearance aids in acceptance. There is nothing wrong with aiming to have a pleasant appearance, rather than one that offends. Good grooming is as important for a woman advocate as for a male attorney. Unkempt hair or a disheveled

appearance suggest similar sloppiness of thought and hurt the client's case.[3]

Just what "professional" is has been a matter of great debate amongst women lawyers. Many find it hard to agree upon what is acceptable and what is unprofessional. Through the years, women lawyers have been rebels and conformers to fashion demands in their attempts to find the right attire: not too sexy, not too dowdy, not too masculine, and not too feminine. Finding the right balance within this fashion box is the ultimate challenge.

My divorce clients come to me and say that in settling with their spouses they want to be "fair." Fair is one of those subjective words. It means different things to different people. The same applies to women lawyers' professional appearances. Like pornography, we may not be able to define it, but we know it when we see it.

"To be a professional is to always appear professional," offers U.S. Tax Court Judge Cohen. "Dress like a lawyer; set the tone; be professional," offers Pennsylvania Superior Court Judge Beck. It is basic advice for the woman who enters the legal profession. Until she can wear the judicial black robes, a woman must wear professional lawyer attire—stylish but not playful. If only it were as simple as donning a barrister's white wig and gown.

Serving the Needs of the Client

During the close of the nineteenth century, when women were first admitted to the bar, it was the fashion of the day to wear a bonnet in public. Finding bonnets frivolous and cumbersome, some women lawyers rebelled. Risking the disapproval of the court and society, women lawyers in Illinois and elsewhere took a stand and removed their bonnets. Lawyer Margaret L. Wilcox gave her opinion on the bonnet debate in an article published on June 1, 1889, in *Dear Equity Club:*

I give you fair warning that I shall wage unending warfare for the free-dom of women lawyers. If one should choose to lay aside her bonnet in the courtroom, whether on account of a heated atmosphere, or the shabbiness of the bonnet, or because she knows, intuitively, that the jury to be addressed would be prejudiced against her argument by either the extremely fashionable style of her hat, or its lack of style; whether one should plead with bonnet on, feeling confident that its beauty and becoming style lends persuasion to her tongue, or conscious that her hair needs the friendly concealment of a hat, in either case, I maintain that it is the inalienable right of each lady to follow her "own sweet will." Her keen intuition will guide her aright.[4]

Margaret Wilcox's words are worth remembering. She spoke of bonnets, but her wisdom can be heeded today when considering the choice of dresses, suits, pants, or heel size. Margaret Wilcox reminds us that the purpose of a single fashion item is to serve the needs of the client, not the lawyer. This distinction is one that women lawyers should bear in mind when deciding whether to accept or reject a fashion statement that may be acceptable outside the office, but completely wrong for the work that needs to be accomplished and the image to be created.

Feminine — Not Sexy

By entering a profession that has traditionally been all male, women have struggled with choosing between blending in, or somehow holding on to their femininity, bringing something new to the pro-fession. For a long time, we wound up wearing suits with men's fab-rics but dressed up with bows—the ultimate schizophrenic fashion statement. I read with great interest the comments collected from Philadelphia's senior women lawyers (law school graduates before 1960) on matters of appearance and dress. I would have assumed (incorrectly, it appears) that the women of the 1930s, 1940s, and 1950s would have downplayed their appearance as women and sought serious attire, to distinguish themselves from the administrative staff where men employers wished to confine them. On the contrary, I read comments such as these:

> I personally believe that wearing men's-style clothing, suits and ties, and otherwise imitating men is not helpful; I think women should look like they are: female.[5]
>
> Too many women try to look like men.[6]
>
> Be firm and fair, and look like a woman.[7]

These insights come from longtime observers of fashion trends, who came into the profession decades before women's work suits were even available. Their comments reflect their observations of the fashion garb of the 1960s and 1970s, when women lawyers struggled with some fairly awful style changes that included dark suits (with skirts only) and, for a brief time, male neckties. The ties gave way to floppy bows and then short bows in primary colors from male necktie material. The yin and yang of male and female: severe suits with ruffles. Today the bows are gone, but there is still much confusion about professional appearances. What we have learned is that to command respect, it is not necessary to imitate men in their manner and attire. Women do not have to jettison style and personal expression entirely.

In crafting and projecting an image to others, women lawyers suffer the examples projected for the masses on our television screens at home. In earlier days, Katharine Hepburn in the 1949 film *Adam's Rib*, Debra Winger in the 1986 film *Legal Eagles*, and Glenn Close in the 1985 film *Jagged Edge* were among the first modern women lawyers portrayed on screen. Katharine Hepburn wore a pantsuit and Debra Winger and Glenn Close wore suits with skirts and bows. The image of the woman lawyer today—rake-thin, in miniskirt, plunging neckline, high heels, and ruffled shirt, as played on television in *Philly* and *Ally McBeal*—is, to me, evidence of the ongoing fight real women lawyers face to engender respect as professionals. Reese Witherspoon's pink Barbie-doll lawyer imitation in *Legally Blonde 2* challenges my sense of humor. The sight of nine-year-old girls entering the theater to watch her heroically mock women lawyers repulses me. Are these the role models for the next generation of young women lawyers?

As many know, Ally McBeal was a Boston lawyer portrayed by Calista Flockhart in the television series bearing that name. A *New York Times* article marking the demise of the series commented that "Ally came to symbolize the nation's collective fatigue over old-style Gloria Steinemish concerns." The author notes further that the character's success was largely an element of this "post-feminist" period and that "[i]t had become simply unfashionable to call too much attention to the dusty old hurdles that had galvanized the women's movement in the 1960s and '70s, like equal pay, the glass ceiling and child-care tax credits."[8] For real women lawyers, these issues have never become shopworn or tiresome. It is the ditsy, sexy, on-screen lawyer who real women lawyers need to dress against.

Wearing the Pants

I know it sounds trite, but nothing provoked such a passionate reaction from my interviews as my question about wearing pants to work. It was an issue I stumbled upon while watching the television program *Philly* (now off the air). Maggie, the show's star lawyer, argued a motion in court wearing a tailored, navy-blue pantsuit and blue shirt. It struck me as unreal, unresearched. Women do not wear pants to court, I thought. It occurred to me to solicit other views on the issue of wearing pants. Maybe it was I who was out of touch with the times.

Wearing pants has been a preoccupation of women in this country since at least the nineteenth century. Understandably, women's attire in the nineteenth and early twentieth centuries inspired much cause for rebellion. A dress usually consisted of several layers of petticoats and a hard frame of bone, wire, or straw to keep a bowl shape to the ground, whereupon the dress spilled over and behind to drag upon the ground. Waist supports and petticoats were tightened to maintain an hourglass figure. While wearing such garments, women were expected to cook, clean, carry, garden, bend, and climb. They would also be expected to practice law in the same outfit.

The woman responsible for introducing a pant-like outfit to women of the midnineteenth century was Elizabeth Susan Miller, a cousin of activist Elizabeth Cady Stanton. Elizabeth Miller had been to Switzerland and observed women in sanitariums wearing outfits that resembled loose pants. Encouraged by her activist mother, Gerrit Smith, and her father, Elizabeth Miller designed an outfit for herself and her cousin Elizabeth Stanton. The new outfit consisted of long billowing pants tied tightly at the ankles with a below-the-knee overlay skirt. Making a sensation in their new outfits, the two Elizabeths walked the streets of Seneca Falls, New York, where they were noticed by Amelia Bloomer. Amelia was immediately converted and popularized the new outfit in her activist newsletter, the *Lily*. From there sprung an entire movement entitled "bloomerism." Any woman wearing bloomers was nicknamed "Dolly Bloomer." Bloomers came to describe any split-skirt outfit, which became all the more in demand as a result of a new craze for bicycle riding. Bloomers in another shape were worn by women professional baseball players in leagues that competed between 1890 and 1934. The New York Bloomers competed with the Philadelphia Bobbies, so named for their bobbed, short hairstyles. In 1944, Edgar Yip Harburg and Harold Arlen, score writers for the *Wizard of Oz*, wrote a popular Broadway musical, *Bloomer Girls*, starring Celeste Holm, which dramatized the bloomer movement of the previous century. Revivals have run off-Broadway as recently as 2002.

The movement was short-lived. Elizabeth Stanton hastened its demise because she felt that the furor over women's attire outweighed its benefits for women's rights. She wrote to Susan Anthony that "[i]t is not wise to use up so much energy and feeling in that way. You can put them to better use."[9] Susan Anthony also positioned herself against dress reforms while concurrently advocating for women's legal rights, stating that "[b]y urging two, both are injured, as the average mind can grasp and assimilate but one idea at a time."[10]

The debate about pants for women lawyers is about the standard of professional attire, but it is much more than that. Wearing pants is also political—it is about bringing the woman's movement to the male den, the workplace that had been his refuge. No one still debates the propriety of women wearing pants privately. There are some smashing pantsuits that are the essence of glamour. Notwithstanding Katherine Hepburn, however, wearing a pantsuit at work or in court, I must report, is not universally accepted as either professional or serious. More often, a pantsuit is viewed as "dressing down" or dressing casually. When a woman chooses a vocation (like the law) to represent others first, rather than herself, then like it or not, she must adapt to the situation. Keep in mind the words of lawyer Margaret Wilcox when she spoke of bonnets.

I raised the topic of the pantsuit debate with law professor Diane Maleson. At the time, we were both wearing black pantsuits, and yet she related that in all her professional appearances she wears suits, dresses, or skirts. Perhaps this dates us. When Professor Maleson entered the working world in the 1960s, there was no such thing as "the pantsuit" for working women. When it appeared sometime later in the 1970s, it was a revolutionary fashion statement. I recognize that those were the years in which my sensibilities were formed. But even so, Professor Maleson added, sounding very much like a modern-day Susan B. Anthony, "[w]hy unnecessarily raise side issues in our quest for professional advancement and credibility by wearing pants?" And I agree. Younger women, and those not so young, who resent this dress code and vow to wear pants may find themselves using their energies to fight the wrong battle.

Today's women law school graduates often express a desire to wear pantsuits to the office and to court. That this is not entirely acceptable everywhere causes some frustration and even elicits some anger. Temple Law School graduate of 2002, Sara Shubert, offers: "If a judge, client, or attorney has not accepted women wearing pants by this point, he or she has a problem that goes beyond me. I don't think it necessary to cater to his or her anachronistic ways, and I believe a pantsuit is as formal and respectful as one with a skirt." Cynthia Mason joins the pantsuit debate: "It should be [acceptable to wear pants to court]—the skirt thing has always irked me. Why should employers like Lynne Abraham require them?"

Indeed, the district attorney of Philadelphia, Lynne Abraham, established a dress code that required women lawyers in her office to wear suits with skirts of appropriate length. She required all male lawyers on her staff to also wear suits and ties. Her dress code precluded skirts and tops, dresses, and sport jackets. When I apologized for raising an issue that may seem "trite" to many, District Attorney Abraham strongly disagreed. "We are," she said, "what we appear to be." It is extremely important, she continued, that victims, witnesses, jurors, and defendants readily identify the person who is the district attorney in a courtroom. Indeed, she declared, the public, who come to rely upon the services of the district attorney's office in times of misfortune, should be entitled to the same representation as those who pay $650 an hour for defense lawyers. For Lynne Abraham, requiring a "dress code" is a matter of professionalism, not feminism.

District Attorney Abraham explained her views: In a courtroom, the judge is easily identified by the robes he or she wears. And so, like any other professional, a lawyer has an appearance to present. We expect our doctors and dentists to wear certain attire. Imagine our reactions, she explained, if a surgeon appeared to discuss a future operation sporting green hair, cutoffs, and nose rings. Complementing the advice of Judge Norma Shapiro earlier in this chapter, Lynne Abraham added her insights on hair and jewelry: Hair in the eyes, hair that is played with constantly, hand motions to put hair back over the ears, earrings that dangle—all these things detract from the message the lawyer is delivering. District Attorney Abraham does not spare the men in her criticisms: A beard with food in it or a mustache that is played with detracts from a lawyer's effectiveness. A juror's focus should be upon the lawyer's words and nothing else.

There is another, more important reason behind what some see as Lynne Abraham's "strict" code of attire: respect—for the system and for the participants in the system. As a judge, Lynne Abraham insisted that even the jurors dress with respect for the occasion. She recalled instances of sending jurors home to change if they appeared in flip-flops or undershirts and shorts. In criminal court particularly, lives and liberty are at stake. The judiciary is our third branch of government, protected and created by our Constitution. Why not bring to our judicial proceedings our full respect for law and democracy?

But then, lo and behold, in its November 26, 2003, issue, the *Philadelphia Inquirer* reported that District Attorney Abraham announced at a staff meeting that her prohibition of pantsuits was a thing of the past. As the *Inquirer* quoted District Attorney Abraham, "I went to New York with my husband last weekend and shopped around. . . . It's apparent to me that it's harder and harder to find suits with skirts—and then the skirts are way too short!" So now, women in the Philadelphia district attorney's office are permitted to wear business pantsuits, with pants and jackets tailored from the same fabric (no khakis and blazers). Nevertheless, District Attorney Abraham's standards remain high for both women and men. No one can argue with her motives and frankly, after some observations of my own, I agree with her message.

When I visited with Eastern District Court Judge Norma Shapiro, she noted that it had come to her attention recently that women were questioning the appropriateness of various attire. Her law clerks wanted to know if they had permission to wear *dresses* instead of suits with skirts. They feared dresses would be too informal for work at the court. Judge Shapiro wears dresses all the time and so, of course, she said that dresses would be appropriate for her clerks. She was impressed by the amount of confusion women find for themselves over this issue. I learned that the women judges of the Eastern District Court of Pennsylvania recently decided among themselves that pants would be acceptable under judicial robes, a practice Judge Shapiro has decided to forgo due to lack of comfort.

Hillary Rodham Clinton wore black pantsuits routinely during her campaign for the U.S. Senate, and Pennsylvania Superior Court Judge Phyllis Beck wears them. Barbara Vetri, one of Philadelphia's senior lawyers, wears them to the office and gives a glamorous professional appearance. Some do and some do not. The problem for women is knowing whether a particular judge or partner or client may take offense, and by then it may be too late. Twenty-five years ago, my law partner witnessed a senior judge berating a woman lawyer for wearing a pantsuit to court. A judge today may not articulate disapproval so vehemently, but the sentiments may still be there. Philadelphia Court of Common Pleas Senior Judge Richette admires the articulate women lawyers practicing before her, without being put off by their wearing pants. She may not be in the majority.

Most women want to wear pants to work because they are comfortable, practical, and warm. Before you wear pants on every occasion, I suggest using the intuitive—yet cautious—approach advocated by Arlyn Katzen Landau, a 2002 law school graduate. She wisely reflected in our conversation that although she would like to be able to wear appropriate pantsuits to court or work, she did not know if every judge or employer would be accepting. And if for no reason other than that, she planned to start work the following September wearing suits with skirts.

Hemlines

Most women will agree: If you walk down the street in a miniskirt, there is a good chance heads will turn and hardhats will whistle. Walk down the hall of your law firm in the same skirt, and chances are your legs will attract more attention than your well-reasoned arguments. I recently shared a teaching panel with a woman in a loud, micro-mini suit that set off my radar for inappropriate dress.

Rather than a "mini," a hemline at midcalf (the "midi") or near the knee is the hemline of choice for the working woman, and with good reason. Aside from the discomfort that many will recall of sitting and bending in a "mini" without becoming obscene, short skirts create an opportunity for others to notice outward appearances with a negative, less serious connotation rather than a positive, professional one.

There is irony in the fact that pants may be too casual for the office and skirts the outfit of choice. But clearly, not just any skirt will do. Fashion masters attempted to revive the miniskirt in spring 2003, after an absence from the clothes rack for more than three decades. But manufacturers concede that professional women will not sport miniskirts to work. Most manufacturers are also promoting longer, straight skirts for the working woman, with hemlines that stop just above or below the knee.

Criticisms about hemlines may not be fair, and may reflect upon the anti-female biases of the detractors. In the 1970s, when a woman law professor was still a rare sighting, Professor Maleson of Temple University Law School solicited feedback about her teaching in year-end student questionnaires; she recalls receiving feedback that derided her appearance with comments such as these: "She always looks like her clothes come from Bonwit Teller" (a now-closed fashionable women's clothing store), and, "Her skirts show too much leg." Professor Maleson did not wear miniskirts, but male resentment of her youth, sex, brains, good looks, and authority focused upon her attire. Fair or unfair, a woman's hemline projects a certain stereotype about her professionalism and targets her for criticism that can stand in the way of her success.

Shoes

I have one other issue to lay down before my sisters in the profession—the matter of shoes. When I began practicing law in 1980, spiked heels—anywhere from one to three inches high—were the norm. After a few years, and I cannot quite recall when this occurred, women who worked in cities got smart and started wearing sneakers with their suits, at least outside the office. Most changed back to spiked heels inside the office. Then women got even smarter and flat shoes became the acceptable style. In August 2002, I personally tossed a large bag of spiked pumps in the trash, considering them relics of an earlier era. Now, imagine my dismay when I strolled through Bloomingdale's at the mall and discovered shoe after shoe with two- to three-inch spiked heels. It is my fervent hope that the women graduating today will not repeat the errant ways of my generation and rush into stores to buy spiked heels.

On a somber note, I, like the rest of the nation, watched programs about the fall of the World Trade Center Towers and, while the entire event is tragic and sorrowful, I was struck by a minor fact. One documentary showed women rushing out of the buildings and down stairwells, barefoot with their feet bloody from glass. Their shoes, unlike men's practical shoes, had restricted their walking and endangered their very lives and so were discarded. Spike heels, in my opinion, are neither professional nor sensible.

What to Wear to Court

Men and women benefit from the same advice on court appearances. The goal is to demonstrate respect for the court, in manner and appearance. Joe Pesci portrays a lawyer in the film, *My Cousin Vinnie*. By a series of mishaps, he appears without his good suit in a small country courthouse with a fearsome judge. Throughout the film, he appears in one bad outfit after the next, all to the consternation of the judge, who is convinced that the lawyer is intentionally showing disrespect for the judge and the judicial process. It is no different today in real-life court, for both sexes. A woman who appears in court in a miniskirt is likely to undermine her case and draw untoward attention to her person, just as a man would do in a loud sport jacket. My husband recalls being advised by his senior mentor, Max

Verlin, to never go to court without wearing a dark-blue, three-piece suit. He adds, "I saw Judge Charles Klein [of the Philadelphia Common Pleas Court] throw a lawyer out of the courtroom for wearing a sport jacket."

Do you wear skirts or pants to court? Judge Cohen, Judge Shapiro, and District Attorney Abraham advise skirts. Common Pleas Court Judge Richette does not mind women lawyers appearing in court in pantsuits. The difficulty is knowing your judge's bias. Because it is impossible to always know how a judge (or, for that matter, a jury) might react to a pantsuit, my suggestion would be to dress more traditionally. Also remember that judges are generally older and from a different generation, one that predates the pantsuit as acceptable courtroom attire. One day this may all change, but it hasn't yet. Remember, your work and your appearance are not about your clothes or you. They are about your client and your case. Anything that detracts from your case or distracts the judge or jury has to go.

Lawyerism Trumps Feminism

A woman lawyer is not an advocate for women, she is an advocate for her client. At work, the woman lawyer must sublimate her own fashion agenda for the agenda of her client. This requires flexibility, depending upon the client and the situation. Certain attire may be more appropriate with Fortune 500 corporate clients than with blue-collar clients. In the office, a lawyer should try to gain the respect of a client and appear as someone the client can entrust with problems and confidences.

Sitting in a courtroom packed with lawyers for a call of the calendar, I looked around at the women and was dismayed at so many disheveled appearances. I believe that women lawyers should never forget the reason they are there and must be prepared to forfeit their personal styles, to some extent. I say this having been raised in the 1960s, when my one favorite piece of attire was hip-hugger bellbottoms (sweeping the floor, of course). People in suits were "square." My clothes were an extension of my personality, my politics, and my sense of art and style. Finding myself in an occupation that required conformity instilled me with inner dread and horror. I remember hating the way I looked on my first day at work. Wearing pants today is merely an issue of comfort and, in my mind, is indicative of how comfortable many women feel with their acceptance as lawyers. This is good news. That being said, from my twenty-some years in this profession and my conversations with a number of women lawyers with more years of experience than I, I offer my conclusions. Forget the short skirts, the little back dresses, the plunging necklines, and the sleeveless, jacketless T-shirts, all of which were represented during my visit to the courtroom. Women would be well advised to dress both respectfully and appropriately. Although it is my personal belief that women lawyers should dress up rather than down every day, certainly talking like a lawyer and dressing like a lawyer should be the rule when in court or meeting clients, even if it means only passing them in the hall. After all, you are your own best salesperson, and the look you convey should be one of success and confidence. I do not mean to advocate sublimating all personal style. I am not opposed to a touch of flamboyance or signature accessories. There are notable lawyers whose identities are forever linked to individual accoutrements: a red bowtie (Thatcher Longstreth), a cowboy jacket (Gerry Spence), or a black hat (Miriam Gafni). I am certain others come to your mind. As Delaware lawyer Ellisa Habbart aptly pointed out, one of the measures of success is wearing what suits you best. In her opinion, there is no hard-and-fast right or wrong way to dress; it's more about how you carry yourself. That can mean opting for a navy suit with an Oxford shirt, if that's your style, or perhaps a stylish knit suit and important jewelry or any other fashionable selection within the range of appropriate garb. Ellisa holds that cultivating a distinctive image and being comfortable in your appearance can affect your entire performance.

Yes, it is true that the Queen of England has been seen wearing pants—but I am certain that it has not been on royal occasions. The woman lawyer must also dress for the occasion.

Conclusion

In conclusion, I offer an anecdote told to me by the former Philadelphia Bar Association Chancellor. In a conversation in which Chancellor Audrey Talley shared my apprehensions about wearing pants to court and work, she told me a story of her early days at work in a large firm. As part of the unspoken dress code then, women did not wear opaque or colored hosiery. One day, she wore black hosiery instead of clear. One of the senior partners took one look at her and commented that she looked like she was on her way to work out at the gym. There is nothing we do or wear that goes unnoticed. Recall Marcia Clark, the prosecuting attorney in the O.J. Simpson trial—she made headlines just by changing her hairstyle from straight to curly.

Women's initial struggles concerning what to wear had to do with countering the general assumption that they were support staff and secretaries rather than lawyers. In most venues, the presence of women around courtrooms and law offices in the capacity of lawyer or judge is no longer groundbreaking. But gender undeniably remains an issue for women. By appearing professional, women demand respect for themselves as professionals. Appearance is an important factor in how we are judged by the public. Our choice of clothing should not be based upon what might make us look good at a social occasion, but rather upon the image we want to project as lawyers. By appearing professional, women declare themselves worthy of the respect and confidence of judges, juries, their peers, and, not the least, their paying clients.

ENDNOTES

1. MIRIAM GURKO, THE LADIES OF SENECA FALLS, THE BIRTH OF THE WOMAN'S RIGHTS MOVEMENT 154 (1974).

2. ABA COMM'N ON WOMEN IN THE PROFESSION, THE UNFINISHED AGENDA, WOMEN AND THE LEGAL PROFESSION 15 (2001) (prepared by Deborah L. Rhode). Reprinted with permission.

3. Norma Shapiro, *Bench with a Point of View: How to Create Confidence in the Courtroom,* in THE WOMAN ADVOCATE 215, 216 (Jean Maclean Snyder & Andra Barmash Greene eds., ABA 1996).

4. GWEN HOERR MCNAMEE, *Practical Concerns, in* BAR NONE 31 (Gwen Hoerr McNamee ed., Chicago Bar Association (1998) (quoting Margaret Wilcox, in *Dear Equity Club,* June 1, 1889, reprinted in VIRGINIA G. DRACHMAN, SISTERS IN LAW, WOMEN LAWYERS IN MODERN AMERICAN HISTORY 177–78 (1998)).

5. PHILA. BAR ASS'N COMM. ON WOMEN IN THE PROFESSION, CELEBRATING MORE THAN A CENTURY OF WOMEN LAWYERS IN PHILADELPHIA 1883–1997 31 (1997) (quoting C. Dowben).

6. *Id.* at 34 (quoting B. C. Molinsky).

7. *Id.* (quoting Hon. L. A. Richette).

8. Ginia Bellafante, *Sic Transit Ally: A '90s Feminist Is Bowing Out,* N.Y. TIMES, Apr. 21, 2002, at sec. 9, 1.

9. GURKO, *supra* note 1, at 153.

10. *Id.* at 154.

"A Day in the Life"
A lawyer in St. Petersburg, Florida

My practice is in civil trial work, mainly plaintiff's first-party property and casualty insurance law, and I practice alone.

Since I can't get my practice to work around my "real life," my life has to work around my practice. For example, I have at least twice the "normal" amount of underwear because it is sometimes weeks before I can find the time to do the laundry. When looking for a dog, I chose a Yorkie because being small, he could get sufficient exercise running around the house, and I installed a doggie door to my fenced patio so he can go outside himself as I am often not around to walk him or to take him to the dog park to run.

I used to be a really good cook and enjoyed making complex dishes and meals. Now, the most adventurous I get in the kitchen is to broil a steak, chop, or chicken breast. I mainly survive on prepared or packaged foods, along with bags of salad, gallons of juice, and fresh fruit.

I make a deliberate effort not to look at my floors most of the time because I do not have time to give them the attention they need, and they can be quite awful for extended periods of time. My friends have become used to voice mail and have come to understand that my legal schedule trumps everything else. I often do my grocery shopping late at night at the twenty-four-hour Kash & Karry, and stop at Home Depot, which is open until midnight, on my way home.

I seem to own only shorts, jeans, and "court clothes." I seldom get the opportunity to shop for new clothes and shoes. When I do shop, it is often hurried. I seldom shop with my friends because they want to wander around the store looking at stuff in a leisurely way. I also like to do that, but I am seldom able to make the time. I am good at ironing and used to do my own. Now, anything that won't make it through the washer and dryer in condition to be worn immediately without further ado goes to the cleaners, and I make an effort not to purchase such items.

Chapter Eight

Dating and Romance

The law is a jealous mistress, and requires a long and constant
courtship. It is not to be won by trifling favors, but by lavish homage.

Joseph Story (1779–1845)
former U.S. Supreme Court Justice
and educator at Harvard Law School

Who Wants to Date a Woman Lawyer?

Once you head down the career path of becoming a lawyer, there is
no turning back. Changes in the way you think and talk overtake
you, and changes also occur in the way others perceive you. Law
school changes you. This has a serious impact—either positive or negative—upon dating and romance. Being a lawyer is not a neutral
event. It makes a difference in whom you meet and whether sparks
or daggers fly in your direction.

Lawyers are smart and generally verbal. That much we know.
From here, the stereotypes begin. The worst of these are that lawyers
are argumentative, tricky, aggressive, self-involved, and opportunistic. These are qualities that, at best, look well on a man if held up to
a different light. "Aggressive" mutates into "assertive": translation—a

guy who won't get pushed around by the garage mechanic. "Opportunistic" and "self-involved" mean "professionally driven": translation—a guy who offers financial security. For women, these qualities can be the kiss of death. "Argumentative" and "aggressive" have no ameliorating side for women, and not much to offer in the way of romance. Caroline Vincent of Los Angeles adds:

> I completely identify with Miranda on *Sex and the City*. It's hard to be smart, considered powerful because of your lawyer title, and convince men that you can be nonthreatening and feminine at the same time.

No wonder that on first dates, many women hold back revealing what they do. I remember those first dates when sometime over the dinner table, or maybe just standing in line at the movies, the subject of "What do you do?" came up. I was a law student at the time. Sometimes the response was subtle and sometimes not so subtle. I recall one person who rolled back his eyes and declared in flat tones, "Oh, . . . you're going to law school." Another was a little less subtle: "Oh, you're one of those." Need I add that there was rarely a second date. That was in the 1980s, but even today, many women lawyers report the same tepid response from men.

Mary, a 1994 law school graduate residing in Salt Lake City, Utah, adds, "I have to admit it's harder to get a date now that I'm a lawyer than it was when I was an art historian. Guys are kind of intimidated by women attorneys." It is the fear that we will win our way in every argument. The fear that we will have them on the witness stand answering rapid-fire questions about whose turn it is to take out the trash. One criminal prosecutor confesses, "I don't disclose my occupation at first; it tends to frighten men off." Amy Packer of Denver, Colorado, a 2000 graduate of the University of Denver College of Law, agrees: "It took me quite a long time to find someone who was not threatened." And from Amber Anderson of Fort Worth, Texas, a 1997 graduate of the University of Texas: "[It took] me a while to figure out that there are few men who can handle or want a smart woman." Some men, the ones women lawyers should have no interest in, simply shy away from smart women. A woman lawyer's desire for intellectual compatibility may also narrow the playing field.

Even in this day, a woman's career or financial success can be intimidating or off-putting to many a man who still likes the idea that he earns more and is more "successful" in his career. Many women lawyers are successful to the same degree as men, or more so. They earn big salaries, hold respectable titles where they work, and command wide networks of professional contacts. Christina Lewis, a 1983 graduate of the University of Texas Law School and plaintiffs' personal injury lawyer, shares her experience:

> I found that some men found it interesting and attractive that I was an attorney, but when [they realized] that I made more money and/or was more successful than they thought they were, it became a real problem.

The issue raised by competing careers is not just one of adjusting egos to comparative success. A woman's success threatens the traditional balance of power at home. When the primary family breadwinner becomes the female rather than the male, an equal division or complete shift of domestic labors is compulsory.

My husband reflected upon the days when I was dating with mixed success and frustration. He offered these thoughts, with an uplifting conclusion:

> I recall being told how difficult dating was for a woman lawyer, and indeed a tax lawyer—how her dates would be put off by the fact that she was a lawyer and how even lawyers would be frightened by the fact that she was a tax lawyer. Men, it seems, are often afraid of smart and successful women. But what may have been frightening for them turned out to be good for me. As Mark Twain has written, "Let us be thankful for the fools. But for them, the rest of us could not succeed."

Being honest with ourselves and with others about our expectations for time, comfort, support, and housework is key to finding compatible mates. Thiele Branham of Columbia, South Carolina, a

2000 graduate of the University of South Carolina Law School, notices that some men undervalue her career commitment:

> I think that men that I date have to understand that my career is just as time consuming and important to me as their career is to them. That is hard to explain and even harder to find.

Creating a nontraditional relationship today is one of the greatest challenges facing a woman lawyer. It requires a mutual respect that each person must have for the career of the other, and a mutual willingness to accommodate for the common good.

Unfortunately, one of the greatest impediments to dating is not a lack of men, but a lack of time. When a single woman finishes law school and begins to practice law, her life is consumed by full-time work that can command sixty or more hours a week. She may look up from her work ten years later and discover that all the "eligible" men are gone. It is axiomatic that the women's pool of eligible men diminishes with age, while the men's pool of eligible women increases. As one Indiana lawyer offers, "Thankfully I did not have a terrible work schedule and was able to socialize, allowing me to marry my husband." A sixty-hour-plus workweek does not leave much time for anything else. Cynthia Mason, a recent graduate of Temple's Beasley School of Law, is in her late twenties. Still single, she writes about how her busy life has crowded out time for socializing: "Law school took over and made it difficult to have meaningful relationships."

Once a woman crosses the Rubicon, there is no turning back, and it becomes time to consider the positives and not just the negatives. After all, most of us went to law school to enter a new world and leave the old one behind. Being a lawyer creates infinite opportunities to meet interesting men in the office and at bar association functions, just to start the list of professional and social opportunities.

It is logical that single women lawyers will date other lawyers. That is who they meet and contact every day. When successful women lawyers go looking for companionship, particularly if they are in one of those sixty-hour-a-week jobs, it makes sense that their search would take them to other lawyers. One 1999 University of Florida graduate comments:

> I date almost exclusively other lawyers. Other men seem to be threatened by my degree of education. Also, a lot of men in less demanding jobs seem incapable of being supportive about long hours, stress, etc. Many men don't seem to care what women do for a living. I've had men suggest I quit my job many times, rather than understanding that I want to work through the challenges.

Others feel exactly the opposite. One Montana lawyer retorts:

> I won't date lawyers—why have two people in a relationship with debating skills?

Dating a fellow law student is not the obvious solution it might otherwise appear to be. In the 1940s, 1950s, and 1960s, women who attended law school were few in number. These women often experienced hostility from many of their male counterparts. They were excluded from study groups, and openly castigated for "taking the place" of men. Philadelphia Common Pleas Court Judge Carolyn Engel Temin, a 1958 graduate of the University of Pennsylvania Law School, offers the story of being excluded from all-male study groups. The men claimed they preferred to study in their underwear. Judge Temin's mother warned her that if she did not marry before graduating, she would never marry.

Years later, the men of my 1980 law school class, with a few exceptions, did not marry the women lawyers they met in school. Although I never felt excluded from a study group because of my gender, I did sense that most of the men did not regard the women of our class romantically. It was not the same resentment that was felt in earlier decades. It was more that the mystery of what the men did—the sheer impressiveness of being "a lawyer"—faded against the mirror image of a spouse doing the same thing. The men were young, and they needed to impress.

The reality is that many women lawyers find their soul mates in other lawyers because they understand the work, the hours, and the lifestyle. I think that once initial feelings of competition subside, law school finally ends, and everyone has a job, men and women lawyers find they have much in common. Many women lawyers with whom I spoke are married to lawyers. Karen, of San Fernando, California, and her husband are both criminal lawyers. Some, including yours truly, married a law partner. Others, I know, feel that two lawyers under the same roof is an explosive combination.

Women are less willing to downplay their achievements in social settings than they may have been twenty-five years ago. Los Angeles lawyer Naomi Norwood offers the best advice: "It's possible that some men are afraid of really capable, successful lawyers. But who would want them, anyway?" One terrifically romantic story came to me from Somerville, New Jersey. Susan D. Mario found happiness with her new mate:

> When I first met my fiancé at a party, he was thrilled to find out I was a lawyer because, as he puts it, the rest of the package was so perfect that it's all I needed to win him over. He says that nothing turns him on like a smart woman. Mind you, the man is a master mechanic in a public-works garage—he turns every stereotype there is upside down. He has always applauded the successes I've had. His theory is that women should run the world, men should pick up the trash and deliver the mail, and women should arrive home from work every night to find dinner on the table. And did I mention he is a phenomenal cook?

The qualities of a lawyer and woman need not be perceived as mutually exclusive. Think about the positive qualities of a lawyer that complete the image: problem solver, competent, hard worker, champion of the less empowered, advocate, thoughtful. These qualities are consistent with being an attractive woman. Some may see only the negative qualities, but others more enlightened will recognize the positive strengths of a woman lawyer. As Moi Vienneau of Ontario, Canada, confirms, "I think if you're comfortable enough with who you are, there is no need to downplay anything." Being comfortable with ourselves as women and as lawyers is what it is all about.

Professional Women on Their Own

The inability to engage fully in one's career and marry is a common concern of many prospective women lawyers. Statistics confirm their fears. For the year 2001, the ABA Commission on Women in the Profession reports that "[a]lmost half of women in legal practice are currently unmarried, compared with 15 percent of men, and few women have partners who are primary caretakers."[1] The Philadelphia Bar Association's 1990 survey reported that 37.3 percent of Philadelphia's women lawyers were single and had never been married. For 2000, the Philadelphia Bar Association's survey showed that, of the women responding, 41 percent under the age of thirty-five were single, never having been married (compared with 32 percent of the men). Twenty-two percent of the women between the ages of thirty-six and fifty remained unmarried, compared with 9 percent of the men in this age bracket.

How does this happen? Both by choice and by circumstance. Societal and family pressures play a large part in when—and whether—we choose to marry. Marina Angel, a Temple University law professor, offers this soul-searching description of her reasons for remaining single:

> I began to think about the abstract possibility of marriage and children. It was clear to me that I was working incredibly hard with very long hours to maintain the kind of grades that I had been achieving. Coming from a traditional Greek-American background, it had also been made clear to me that the roles of wife and mother were difficult and time consuming. I realized it would be impossible to find a man to share even half the job of running a home and raising children. And even if I managed, I would be competing professionally with men married to women who were carrying 100 percent of the job of running a home and raising children. It seemed clear that the possibility of combining marriage and children with a successful legal career was close to zero. Given a choice between the two, I decided that I would make a miserable wife and mother if I were unhappy, and therefore, those goals would probably have to be set aside in favor of a professional career.

Although I consciously reached this conclusion at an early age, I don't believe most professional women do. The statistics indicating the differences between professional men and women in marriage rates and parental status show that most professional women learned this lesson the hard way, because they didn't think it out ahead of time.[2]

Marina Angel's articulation of her personal life choice perhaps can be retold many times by many other women lawyers. Many women fear that a law career and marriage will obliterate—rather than accommodate—one another.

Some women are single by choice for a variety of personal reasons. Some simply fail to find that perfect mate. Many, I am certain, are too busy to look around. In her book *Creating a Life,* author Sylvia Hewlett advocates that professional women bring the same energy and focus to finding husbands that they bring to their schooling and careers. I fear this adds to the burdens of these young women and unfairly adds to their sense of personal fault in matters of the heart. If nearly half of women lawyers nationally are unmarried[3] (and statistics point out that 49 percent of all professional women are childless), that circumstance cannot be attributed solely to a failure to make an effort. Something else is at work to create these statistics.

Changing Aspirations

Whether they are aware of these reported projections about love and marriage, or whether they are responding to more personal impulses or observations, younger women are rebelling. Many expressed to me scaled-back career aspirations, sensing that full-time, high-powered careers would be of short-term duration, giving way to some other work that would allow time for families. You can almost see the skid marks and hear the screech as hard-driving women slam on the brakes. Women who pushed themselves toward academic excellence in grade school, high school, and college hit the wall.

The aspirations of these women on the cusp of their legal careers were uncertain and short-term. The Philadelphia Bar Association membership survey of 2000 indicates that 24 percent of men under the age of thirty-five and 42.9 percent between the ages of thirty-six and fifty aspire to be equity partners or shareholders in a law firm within the next five years, compared with the hopes of only 12.8 percent of women under age thirty-five and 15.4 percent of women between the ages of thirty-six and fifty. Nearly 22 percent of the women under age thirty-five did not know where they would be professionally in five years, and had not yet formed their aspirations.[4]

This ambivalence about work may be explained by another response in the same survey. When asked if they agree with the following statement, a full 38.7 percent of women responded affirmatively: "The stress and long hours of my job are disrupting my family and social life." Of the women who responded positively to this statement, the largest group was in the under-age-thirty-five category, at 48.7 percent. It is interesting that in the next age category, thirty-six to fifty, the percentage of women responding affirmatively drops to 36.3 percent. Younger women, who are the most ambivalent about their futures and yet most nearly on parity economically with their male counterparts, are questioning the balance of their lives. By the time these women reach their midthirties, the dissatisfaction is less. Perhaps, like my classmates, these women have found accommodations that permit them to restore some balance to their lives with less stress. They have learned how to compromise and integrate, albeit at an economic and professional cost.

Thoughts about the Future

Alice Abreu, Temple University law professor, believes that "women today are more savvy, more centered." Many women, and men, are less willing to climb the ladder and sacrifice other meaningful parts of their lives. Arlyn Katzen Landau, one of Temple's 2002 graduates, expresses an equally passionate desire to have a family and pursue a career. She sees that her husband's friends are having babies and that their wives, all nonprofessionals, are working a day or two, if at all. Arlyn cannot imagine herself working part-time. She has put in too much effort through high school and law school to consider part-time work for now. Still, Arlyn does not envision a life for herself in a large firm, at least not forever. She interviewed at two large firms in the city and neither seemed attractive for women. In one, she was interviewed by a female associate who claimed that her work was flexible. It allowed her to go home at 7:30 to spend some time with her children, after which she could put in three hours of work at home. In a second firm, she never saw a female partner. When she inquired about this, a female associate told her that most women did not stay with the firm long enough to become partners, because of the long hours and desire to have family lives as well. Both situations seemed highly undesirable.

When I interviewed Arlyn, she was looking forward to clerking for Pennsylvania Superior Court Judge Phyllis Beck. She has struggled with the idea of when to start a family. One classmate at school, already a mother, advised her that "there is no good time to have a baby. Just less inconvenient times." Sara Shubert, another law school graduate of Temple's 2002 class, had similar impressions of large law firm practices:

> I think large law firms, from what I've seen, are not conducive to the level of involvement I want to have with my family. Therefore, I could see myself leaving a large firm, after a few years, and once I have children, in order to practice in an environment more conducive to family, but I'm not yet sure what that will be. Perhaps, since I want to teach eventually, I would try to clerk or move into teaching around the time that I start a family. I would, if given the option, take advantage of family leave or part-time policies. . . . I would be willing to "lower" my career expectations for a family.

Cynthia Mason, a 2002 graduate of Temple Law School, believes her life will be a "success" if she is able to do the following:

[Find] a way to work part-time in a legal job, doing something related to women's issues that is intellectually challenging, and [play] music part-time. Also, I'd like to have a family sometime over the next ten years.

Amanda, also a 2002 graduate of Temple Law School, envisions that five years from now, she will be married and planning her first child. She looks forward to working a schedule that allows her to have a family. She expects that balancing work and family will be easier in a small firm. She does not expect to take time off from work to raise children, but answers "yes" when asked if she would trade off income and compromise her professional goals for time to raise her children. She expects to take a maternity leave *and* get her job back afterward.

Cynthia Mason's professional aspirations will require a different kind of balancing. She would like to find "part-time work doing research or policy work related to women's issues and continue playing music [guitar] professionally for the rest of the time." She has been playing music "semiprofessionally" for nearly ten years and wants to incorporate music and law into her life. She envisions having a family in the future and believes that part-time work will be the way she "integrates" all her interests. Her prediction: "A small firm would probably be more suitable to me. I'm not interested in working for a big firm, and though I'd like to be able to pay back my student loans sooner rather than later, I value my free time more than anything."

Cynthia Mason is optimistic about sharing domestic responsibilities with her future unknown husband. Her vision of equality is not one that many women have had until now. Cynthia declares she would take time off to raise children "if necessary." She elaborates: "It depends on what my future spouse's work situation was. If we could share responsibilities, obviously that would be ideal, but who knows." Cynthia believes "absolutely" that women should expect their jobs to be there for them after maternity leaves but, in the final analysis, Cynthia is clear that she would compromise her professional goals and trade off income for time to raise children. She writes, "I am not interested in prestige or making a lot of money. My time and family/friends take top priority always." And yet, Cynthia has expressed the heart of the issue facing all women: "I wish it was not necessary to sacrifice one for the other."

Conclusion

There are plenty of terrific men out there who are attracted to smart women and are willing to do their share of domestic duties. There are also plenty of men who really are happier in a traditional situation where a wife picks up his shirts from the laundry while he works, prepares his dinner, and makes sure the kids are groomed and educated. I have seen them both and I have dated them both (the latter not for long). Not all the traditional men are of an older generation. I know plenty of young men who lead very conformist lives and plenty of young women who are housewives with no other aspirations of their own. On the other hand, I can point to men of an earlier generation who have transformed themselves to become involved at home and supportive of their wives' careers. Finding the perfect mate is a tall order. Clear away those who are intimidated by the very notion of a woman lawyer, clear away those who are put off by a woman who makes more money than they do, clear away those with whom you may not be intellectually compatible, and you are ready to skim the cream off the top.

For women lawyers in search of companionship, the remaining impediment to finding friends and romance is time. The lack of time is a very real issue for women lawyers working full-time. This becomes immediately obvious to young women just out of law school. Establishing careers can require long hours and weekend work in offices that do not provide much opportunity for finding companionship. Young women, unlike young men, begin to doubt they can do both at the same time. It is at this point that most women begin to understand that life requires compromises, and the adjustment of goals and priorities. But with a little planning, and a long-range perspective on life, women should not be discouraged and abandon all hope for social lives. The law may be a jealous mistress, but she will not always need *all* our attention *all* the time, and she will always take us back if we abandon her for a short time.

ENDNOTES

1. ABA COMM'N ON WOMEN IN THE PROFESSION, BALANCED LIVES, CHANGING THE CULTURE OF LEGAL PRACTICE 17 (2001) (prepared by Deborah L. Rhode). Reprinted with permission.

2. Marina Angel, *Women in Legal Education: What It's Like to Be Part of a Perpetual First Wave or the Case of the Disappearing Women*, 61 TEMP. L. REV. 799, 815 (1988).

3. SYLVIA HEWLITT, CREATING A LIFE (2002) (book relies heavily upon accumulated statistics of survey entitled, "High-Achieving Women, 2001," conducted by Harris Interactive under auspices of National Parenting Association, a nonprofit research organization; "high-achieving" career women defined as those who either have professional degree or doctorate or who earn at least $55,000 per year in the twenty-eight to forty age bracket, or at least $65,000 per year in the forty-one to fifty-five age bracket).

4. PHILA. BAR ASS'N, PHILADELPHIA BAR ASSOCIATION MEMBERSHIP SURVEY 2000, Table 131 (2000).

"A Day in the Life"
Nancy, counsel to the court in Florida

My job is to advise the trial judges on pending case files and draft orders if they request that. Our court handles felonies, family law civil matters involving over $15,000, and probate cases. Because the state capital is in our county, we get administrative matters from all over the state (mostly injunctive relief cases). This gives me a nice variety of work! I also help the chief judge with administrative matters such as public records requests to the court, judicial personnel questions, composing checklists for the judicial assistants (legal secretaries) to use for screening certain types of cases, monitoring legislation affecting the courts, and anything else the judge asks me to do. I supervise a staff of four attorneys and the five of us do legal work for the fifteen trial court judges in our six-county area (Florida's Second Judicial Circuit, which includes the state capital, Tallahassee).

I enjoy the variety of legal issues presented in my work, and I enjoy taking large piles of paper and turning them into well-organized, legally sound orders.

My exact role with the court is—well, my title is Senior Trial Court Staff Attorney, and I am under the direct supervision of the chief judge of our circuit. Our circuit does not have the traditional "law clerk" positions present in some appellate courts, but the staff attorneys do similar legal research and case summaries for the trial judges as requested. Unlike the traditional "law clerk" position, we have more than one judge to work for, and we must be generalists rather than specialists. The advantages to a trial court staff attorney job for a family-oriented person are (1) we work a fixed number of hours per week for a fixed salary, not billable hours, (2) we are government employees, so our offices are closed for holidays and we accrue some paid vacation and sick leave, (3) the variety of work keeps the mind flexible, but the amount of pressure from deadlines, workload, etc. is manageable, and (4) our judges are generally willing to accommodate us on time issues such as leave without pay for maternity leave, relatively flexible schedules, and telecommuting from home when necessary. In my position with four small children, these advantages easily offset the lack of salary potential. My children are now ages ten, six (twins—so much for planning everything in our lives), and almost four. I have been with the court since before the ten-year-old was born, so that shows how this job has allowed me to adapt! I have spent tens of thousands on day care, after-school programs, and summer camps. My parents helped a great deal (until my mom passed away this February) and I get by without much leisure time. It's a juggling act, but it's worth it to me.

Chapter Nine

The Name Game

To name oneself is the first act of both the poet and the revolutionary. When we take away the right to an individual name, we symbolically take away the right to be an individual. Immigration officials did this to refugees; husbands routinely do it to wives.[1]

Erica Jong

"A rose by any other name . . ."—ever since Shakespeare penned those immortal words, men and women have contemplated and debated the power and significance of a woman's surname. As Romeo pined away for his Juliet, another powerful woman of the day doffed her name and shunned marriage for the simple, "Queen Elizabeth." Preceded by Cleopatra, and followed by Madonna and Cher, some women of power and fame have answered the name debate by dropping their surnames altogether. Who we are, and how we project ourselves to others, is very much revealed by what we call ourselves. As lawyers, our names send a message to prospective clients, coworkers, judges, and juries about how we perceive ourselves. As advocates for others, our selection of names tells much about how we assert our individuality.

With women's coming-of-age in the midtwentieth century and the revolution of the 1960s, women began questioning the custom of changing their last names, just as they were devising an alternative to

Miss and Mrs. The conflict felt then was artfully articulated by author Erica Jong in 1977:

> Perhaps I should show my commitment to the marriage by taking his name. And yet, it seems so illogical. My maiden name feels right: an old shoe. It is my identity. To give it up seems like an amputation. . . . Why should I take this fluke of history as my identity simply because I happen to go to bed with its bearer?[2]

The Right to Choose

By 1980, assuming a husband's last name was a considered choice rather than a given. It had not always been so. Lucy Stone, a feminist and suffragist of the nineteenth century, has been credited with being the first married American woman to retain her birth name.

Lucy Stone was born August 13, 1878, in Massachusetts, and observed at an early age the inequalities of married life for women in general and her mother in particular, living under the stern, parsimonious rule of her father. Vowing not to live without basic rights of property and humanity, she eventually relented to marry Henry Blackwell—a Cincinnati businessperson, poet, and supporter of rights for women (two of his sisters were physicians)—under the terms of their own written marriage vows that promised Lucy a marriage without male "privilege" and "degradation." At the altar, Lucy vowed to "honor" but not "obey." She also kept her maiden name. Reportedly, Lucy Stone corresponded with her future husband expressing her views:

> A wife should no more take her husband's name than he should hers. My name is my identity and must not be lost.

On weekends, Lucy Stone was an active lecturer for abolition of slavery and, on weekdays, for women's suffrage. She was a colleague of Susan B. Anthony and Elizabeth Cady Stanton until their split over whether to lend support to passage of the Fourteenth and Fifteenth Amendments that enfranchised black men yet excluded women from the right to vote. Lucy's daughter, Alice Stone Blackwell, shared the surnames of both her mother and her father, as has become customary today in elementary schools across the country for children with parents who have different last names.

In 1974, Philadelphia Common Pleas Court Judge Lisa Richette was taken to court by her former husband to stop her from using his surname, "Richette." Even though she had remarried, the judge kept the last name of her former husband and did not wish to relinquish it for her maiden name or new husband's name. By the time of the lawsuit, Judge Richette had established a prominent career as a judge, author, lecturer, and lawyer, all by the name of Richette. The court, under the opinion of Judge Meyer, acknowledged the growing trend among women to keep their birth names:

> More and more women today are concerned with maintaining their own identity after marriage. There are many reasons for this. To name a few, women who have jobs find it less confusing to continue to use the same name by which they are known to their associates, clients, patients, etc. Many have established credit and want to have an independent credit rating, and do not want to go to the trouble of changing Social Security cards, drivers' licenses, and other forms of identification. There are organizations such as "NAME CHANGE" in Massachusetts and "WOMEN'S OWN NAME" in Illinois whose purpose is to advise women on their rights as to the use of surnames. Few performers on stage or screen are known by their own names before or after marriage. Many professional women do not use their [husbands' surnames].

Concluding this case in Judge Richette's favor, the court held that absent a finding of fraud or intent to deceive, any woman, or any man, has the right in Pennsylvania to "use any name he or she chooses."[3] In support of its conclusion, the court cited the 1961 case of *State of Ohio ex rel. Joseph Cyrill KRUPA, Relator v. Green*, and chose to incorporate the following language in full:

> If any question of public policy should be advanced seeking to hold that a married woman has been bound by custom to take the name of her

husband in all events and for all purposes, there being no statute requiring it, it should be noted that the trend against the loss of the identity of a woman by marriage has received common acceptance. An examination of the statutes shows the trend toward emancipation of married women from the common law rules of bondage, from complete deprivation of all property rights, to that of being accorded the right to contract with her husband and others, to own property separate and apart from her husband, and to have the right of franchise, being limited only to the extent that her marital status cannot be changed or altered by common consent. From these facts, it must be evident that many unnecessary restrictive customs have fallen by the wayside. Certainly, if public policy sanctions commercial activities by married women, which of necessity are in no way concerned with her domestic life, then her family name, by which she is known in domestic circles, will not be harmed by whatever name she used in her commercial activities.[4]

Also cited as precedent was an Illinois case from 1945, in which a woman lawyer who practiced law under her maiden name was permitted by the court to register to vote in her maiden name, contrary to the Illinois election code at that time.[5] And so the legal right of a woman to continue the use of her maiden name, or any other name, is not one that should be taken for granted. As late as 1974, a Philadelphia Court of Common Pleas judge articulated the right of each woman to choose her own name and identity in all spheres. This right was granted as part of a continuum of rights that have been hard-won and fought for since the nineteenth century: the right to own property, to practice law, to vote, and yes, to keep one's very name.

The message from this history should not be overlooked by women entering the practice of law. Once a woman begins the practice of law under a particular name—whatever it may be—she will be known in the legal community by that name, and changing a name in midcareer cannot come without a loss of personal history and recognition. One's name and identity quickly become inextricably linked.

Regardless of whether a woman chooses her maiden name or married name, or some combination of the two, the path has been cleared for women to explore ways to keep their identities, both personally and professionally. Moreover, women have the right by law to choose.

Growing up in the 1950s and early 1960s, young girls dreamed about getting married and taking their husbands' names. A name change was proof of marriage, which was the epitome of life as we knew it. You would *want* to change your name rather than acknowledge publicly you were "still single." Young girls played games with the names of cute boys. Would their names "go" with theirs? Could you live with being Mrs. So-and-so? The world has certainly changed.

All women today, when they marry, choose to either follow custom and take their husbands' surnames or keep their "maiden" names, in whole or in part. If Jane Smith marries Bob Jones, the choices of names, as I see them, are as follows:

- Jones
- Smith
- Smith-Jones
- Jones-Smith
- SmithJones
- Smith Jones

All the above require a lifetime of explanation*: "One word, no hyphen." "Two words, with a hyphen." And so on. It is like living on a street with too many letters and syllables. And if someone does not get it quite right, you are doomed to oblivion. For example, I chose to use my maiden name as a middle name. I can be found in some directories under "E" for Epstein and sometimes under "H" for Horn

---

* And, of course, this also raises the question of what last name should be given to children. Should the child be known as Sara Smith-Jones? And what if Sara Smith-Jones should marry Kevin Schwartz-Wolf? Is their child to be known as Robert Smith-Jones-Schwartz-Wolf? Dostoyevsky would love it.

Epstein. Pennsylvania Supreme Court Justice Sandra Schultz Newman told me of similar experiences, including looking for hotel registrations under "S" for Schultz and "N" for Newman. Other women opt to hyphenate their last names by placing either their own names first or their husbands' names first. The benefit of placing a husband's name first is that both people can be found in the same place in the telephone book or school directory without a search.

I know that many professional women do not change their names after they marry, often because they have already established themselves under their maiden names. Perhaps this is a growing trend. The women I know who have retained their maiden names—writers, doctors, and lawyers—spend a fair amount of time explaining their connections to their husbands and children and often forgo their separateness when hard pressed by medical providers, school directories, or similar family situations. In earlier days, when a child and parent did not share a last name, it was assumed that the family was blended as a result of a divorce or two. Today, that is no longer the assumption. Once pervasive, the stigma of a different name is no longer there. At the same time, the divergence of names can be confusing, especially for younger children.

My research for this book took me to the Philadelphia Bar Association Jenkins Law Library, where the legal directory for 1980, the year I began practicing, was retrieved for me from the "rare" book room. Hmmm!!! You can imagine, dear reader, how that felt. At a glance, I noticed that for Philadelphia and the surrounding counties of Bucks, Montgomery, Chester, and Delaware, I could find only one woman using two last names (one as a middle name) and only one with a hyphenated name. There may have been one or two others that I missed, but not many. Today's legal directories have numerous examples of double last names and hyphenated names. I have to believe that many married women listed in the directory are using their maiden names.

The young women law school graduates with whom I spoke remain divided over what they will do. Cynthia Mason, a law graduate of 2002, insists that she intends to keep her maiden name.

Sounding eerily similar to the sentiments Erica Jong wrote less than thirty years ago, Cynthia writes, "I would never give up that part of my identity to marry. My name is my name, and I'm never going to change it." This is in direct contrast to the statement of a fellow grad: "I want me, my husband, and children to have the same last name." Sara Shubert expressed indecision—because she has already published an article in the Temple Law Review, she speculates that she "may want to keep [her] maiden name for simplicity and consistency."

Arlyn Katzen Landau has also struggled with her name. She adopted her husband's name but kept her maiden name as a middle name. Throughout law school, she kept her original surname but felt compelled to decide "officially" when applying for the bar exam. She concedes that adopting her husband's name was what he wanted and that she underestimated the impact changing her name would have upon her emotionally. In changing her last name, Arlyn felt she had lost part of her identity. Years earlier, Professor Diane Maleson gave up her maiden name when she married, and recalls vividly the same loss of identity. She believes that if she were a younger woman marrying today, she would not make the same decision.

Looking over the list of my fellow law school graduates of 1980, I count four women with hyphenated names out of ninety-nine women in all, and twenty-two women with two last names. I go by the name of Phyllis Horn Epstein: first name, maiden name, husband's name. I was thirty years old when I married in 1986. I had been out of law school for six years. I had worked independently the first year and a half. In January 1982, I became an associate of my husband-to-be. Four years later, after having been known as Phyllis Horn, I made the decision to change my name personally and professionally.

So why did I take my husband's name? First, I did not believe I had sufficiently staked out my professional reputation under the name "Horn," although all my diplomas and court admission documents had that name written on them in beautiful writing. I thought I was on the cusp of my career and would not create big waves by adding another name. Second, I worked with my husband and my professional reputation was already tied to his. We shared clients and work. Many of those clients were older and traditional, and probably (I believed, rightly or wrongly) would be more comfortable with my becoming an Epstein. Moreover, and more compelling, I also felt at the time that I did not want to live a double life. I wanted my life simplified, not complicated by marriage. I did not want to be Epstein here, Horn there. I thought of my driver's license, health insurance policy, credit cards, and future children. Lucy Stone, throughout her years, was plagued by officialdom in government and officiousness in hotel clerks who required her to sign her name as "Lucy Stone, married to Henry Blackwell."

I also did not want a life trying to remember what name I used when. Is my driver's license in one name, while my credit cards are in another? I am not that organized. So I kept my name as my middle name in print for all to see. I kept it on my cards, on my stationery, and in my signature. Would I make the same decision today, looking back? I think so.

From speaking with many women while writing this book, I have come to this conclusion: We are each different and bring to our lives our own sets of values and necessities. How we are to be known and named is within our power as a result of the struggles and legal battles of our predecessors. Each woman's exercise of that power is its own validation.

ENDNOTES

1. Erica Jong, How to Save Your Own Life 123 (1977).
2. Id. at 129.
3. Richette v. Ajello, 72 Pa. D. & C.2d 22, 29 (Philadelphia Court of Common Pleas 1974).
4. State of Ohio ex rel. Joseph Cyrill KRUPA, Relator v. Green, 177 N.E.2d 616 (Court of Appeals of Ohio, Eighth District, Cuyahoga County 1961).
5. People ex rel. Rago v. Lipsky, 63 N.E.2d 642 (Court of Appeals of Illinois 1945).

"A DAY IN THE LIFE"
SUSAN, A LAWYER SPECIALIZING IN LAND-USE LAW IN NEW JERSEY

I am a single parent to an eleven-year-old daughter and a nine-year-old son, and working as the only woman in a medium-sized suburban firm. I had been married for twenty years and when I was divorced, I decided to retain my married name, which I had been using professionally.

Since my former husband is not much practical help with the children, I do not have the time to be either the kind of mother I want to be—spending lots of consistent time with my children—or the kind of lawyer I want to be—getting everything done on time and with the level of competence I can easily achieve. In fact, I am the queen of missed deadlines at work. I commute at least an hour each way. Since I do land use, and planning boards meet in the evening, sometimes I am out of the house for fifteen hours a day. There is no balance that is going to make everybody happy. I go through my days knowing that no matter how hard I try, I will not accomplish everything on my "to-do" list, and someone will be unhappy with my performance.

As an attorney friend with three kids said to me once, "I wake up every morning, think about all I've got to do for the kids, for work, and for the house, and I concede defeat before I ever lift my head from the pillow." I am totally disgusted with law firm life and with the practice of law, and I am seriously considering chucking the whole thing and doing something else with my life.

Chapter Ten

Having It All

Success and satisfaction are attained by developing your own skills to serve others.[1]

Senior Judge Norma Shapiro
Eastern District Court

We need to understand that there is no formula for how women should lead their lives. That is why we must respect the choices that each woman makes for herself and her family.

Hillary Rodham Clinton
Senator and Former First Lady of the United States
Remarks to the United Nations Fourth World Conference on Women
Plenary Session in Beijing, China, September 5, 1995

Not Enough Time in the Day

Is there ever enough time to work, mother, cook, clean, do laundry, read the paper, keep up with professional journals, network, have a hobby, keep friends, and be there for a husband, aging parent, or the class play? No! For the woman who chooses the law as a profession, there is not enough time in the day for everything, and something must give way. Professor Alice Abreu of Temple Law School states, "We were of a generation that believed we could have it all. We had to figure out for ourselves that we had to make choices." As she rightfully observes, "the day only has twenty-four hours and in that time we have to fit in our work, our families, our gardening, everything."

Life offers a plethora of choices: marriage, single life, divorce, cohabitation, parenthood. A law career offers an array of choices as well. A law graduate may work in private practice, in a large firm, in a small firm, in local or federal government, as in-house counsel, as corporate counsel, as a teacher, and on and on. Legal fields also vary; there is criminal work, litigation, corporate transactions, family law, tax, pro bono, civil rights, the judiciary—the options are endless. It is a veritable Automat of choices. Combine all this with personal pleasures of travel, music, cooking, and hobbies, and life is full. Overlay the expectations of others about what defines success, and it is easy to lose one's way. Most would agree that "having it all" requires choices in life. When the choices you make flow from an inner compass, then you can "have it all."

What Is "All"?

"Having it all" has come to mean having time for personal interests, family, friends, and work, but not all in the same degree or at the same time. "As for 'having it all'—it depends what one considers 'all,'" Barbara Kron Zimmerman wrote to me. She adds:

> Having a good life is having it all, and one must know what that means for her. For me, doing things serially rather than all at the same time worked out best. In fact, I chose part-time activity even before I had children because my full-time work did not allow time for so many of my other interests. For some, having a successful career could well be "all."

"Having it all" means abandoning any preconceived, single standard of success, and requires each woman to redefine for herself the meaning of the phrase. The women with whom I spoke, women of experience, all encouraged other women lawyers to begin by redefining for themselves the meaning of "success."

Married without Children

Women lawyers have long struggled with the question of whether it is possible to be both a lawyer and mother. Leslie Miller, past president of the Pennsylvania Bar Association and currently counsel to Pennsylvania's Governor Ed Rendell, revealed to me that her decision to not have children was a conscious one, resulting from the demands of her career choice.

History bears out how difficult it has been for women to raise children while pursuing careers in the law. In 1939, an astonishing 76 percent of women lawyers, a huge number, had no children. Thirteen percent had one child. Matters changed only slightly by 1949: 70 percent of women lawyers had no children and 14 percent had one child.[2] The *ABA Journal* compiled more current statistics in 1983, showing that 59 percent of women lawyers had no children, compared with 24 percent of male lawyers.[3] Given these statistics, it is no wonder that many women have begun thinking about the meaning of success in other than purely financial terms. That means finding the job that affords an opportunity to devote time to both family and law without feeling the need to sacrifice one for the other.

Delayed Marriages, Stress, and Infertility

A 1997 study by the U.C. Davis School of Medicine & Medical Center reported that women lawyers who worked more than forty-five hours a week were more likely to suffer miscarriages brought on by the stress of work and home.[4] The study reports that "[w]omen working longer than [forty-five] hours a week experienced miscarriages three times as often, even after researchers adjusted for age, smoking, alcohol intake, and previous miscarriage." The greatest degree of stress was experienced by women lawyers who were partners or associates in their firms, specializing in criminal law or litigation. The study linked its findings to those the ABA prepared in 1990, which concluded that women felt greater stress at work than men in equal positions, as a result of "political intrigue, back-biting, sexual harassment, lack of opportunity for advancement, advancement not determined by quality of work, and lack of respect by superiors."

Women who exit law school in their late twenties, as most do, have devoted most of their fertile years to the all-consuming study of law, rather than dating. The next few years are devoted to finding employment and then working like crazy to keep that job. Given that new studies mark women's decline in fertility at the age of twenty-seven, it is highly likely that these "high-achieving" women will have some trouble conceiving.[5] The same studies report that men's fertility does not begin to decline until age thirty-five.

What this means for young women lawyers is unsettling. Going straight from undergraduate school at age twenty-one or twenty-two to law school, and graduating three years later at age twenty-five does not leave much time for women to date, marry, and start having children before their fertility declines. For men, these are the years when they are putting their energies into school and establishing careers with the long hours and focus that both demand. But unlike women, men are not "under the gun" at the same time over the future ability to have families. In fact, most would argue that men's social "marketability" increases with age and success. On the other hand, the statistics are telling us that half the women who devoted the same time and focus to establishing their law careers as men will be unmarried and childless. While I was pregnant, an acquaintance casually stated that if a woman miscarried she could "just have another one." Not, apparently, if she keeps her forty-five-plus-billable-hour-a-week job.

A Woman's Evolution

Pennsylvania Superior Court Judge Phyllis Beck welcomed me into her office for a long conversation that would change the way I saw my life. In her unassuming and comfortable manner, she took me into her confidence and shared her perspectives on work and life. "Success," she said, "has been defined by men all these years as movement high up the ladder. Women have to define success differently. It isn't necessary to be the top person to be successful," she explained. To Judge Beck, "success" is having work in your field that permits you to have a life as well. That might mean taking a job that has less pay and prestige, but that allows you to take time to see the school play. In her view, it is an intractable fact that children are women's primary responsibility. It follows that women with children will have to devote time to them. But, she urges, while taking the time to do this, women should not worry about "catching up" professionally. Judge Beck motions horizontally with her hand to explain her theory that life is a continuum—a horizontal journey rather than a vertical climb. Her hand, still level with the ground moves higher and lower as she continues: "There are highs and lows but always a continuum. Unlike men, women will have to face certain compromises." Judge Beck is a mother of four who entered the law after years devoted primarily to raising her children. From her vantage point, she proffers this: "Women should understand that they can miss the young years of their children and their children will probably turn out fine, but the mothers will have missed something precious and special. The mothers will suffer rather than the children. If possible," she advises, "try to work through the years children are young, set priorities (and reset them when necessary), and be prepared to work hard, from the bottom up."

Grace Kennedy, Fordham Law School graduate of 1940, feels fortunate that she was not working when she had her children, and she confides that her husband's income was sufficient—she never felt she needed to make a lot of money on her own. Like Judge Beck, Grace Kennedy motions up and down with her hand and says that she suspects most women's lives are like that. "Women find ways to work and raise families and learn that it can be done. Men's lives are flatter," she tells me, "with fewer choices and roles to play. A law career has been a wonderful career for me," Grace reflects. Her experiences have been varied and fulfilling.

Redefining Success

I asked many women of all generations how they would define "success." The answers I received were remarkably similar. Most women defined success as just the right blend of work, family, and financial comfort. Success is a cocktail of these factors, custom-made for each individual, subject to change in tastes, and contingent upon the quality of each ingredient.

If we were to define success empirically, such as by how much money a person earned, that would make our discussion much easier. But, for most women lawyers, success is not defined by money, at least not by money alone. Success is happiness in three basic areas of life, in the right amounts at different times. Happiness at work is equated with several things: doing the best one can for a client, taking pride in doing a good job, enjoying one's work, and earning the trust of one's clients and the respect of one's peers in the profession. Included in the mix is the opportunity to achieve justice. For one Wyoming lawyer, success means the chance "to have contributed in some positive way to [the] community, to have followed through on those things that we say 'someone ought to do something about that.'" Financially, women express the desire to make enough money to live comfortably or to provide for family needs, but not at the cost of other important ingredients to success. Personal contentment includes time for friends, family, and personal pursuits. For some, but not all, this means taking years away from work or working fewer days or hours. Ultimately, "success" is being able to combine the best of these elements in a way that brings personal happiness. For one Benjamin Cardozo Law School graduate, it is as simple as "[h]aving happy and healthy children and a husband and some opportunity to use [her] brain outside the home."

Defining "success" is so personal that one woman wrote, "When you find out the definition, let me know, because I'll be sure not to read it." I spoke with several women lawyers who achieved personal satisfaction with their lives and careers in very personal ways.

Ask District Attorney Lynne Abraham if she "has it all" and she will wholeheartedly answer in the affirmative. I met with her in her large and eclectic office at the top of the city office building that is the home of her department. During our talk, one of her very large cats that inhabits the office perched on my shoulder and purred contentedly. Yes, District Attorney Abraham muses, she could be earning much more money in a large firm, but she is enormously content with her work . . . *and* her personal life. "I love what I do," she says. "Every day, you get up to bat, and you have to make difficult decisions that practically please nobody. That's what a prosecutor does, you make difficult decisions. I'm only driven by, 'Are we doing a good job, are we giving justice to each individual case?' We'll win a large number of cases but we're going to do it right. That's the measure of success."[6]

Ask the same question of the woman who broke the gender barrier to become Philadelphia Bar Association Chancellor, Deborah Willig, and she will also answer in the affirmative. Yes, she says, she could move into a large firm and earn more money, but that would not be her personal idea of "success." She is happiest being the managing partner of her own firm, representing labor unions and individuals rather than management in labor disputes, and she is content with the level of independence she has in the way she chooses to practice law. Her personal life is happy and settled as well. Deborah's "success" is defined by the satisfaction achieved in both spheres of her life and her feeling of control over how she manages to accommodate both.

Equity partnership is not the brass ring for everyone, nor is it the only way to achieve a comfortable level of financial success. Lila Roomberg, a senior partner with Ballad Spahr Andrews & Ingersoll, has worked these past fifty years to reach the upper echelons of her law firm. From her perspective, women have come this far to have *more* choices (including equity partnership), not to have a single model of success sold to them. Success—financial or otherwise—is not simply a number and does not come in one model, packaged and labeled as an equity partnership.

I am struck by the early wisdom of Sara Schubert, a 2002 Temple Law School graduate, who writes:

> I guess for me, success is achieving a balance in your life such that you have at least a taste of everything you want. For me, it would be raising a happy family as well as nurturing a sense of my individual self.

Success is an "evolution"—a fluid shifting of priorities as life unfolds. Perhaps U.S. Tax Court Judge Mary Ann Cohen was on the mark when she offered this: "Life is a series of choices and sometimes your life unfolds in ways you haven't actually chosen. Be flexible and open to opportunities and experiences."

The Anxiety of Doing It All

The greatest challenge for today's women is to find happiness and the circumstances to achieve that happiness. After the birth of my son, I found that trying to be a good lawyer, a good wife, and an on-site mother was exhausting. Women with children are constantly checking the time to see when their children are up from naps or home from school. I became one of those women. I would live in terror about selecting the right sitter for my infant. At the same time, I would agonize that I was not devoting enough time to perfecting my legal skills. I would never know enough or be good enough, I thought. I would be found out—discovered and disbarred. I am sorry to say, I found that I was not alone. The ABA-sponsored publication, *Balanced Lives*, gives us the following:

> For employed women, who still spend about twice as much time on domestic matters as employed men, extended hours result in "double

binds and double standards. Working mothers are held to higher standards than working fathers and are often criticized for being insufficiently committed either as parents or as professionals." Those who seem willing to sacrifice family needs to workplace demands appear lacking as mothers. Those who want extended leaves or reduced schedules appear lacking as lawyers. Those mixed messages leave many women with high levels of stress, and the uncomfortable sense that, whatever they are doing, they should be doing something else. "Good mothers" should be home; "good lawyers" should not.[7]

I can relate. I am married now for seventeen years to my law partner, we have a thirteen-year-old son, and I practice law in the office every day. The words "balance and compromise" are my mantra, and I still struggle against self-criticism for the choices I make. When I leave work midafternoon to pick up my son from school and do homework with him, I feel guilty about not working, but I also know that this is the time I will know immediately if my son had a good day or bad, or if his backpack is too heavy; this is the time when I can be most in tune with his well-being. When I need to work late, I feel apologetic toward my husband and son, asking them to fend for themselves (although they somehow seem to enjoy this private time together). When I work late, I am rushed because I have not been home to shop for food or do the laundry or check homework. When I pass up a professional meeting because it means too much time away from family, I agonize about being out of the loop for professional advancement. I lapse into fantasies of complete dependence: long days when I can organize the house and attic, return items to the store within hours of purchase, match socks, lunch with friends, always have fresh milk in the fridge, exercise, and keep my roots from growing in. I long for the world of *Leave It to Beaver*. More often, I long for the life of Mr. Donna Reed: having someone there who will cook my dinner, do my laundry, take sick children to the doctor, and be up all night with the kids so that I can be fresh for work in the morning. And yet I do not want to be that young male lawyer in my office who proudly compartmentalized his work and family. The reality is that most men do not make dinner and do not initiate chores around the house, while the woman at work struggles to cover all territories no matter how much "help" she gets. Some of this comes down to the simple nuts-and-bolts of family finances. Who makes the most money? If someone has to miss work for a doctor visit, the spouse with the lower billable rate stays home. Most of the time, albeit not all of the time, it is the woman lawyer.

But let me digress. I will confess that just now, my mother looked up at me and wondered why all these professional women were cleaning house and cooking. Why didn't they have help? My answer is, the cost. If I worked full-time in a large firm and pulled down a salary in the upper six figures, I could have lots of backup help. But most women are not bringing in that kind of income, even if they are working full-time. Women in government, in the district attorney's office, or even in private practice can ill-afford extensive home help.[8] Moreover, since the days of President Clinton's failed nominees for the Supreme Court, cleaning services cannot be run as cash businesses and cleaning expenses are most certainly not tax-deductible business expenses, though perhaps they should be. An additional 7.65 percent of any salary paid for help must be added to the base salary, in addition to employee withholding paid to the government for taxes and Social Security. The paperwork, the accounting, and the costs are prohibitive for many working women, leaving them to demand more of their husbands and children around the house.

Feeling Guilty

When women feel compelled to choose between families and careers, it is nothing less than tragic. This dichotomy has historically been framed as a noble "natural" pull for children, pitting family against "unnatural" selfish needs for intellectual and financial rewards. The feminists of the past half century tried to free women from the guilt trip that children would suffer if women worked, sometimes taking extreme positions. The 1960s feminist Germaine Greer attacked the traditional segregation of proper roles:

> Childbearing was never intended by biology as a compensation for neglecting all other forms of fulfillment and achievement. It was never intended to be as time-consuming and self-conscious a process as it is. One of the deepest evils in our society is tyrannical nurturance.[9]

Justice Newman of the Pennsylvania Supreme Court confessed to me that during law school, with her young children at home, not a day went by when she did not feel guilty pursuing her degree. How many of us still debate the benefits of quality-versus-quantity time spent with our children? The struggle between work and family, even if resolved in favor of more time with family, no matter how temporary, leaves more than one woman with an unsatisfied feeling that she is then letting herself down. Caroline Vincent reflects upon how her own choice has made her feel:

> For me, learning to accept what works in my life and what I enjoy doing has been hard, because the reality is that I have chosen quality of life over a large salary and being a workaholic. This has required me to deal with my ego, which tells me that as a lawyer I have to achieve a certain level of wealth to be successful.

What we know in our heads, and what we feel in our hearts, may not always go together. Giving ourselves permission to accent work or family is the most difficult challenge of all. Sometimes I fall into thinking I should network more; I should write more; I should be busier; I should be making more money; I should be a better housewife; I should have infinite patience for everyone. My classmate Susan Holmes offers a prescription for this self-defeating cycle: "I guess what I've learned is that it's okay to say I need help or that I can't do it all, all the time. It has been a hard lesson to learn and often I feel like saying, 'Stop the world, I want to get off.' " The cycle of guilt can be alleviated by recognizing the enormous external pressures that make "doing it all"—all at the same time—so difficult.

Having Outside Interests

Be creative in developing your own life.

Professor Laura Little

Judge Carolyn Engel Temin is a dancer at heart and participates as a board member in local Philadelphia dance organizations. Judge Norma Shapiro is on the board of the Jewish Publication Society. Leslie Miller is on the board of Philadelphia's performance hall, the Kimmel Center. Having interests outside the law, and outside family, nurtures the individual spirit and enriches life. If that is not reason enough, outside interests are good for business as well. My classmate Susan Schulman advises:

> I don't think there's a different recommendation for men than for women—this career choice is not right for everyone. It helps to have a secondary interest shape the way your legal career develops.

Men have always networked by attending professional sporting events, golfing, or joining wine-tasting clubs. During her hiatus from the full-time practice of law, Judge Shapiro became active with her local school board, from which she began developing a wider circle of contacts that ultimately benefited her when she sought endorsement of her elevation to the bench. To be known by others is to have the makings of a future client base and sources of business referrals.

Women should participate in professional organizations like the American Bar Association, as well as local bar associations. I have been a member of the ABA Tax Section for nearly twenty years and by doing so have expanded my professional network of tax lawyers to men and women across the country. I have been able to refer legal matters to others with specific tax expertise and have had matters referred back to me. The continuing legal education within the organization is at an expert level. There is an energy—a synergy—that emerges from gathering with peers in legal symposiums. Our bar associations have much to offer and a myriad of ways to participate.

Conclusion

You can "have it all" if you, and not someone else, dictate what "all" means. Certain goals may forever elude you as your life unfolds. Judge Shapiro, a woman most would consider a "success" on all accounts—home, children, career, and outside interests—shares with me her disappointment at not becoming a U.S. Supreme Court Justice. Her "setbacks," as she describes them, are balanced by her accomplishments. Any disappointments are lessened by the pride she feels being the first recipient of the Philadelphia Bar Association's Sandra Day O'Connor Award.

Nicole Berklas is a 2001 graduate of New York University, now living in Los Angeles. She suggests a fail-safe barometer for judging "success": "Don't measure the success of your life by the goalposts typically set in the legal field. Don't be afraid to ask, 'Am I really happy doing this?' "

There is an old Hebrew proverb—Gam Zeh Yavo (this, too, shall pass). Homework demands will recede and time for other activities will emerge. I would not trade my time after school with my son for any amount of money. Ultimately, like baby diapers, nothing is forever. You *can* "have it all," but probably not all at the same time. With some effort, women can redirect their lives, their careers, their marriages, and even their interests in the long journey that is a successful life.

ENDNOTES

1. The Honorable Norma Shapiro, Address before Girl Scouts of Greater Philadelphia (Mar. 12, 1990).

2. VIRGINIA G. DRACHMAN, SISTERS IN LAW, WOMEN LAWYERS IN MODERN AMERICAN HISTORY 257 (1998).

3. *Survey: Women Lawyers Work Harder, Are Paid Less, But They're Happy*, 69 A.B.A. J. 1384, 1388, n.2 (1983) (cited by Marina Angel, *Women in Legal Education: What It's Like to Be Part of a Perpetual First Wave or the Case of the Disappearing Women*, 61 TEMP. L. REV. 799, 807, n.44 (1988).

4. J. Occupational & Envtl. Med. (June 1997), cited in online article, Carole F. Gan, contact, "Working More Than 45 Hours Per Week Linked to High Stress, Threefold Increase in Miscarriage Rate in Women Lawyers," News from UC Davis Health System (June 1, 1997), *available at* http://news.ucdmc.usdavis.edu/news/medicalnews/womenlawyers.html.

5. *Id.*; Associated Press, Emma Ross, *Study Examines Human Fertility* (May 1, 2002), *available at* http://www.thedesertsun.com/news/stories/health/1020210807.shtml; Associated Press, *Biological Clocks Starts Ticking in Late 20s—Study* (May 2, 2002), *available at* http://www.reutershealth.com/framez/eline.html.

6. Gwen Shaffer, *Tough Love, Part 2*, Philadelphia Citypaper.net (May 10–17, 2001), *available at* http://citypaper.net/articles/051001/cs.cover.lynne2.shtml (downloaded on July 8, 2002).

7. ABA Comm'n on Women in the Profession, Balanced Lives, Changing the Culture of Legal Practice 17 (2001) (prepared by Deborah L. Rhode).

8. The starting salary in the Philadelphia district attorney's office is $44,823; for the N.Y. Manhattan district attorney, it is $48,000, with "periodic raises" possible "as the budget allows."

9. Germaine Greer, The Female Eunuch 88 (1970).

"A DAY IN THE LIFE"
TERRY, A TRIAL LAWYER FROM TEXAS

I am a plaintiff's personal injury attorney in a solo practice. I think the biggest benefit to my work is getting to help people and having clients who truly need you in a very tough time in their lives. The biggest disadvantage is that it is a very male-dominated area of the law and requires money to finance big cases. I started out working in law firms and I believe it is essential to get experience in this area before striking out on your own. The stakes are very high. The biggest benefit of working solo is control over my time. I have good working relationships and friendships with other lawyers that have helped me. Those were developed in working for firms and other lawyers. I believe I am taken seriously because of my experience and work over the years, but if I had gone out on my own initially it would have been very, very difficult. The best thing about personal injury work is helping people. There have been times when I was disappointed in the fee or bonus I earned in large cases I worked on. It is easy to sink into some bitterness when you see a referring attorney, co-counsel, or other attorney walk away with millions on a case you did most of the work on, and you walk away with your salary and a small bonus. But when I remember the client, and the good that I did for that family, it's easier to accept. Working for myself, I have some control over the fee issues.

Acquiring business is a problem, but I have chosen to limit my practice to one or two big cases a year. I have been fortunate in having friends that refer me just enough cases. I let everyone I encounter know what I do.

My schedule is controlled because I limit my cases. It's usually not too hard because I stay in state court where you have more freedom in scheduling. Defense counsel usually moves to slow things down, so it's more often that I find myself pushing them to get something scheduled.

The only thing that I really do not like about my work is the attitude of some lawyers who think they have to be nasty to represent their clients. I love helping people, and I love research and writing and the daily challenge of moving a case along. The money can be very good but you have to be prepared to weather the times when you don't have it coming in. I take an hourly case every now and then for that reason, but I also save when I have a big settlement. I have always earned a good income; maybe not exactly as much as I feel I should have earned, but again I go back to the clients and it seems like a sweet deal: Earning a good income, control over my life, and helping people!

Chapter Eleven

Part-Time Work: Is It for You?

It is to me surprising that anyone should speak with apprehension of an impending social change by which women are to seek fortune and fame in fields which were formerly denied to them. Such persons should awake from their slumbers. The revolution is over. It was so gradual that perhaps you did not observe it, or not the several steps of the progress. But it is over. It is an accomplished fact.

Judge Thayer, in *In re Kilgore*
18 Am. L. Rev. 478 (1884)

Who Needs Part-Time Work?

Many women trying to fit another dimension into their lives consider part-time work. Part-time work offers certain benefits, the most obvious being fewer work hours with more time for family, hobbies, or school. Part-time work can mean reduced work-related responsibilities that may attend being a large-firm equity partner. There is the possibility of finding work that stays behind in the office and does not overflow into the hours away. Working mothers make up the largest group seeking part-time work. Some see part-time work as the best accommodation to a working mother's dual career. In the words of Third Circuit Judge Dolores Sloviter:

> I think law as a profession is going to have to accommodate part-time work. I think that's one of the most important things to do. I think natural maternal instincts mean that . . . there's going to be a period in a young woman's life, if she's married, or if she has children, married or not, . . . when she wants to spend some of the time on her maternal responsibilities. And it's not fair to say you have to be out of the profession for ten years full time . . . when it would be easy enough in many instances to accommodate the woman with part-time work.[1]

What Is Considered Part-Time?

In the past ten years, many large law firms have tried to accommodate women in part-time positions by having nonpartner tracking. Sometimes these positions are called "of-counsel" or "co-counsel." Whatever they are called, part-time policies generally allow women to work two-thirds or three-fifths time, with a corresponding diminution in pay and benefits. In practice, part-time work is just another name for what has long been identified as the "mommy track."

UNDERSTANDING THE DIFFERENCES: PART-TIME WORK, FAMILY LEAVE, MEDICAL LEAVE

According to an American Bar Association report, a 1997 survey conducted by the National Association for Law Placement determined that approximately 92 percent of the law firms surveyed had part-time work policies and nearly half had parental-leave policies.[2] Most of these new policies were instituted in direct response to the legal compulsion of the Family and Medical Leave Act of 1993. There are some distinctions.

"Family leave" covers time away from work for disability and caretaking. Pregnancy and childbirth must be treated similarly to other temporary disabilities by reason of the Pregnancy Discrimination Act of 1978.[3] The act does not require the institution of a disability policy.

The Family and Medical Leave Act of 1993 (FMLA) covers employers of fifty or more, and requires them to provide unpaid leave for a minimum of twelve weeks for medical and family care needs for events such as birth, adoption, foster-care placement, care of a child, or serious health condition of the employee or employee's spouse, children, or parents. The FMLA requires these larger employers to maintain the health benefits of these employees while absent and to allow them to return to work at the same job or a comparable position.[4]

Part-time work is not legally compelled, and policies, if they exist at all, are relatively new. The American Bar Association, Pennsylvania Bar Association, and Philadelphia Bar Association have adopted similar Model Part-Time Work and Flexible-Work Policies in the past five years. Most, if not all, large firms in Philadelphia now have similar policies. Most bar associations do *not* have similar model policies, the exceptions being (as of this writing) New York, Washington, D.C., Indiana, San Francisco, and Minnesota.

Part-Timers Get No Respect

The pitfalls of part-time work for men and women are the same. Lawyers shy away from part-time work because of the perceived negative consequences to their careers, which include permanent associate status, loss of partnership contention, less prestigious work, and a greater percentage cut in pay than cut in hours. As a result, few lawyers ask to use these policies.

The statistics gathered by the ABA Commission on Women in the Profession (Women's Commission) bear this out: "Although 95 percent of law firms have policies that allow part-time work, only 3 percent of lawyers actually work part-time."[5] The ABA reports:

While the policies exist on paper, though, few lawyers—women or men—are actually using them. According to the same NALP study, only 2.7 percent of lawyers say they work on a part-time basis. The figure seems to hold true whether the work setting is a law firm, the government or a public interest job.

Lawyers are much less likely to work part-time than people in the workforce as a whole, or in more narrowly defined segments of the workforce. About 11 percent of all workers age twenty-five or older who worked in non-agricultural industries during 1997 usually worked part-time, and 13 percent of workers in professional specialties usually worked part-time.[6]

The reasons for avoiding part-time work are, like the policies themselves, gender-neutral, yet women suffer the consequences of part-time work more keenly. That is because women, more so than men, will exercise the part-time option out of needs and desires to find ways to balance childcare with working. Doreen Davis, an equity partner at Morgan, Lewis & Bockius, confirms that the young men in her firm admit to wanting part-time work but none do so. Women associates in her firm were more likely than men to seek part-time status, although this, too, occurred infrequently.

Part-time policies in large firms are "politically correct" these days but, in reality, they stigmatize the women who call themselves part-timers. The Women's Commission drafted a model policy for part-time work, but declined to call it that to avoid "the negative connotation" of those words among lawyers and employers. Instead, the Women's Commission recommends employers rename these policies to either "Alternative Work Policy" or "Flexible Work Policy" to suggest something more positive to men and women lawyers. The Women's Commission acknowledges that because these policies are used mostly by mothers, they are all too often avoided as a "woman's thing." This perception serves to equate flexibility with special treatment for women and, the committee reports, results in the marginalization of those who use them. I doubt trying to dress up a part-time policy in a new coat will fool any savvy lawyer trained to read between the lines.

The Women's Commission report speculated on a few of the reasons part-time work is so resoundingly avoided:

> It is hard to tell what discourages lawyers from taking advantage of part-time policies, whether it is a concern that the part-time lawyer will not be seen as being seriously committed to the law, a concern that a part-time job will grow into near-full-time work with part-time pay, or the belief—realistic or not—that at least certain kinds of legal work can be done only on a full-time basis.[7]

Part-timers sense that regardless of the quality of their work, they do not receive equal respect from their coworkers. "When lawyers assume that a working mother is unlikely to be fully committed to her career, they more easily remember the times when she left early than the times when she stayed late."[8] Jayne Spangler Weiss experienced part-time work at a large Philadelphia law firm. She noticed a subtle feeling in the firm that there are some women who are serious about their work and other women who are "mommies" . . . and therefore less serious. Coworkers complimented her work and expressed surprise, given her part-time status, for her industriousness and work ethic. Thiele Branham, a plaintiff's litigation lawyer in South Carolina, works part-time and shares the view that there is a "perception that you are less of a lawyer for it."

Logically, women who become part-timers for a few years are likely to fall behind economically. Aside from the immediate loss in income from working part-time, the impact can be long-term. In the words of Joan Williams, author of *Unbending Gender*, women starting later than those who work full-time all along have an impossible job of catching up to do:

> Many women who work part-time do so for only a limited period; then they return to full-time work. However, not only are part-timers penalized during the period they work part-time, but they suffer long-term consequences for having done part-time work. Even if someone who has been working part-time later takes a full-time job, she (or he) is likely to earn far less than someone who always worked full-time.[9]

As with women lawyers in large firms, very few women in larger corporations—less than 10 percent, Ms. Williams claims—avail themselves of part-time policies, for similar reasons. Sue Shellenbarger of the *Wall Street Journal* reported on dissatisfaction with part-time work among corporate women working in large companies. The corporate climate has parallels with large law firms:

> Many corporate employees are yearning for flexibility or reduced hours to tend family or pursue off-the-job passions. But people on flexible, work-at-home or part-time setups too often reap unintended consequences. Many become more frazzled than ever as they strain to reconcile their new work styles with rigid workloads and office routines. They face isolation from management and co-workers. All too often, they're branded second-class citizens, stalling careers and rendering them more vulnerable to layoffs.[10]

Yet, even given the drawbacks in loss of prestige, respect, career advancement, and financial rewards, women are more likely than men to choose to compromise and more likely to *have to* compromise to raise a family. The nonprofit group Catalyst confirms these conclusions: "Men and women respondents agree that flexible work arrangements adversely affect advancement. . . . Women law graduates, whether by choice or by necessity, make that trade-off, whereas men do not."[11]

Part-time lawyers sense that stepping down from full-time status, even for a period of time, seriously jeopardizes a climb up the partnership ladder. Seventy-five percent of the women lawyers interviewed by Catalyst across the country believed that if they went on part-time status, it would jeopardize their employment.

For a 1986 article in the *ABA Journal*, several women were interviewed on a variety of subjects, including part-time work. Similar conclusions were shared by these women; namely, that part-time workers are resented by their full-time counterparts, are paid part-time hours but work overtime without compensation, forfeit partnership opportunities, and are given less prestigious work. Women lawyers in the early 1980s, the article reports, were afraid to ask for part-time work because they believed they would be perceived as less serious and less committed.[12]

In this respect, very little has changed in the past twenty years for women considering part-time employment. Regardless of employment safeguards, women perceive, and they appear to be correct in this respect, that the trade-offs required to work part-time are fatal to career advancement, without offsetting career benefits.

What Is Part-Time Work Really Like?

Although the concept of part-time work sounds like the perfect solution for the working mother (or father), the reality is less than ideal. Part-time work has led many to conclude that the system is a "rip-off."

Alexis is a young mother who works in a large firm in Los Angeles. As an "employee," she is not subjected to any minimum billing requirement by the firm. However, if she were to switch to part-time status, she would be required to bill 1,950 hours, hardly a part-time schedule, if you consider that it requires a 40-hour week for 50 weeks of the year, billing every minute, to reach 2,000 hours. Alexis states the obvious: "I can work full-time and bill 1,500 hours or I can work part-time and bill 1,950 hours, but be paid much less."

Mary from Utah reports that she has seen many part-time arrangements where a lawyer who works a percentage of full-time receives an identical percentage of base compensation. These arrangements rarely work well financially for the lawyer, who usually ends up working more than the arranged number of hours but at a reduced salary. In Mary's firm, part-time employees are compensated on an "hours billed" arrangement. It allows for the lawyer to have a flexible schedule and, in her view, "doesn't impose an additional requirement that the lawyer be in the office a certain percentage of the time, which always seemed like a bizarre requirement of a professional in any case." I could not agree more. What it does *not* do is compensate women for the down time they spend in the office, which inevitably creeps into any workday.

In a large firm or corporation, part-time work often means an 8-hour-day on an early shift. Until recently, Jayne Spangler-Weiss was employed "of counsel" in the real estate department of a large Philadelphia firm. In this case, being "of counsel" meant that Jayne was a part-time employee. "Part-time" work for Jayne in a large Philadelphia law firm meant a 40-hour workweek, billing at least 6 hours a day, which translates into 1,250 a year. Jayne chose to work part-time to allow herself time with her daughter after school and time for family. Arriving at work by 7:00 a.m. each morning, she was able to leave by 3:30 p.m. to pick up her daughter from school and supervise homework. Jayne was not in line to be a partner at her firm, but then again, as she pointed out, she did not work until 11:00 p.m. like others in the office. When her work was done she felt free to walk out the door, untethered to work. Those who are "full-time" at her former law firm and pursuing partnership inevitably would work nights and weekends

One of the dangers in part-time employment is the precarious nature of the position in the event of a downturn in available work. Partners, or those on partner track, will scramble for extra work to fill the billable-hour minimums they are required to have each year. They may seize upon the work being done by the part-timers. With less work to go around, the part-time lawyer is going to be the first to be let go.

BEING ASSERTIVE ABOUT SETTING LIMITS ON PART-TIME WORK

The greatest danger in part-time work is that the work actually expands beyond the agreed-upon hours, at a salary based upon a shorter workweek. As one Florida lawyer observes, "[w]omen end up working a forty- to fifty-hour workweek and only get half the pay." Naomi Norwood, a Los Angeles lawyer, commented that she "knew a woman who made one of the early deals (in the mid-1980s) to work what turned out to be two-thirds time (as in, a normal 8:00 to 5:00

day) for half the pay and no credit toward partnership." One Santa Monica lawyer cautions women considering a career in litigation in particular: "You might as well get full pay, since you'll be working full-time anyway."

Rebecca Swan from Los Angeles offers this advice to make part-time arrangements work at all: "I have been part-time (three days) since 1999 and it has worked well for me. The key is to set the ground rules early about the amount of time you are going to put in. Also, it is important to have a good support staff at the office to deal with your cases when you are not there. I am an hourly employee, but I also get health benefits." Theile Branham from Columbia, South Carolina, echoes her advice: "I do think the parameters of the deal need to be clearly defined. I have seen lots of 'part-time' positions turn into 'full-time' positions because partners did not understand the parameters of the arrangements."

PART-TIME MEANS LESS POWER

There is great debate over the benefits of part-time work for women lawyers and the concomitant harm it does to their careers. One outspoken detractor is Marina Angel, a professor at Temple Law School. Professor Angel sees changes in large law firm structure throughout the profession that do not bode well for women. Women in part-time positions at these firms work reduced schedules, but work without recognition, without equal pay, and without a say in the running of the firm. The system is a "rip-off of their talent" in part-time, nonequity positions, harkening back to the days when women worked in rooms hidden from clients, without personal recognition, and without signing their names to their work. In Professor Angel's view, "this is not special treatment." This is "flat-out, outrageous discrimination."

In Professor Angel's words, women are now "jammed into other titles"—"co-counsel," "of counsel"—to accommodate part-time positions. Concurrently, she claims, the "number of women equity partners has shrunk," resulting in "an aggregate of power [in the larger law firms] to fewer white men," with little incentive for change while they at the top are doing terrifically. The work environment in large firms has resulted in few women in positions to influence change. Professor Angel's observations and fears were echoed by the research conducted by Joan Williams in her book, *Unbending Gender*:

> According to Fern Sussman, executive director of the Association of the Bar in New York, "the top tier is the full-time partnership track lawyer who has all the perks and prestige, and the bottom tier is the part-time track, made up largely of women." Some firms have made the mommy track a formal option, instituting a "permanent associate" track. One commentator raised the "frightening possibility" that law firms will evolve into institutions "top-heavy with men and childless women, supported by a pink-collar ghetto of mommy lawyers," often with permanent associate status.[13]

Women working in government and smaller firms might have more manageable hours, support systems, and benefits, but, as Professor Angel cautions, the "power has not traditionally been in those firms." Promotion to bar association leadership roles and government traditionally passes around within larger firms, with their long tentacles of influence and nepotism. Sixteen years ago, Karen Berger Morello concluded her treatise, *The Invisible Bar, 1638 to the Present*, with very similar sentiments:

> We must recognize too that the entry of substantial numbers of women into the law will not necessarily mean that women will move on to the higher levels of the profession. Women are likely to be relegated to a second tier—in much the same way that educators in the elementary school grades are for the most part women, and teachers of higher grades, and principals, primarily are men. The forces that once kept women out of the law altogether simply have shifted now to keeping them out of powerful positions within the law. It is important for women attorneys to know their past and to understand that the struggle for equality is nowhere near completion, for as Belva Lockwood pointed out over a century ago, "We shall never have equal rights until we take them, nor respect until we command it."[14]

Whether women are "relegated" to less-powerful positions (particularly in larger law firms) or happily welcome such positions is a subject of serious debate among women lawyers. The challenge for all lawyers who seek more balanced lives while remaining in large law firms is to structure these new opportunities in ways that offer economic parity, fairness, and professional status.

PART-TIME IN A SMALL FIRM

In large firms, some lawyers rise to the top due to the quality of their own work, and others rise due to the work they bring in for others to do. Midsize and smaller firms necessarily require lawyers to do *both*. Bringing in work requires an equal amount of effort, which is largely performed outside the office at sporting events, dinners, and functions. Economically, women in smaller firms feel the pinch because cutting back on work hours often means cutting back on enormously time-consuming efforts to get business. It is extremely difficult for a mother of young children to go out at night to dinners, functions, and clubs to network. Golfing all day is impossible and lunch is hurried when one eye is always on the clock.

Women in smaller firms scale back their office time and work at home, attend a dozen or more hours of continuing legal education courses each year, and, in most instances, put considerable effort into acquiring work. "Part-time" office schedules in smaller firms may not result in fewer overall work hours, but they do allow for greater flexibility to control personal schedules to accommodate the needs of domesticity. It is this flexibility that is sought by so many women, and it is a primary cause of large law firm attrition even when part-time work is available.

I have always worked around my son's schedule, dropping him at school and picking him up. I have continued to work through it all and participated to a good degree in bar association activities. For a number of years, I was the editor of the ABA Tax Section Newsletter. My son has been to many judicial conferences and bar association conferences. For me, part-time work has meant less money, and now that my son is becoming more independent, I feel like I am starting to build a law practice anew. It has helped to be practicing all these years, even part-time. I would recommend to any woman that she do what she can to stay current and stay visible, rather than disappear altogether, if she hopes to make a career after the kids are grown.

What Is Right with Part-Time Work?

FOR EMPLOYEES

Despite the inherent inequalities that it insures, part-time work remains attractive to women due to its promise of reduced work schedules and the opportunity to work through the young child-raising years, as opposed to dropping out altogether. Some prefer not having the pressure of partnership tracking and are pleased not to have the same responsibilities as others more senior. It is simply a job. Philadelphia Flex-Time Lawyers, an organization founded by part-time lawyer Deborah Epstein Henry, has 250 members (248 of which are women) who sign on to work reduced schedules on a contract basis at other firms. Henry states:

> People who are willing to be flexible are much more attractive. And just because we're part-time doesn't mean we're not available. We are as available, if not more available, than full-time attorneys.[15]

FOR EMPLOYERS

Part-time work may be right for some women, but is it "right" for employers? Enunciating the argument for the opposition, Jeremy D. Musken, committee chair of the Philadelphia Bar Association's Large Firm Management Committee, and managing partner at Montgomery, McCracken, Walker & Rhoads, LLP, was quoted saying the following:

> A law firm makes its living by billing lots of hours. An economically rational law firm would say, "Why should we hire someone who leaves at 3:00 p.m. when we can have a full-timer?"[16]

I posed this question to Doreen Davis, Philadelphia's former chancellor of the bar, who has the benefit of partnership experience in two of Philadelphia's largest large firms, and she agreed. Large firms prefer full-time workers to part-time workers. I would have to assume that whether part-timers are "right" for a firm comes down to the economics of billing out the time of the part-time or full-time worker. In the long run, keeping a good employee by affording maternity leave, part-time work, and greater flexibility can have only positive repercussions for the firm. One Santa Monica lawyer offers a personal observation:

> I've had lots of associates who've worked part-time, including two women now. The positives are for them, personally, and not really for the firm. The negatives are the lack of continuity; sometimes it's just not convenient that Lilly won't be here until Friday, etc. But we live with it, because we want her. And in the balance, it is worth it.

Not Every Job Can Be Part-Time

Part-time work is not always offered or possible in some fields. A woman working in litigation—in a law firm or for the district attorney—cannot take her work home in the evening to complete by computer. Court work can never be made homework, nor can a lawyer leave court in the middle of the trial for a class play. In the district attorney's office in Philadelphia, litigators finish a day in court with hours in the office, writing reports on the day's files, returning calls from lawyers and witnesses, and preparing for the next day in court with another seventy or eighty files. It is hardly a job where work can be performed in multiple locations or on flex-time. In fact, for those reasons, part-time or flex-time positions are not even offered. If part-time work is something you would consider for even a few years, your choice of employer and field of practice may need compromising. Want to go on that all-day class trip? Litigation is probably not for you.

Finding a Firm That Is Part-Time Friendly

In 2002, the Pennsylvania Bar Association's Women's Commission instituted a new award for the Promotion of Women to Leadership Positions. The recipient of this award is selected from among the hundred largest Pennsylvania law firms. Its purpose, as explained by the commission, is as follows:

> The total percentage of women in a firm does not indicate that the firm is making the best use of its talented and able women lawyers unless they are also well represented in leadership positions. Associate and non-equity partner positions may or may not be stepping-stones to true leadership positions in a firm. Part-time positions might be compatible with wholesome family life and provide some women and men with the ability to practice their profession which would not be available if they had to work full time. However, part-time positions should not be dead-end positions that exclude the possibility of equity partnership or other leadership positions. Opportunities for advancement of excellent lawyers should be available in varying circumstances.

The first recipient of this award was the law firm of Willig, Williams & Davidson, a firm of thirty-four lawyers with offices in Philadelphia, Harrisburg, and New Jersey. Name partner Deborah Willig is a 1975 Temple Law School graduate and the first woman Philadelphia Bar Association Chancellor. The firm was recognized for promoting and retaining women in part-time positions. Deborah herself works in overdrive, but on a schedule that permits her to be a night owl and arrive somewhat later in the morning. Her partners and associates often work from out-of-the-office locations and communicate frequently by e-mail. In accepting her firm's award, Deborah made the following remarks:

> [W]e have—in a very gender-blind fashion—always said: We need the best person for the job; in partnership decisions we have always commented that if an attorney has been a talented and valuable part-time associate, her talent and value would not diminish as a partner, just because she works part-time; and we have, not consciously but always, made people aware that soccer games and senior proms are as important as briefs and oral arguments, and that the former, unlike the latter, can never be postponed.
>
> Having been so honored today, I have a series of admissions.
>
> We don't seek out female attorneys. Our majority female partnership, or the record number of female attorneys, was not a goal we affirmatively sought to achieve. We did not create a formula for flex-time or part-time work and then seek candidates who would complement our model. Many women, outstanding applicants sought by bigger firms who frankly could afford to pay them more, chose to join our firm because of our policies.
>
> They were not originally designed to achieve this goal, but the reality is that this approach enabled us to attract and retain the best and the brightest. We reached this position not because of something we were taught in law school, although maybe it should be taught, but by following the most common-sense maxim—hire the best, most talented people, treat them humanely, and you will get the best results.

It is my hope and most optimistic wish that in the years to come, the Pennsylvania Bar Association's Women's Commission will find other worthy recipients upon which to bestow the award for the Promotion of Women to Leadership Positions. Women who are not practicing on their own should shop around to find a firm that is receptive to women working part-time or in flexible arrangements that allow working from outside the office. Ask if there is an office policy, how many other lawyers have used the policy, how many lawyers work part-time currently, and exactly what the impact may be upon career advancement at that firm.

ENDNOTES

1. Interview with Judge Dolores Sloviter, conducted by The Oral Legal History Project of the University of Pennsylvania Law School (Apr. 2, 1999).

2. ABA Div. for Media Relations & Pub. Affairs, Facts About Women and the Law (1998) (Question 8).

3. 42 U.S.C. § 2000e(k) (1978) (amendment to Title VII of the Civil Rights Act of 1964).

4. 29 U.S.C. §§ 2601 (1993).

5. ABA Comm'n on Women in the Profession, Balanced Lives, Changing the Culture of Legal Practice 12 (2001) (prepared by Deborah L. Rhode).

6. ABA Div. for Media Relations & Pub. Affairs, *supra* note 2 (Question 8).

7. *Id.*

8. ABA Comm'n on Women in the Profession, *supra* note 5, at 8.

9. Joan Williams, Unbending Gender, Why Family and Work Conflict and What to Do About It 73 (2000).

10. Sue Shellenbarger, *Perils of Part-Time: Flexible Work Hours Aren't Nearly as Heavenly as They Sound*, Wall St. J., June 27, 2002, at D1.

11. Catalyst, Women in Law: Making the Case, Executive Summary 10 (2001).

12. Deborah Graham, *It's Getting Better, Slowly*, A.B.A. J. Dec. 1, 1986, at 54.

13. Williams, *supra* note 9, at 73.

14. Karen Berger Morello, The Invisible Bar, The Woman Lawyer in America: 1638 to the Present 218 (1986).

15. Jeff Lyons, *The Case for Flex-, Part-Time Attorneys*, 31 Phila. B. Rep. 5 (2002).

16. *Id.*

"A DAY IN THE LIFE"
CALIFORNIA LAWYER KAREN RICHARDSON

After being a nurse for a number of years, I had wanted to get an education past the B.A. level. I was working at my alma mater, University of Maryland Hospital. I thought of going to law school in the early 1970s, but they had no part-time program and I had to work. When my husband and I moved to California in 1973, he started at a part-time program and I soon joined him. It took a number of years to complete law school, as I was working full-time and gave birth to my son prior to graduation. I took some time to pass the bar exam and had my daughter in 1983. When she was five years old, I went back to studying for the state bar exam. I was a school nurse for Los Angeles unified school district at the time. I began my job as a public defender in January 1990. It was difficult at first because of the large amount of law and procedure that I had to learn. I started representing clients accused of misdemeanors. Within four months of being in the office, I started doing trials. Because of my age and past work experience, I think that I was better prepared to tackle the challenge. Not everyone that started in the office made it through the first year. The public defenders office, at the time I was hired, sought people with other job experience and maturity. Therefore my work history was helpful. The office still tries to secure a mix of young, less experienced lawyers and those with prior work experience. Women in my office have been slower in getting management positions, but that is beginning to change.

My work hours are generally Monday through Friday, 8:00 a.m. to 5:00 p.m. I am assigned to one superior court and carry a caseload of about fifty felonies. One day a week I am assigned to a preliminary hearing court where my new cases are either settled by way of plea bargain, or a hearing is done and if the client is held to answer, he or she is then sent to superior court for trial. Trials are generally done on the more serious charges such as murders and other crimes that carry a life sentence. A lot of extra time goes into trial preparation, so often work hours will be later and extend to weekends.

My job involves interviewing persons charged with crimes. These people are usually in custody and so I need to go to jails to see them and conduct interviews. On a daily basis I have contact with judges, prosecutors, other defense attorneys, court staff, and office staff.

Because this is a government job, equal opportunity is probably more available than in the private sector. However, when young women have children, they tend to want to move to less demanding and stressful jobs, such as arraignment court. This has become known as being on the "baby track," and women are sometimes criticized for this.

I do like my job. It is interesting and generally fulfilling. A government job offers job security and good benefits. The disadvantage is having to work with people who are not invested in the job and just coasting, or doing the bare minimum. However, when you have your own caseload, you can handle the work independently.

Chapter Twelve

Time Out

There is a time for some things,
And a time for all things; a time
For great things, and a time for small things.

Miguel de Cervantes Saavedra,
Don Quixote

Some women withdraw from the workforce for a period of time to pursue a family or community work or for other reasons. For the professional woman who expects to pursue a law career at some time in her life, just how damaging is a "time out"?

As an alternative to working part-time or seeking some other compromise, some women elect to be full-time mothers, at least while children are very young. Although full-time mothering is a luxury we cannot all afford or even want, some believe it is in the best interest of the child, while others believe it is in the best interest of the mother.

In earlier decades, women were expected to take time off to raise young children. In 1966, the National Organization for Women (NOW) issued a Statement of Purpose that challenged assumptions and addressed the dilemma of professional women who felt compelled to withdraw from the workforce to raise children, only to struggle to reenter years later:

We do not accept the traditional assumption that a woman has to choose between marriage and motherhood, on the one hand, and serious participation in industry or the professions on the other. We question the present expectation that all normal women will retire from jobs or professions for ten or fifteen years, to devote their full time to raising children, only to reenter the job market at a relatively minor level. This in itself is a deterrent to the aspirations of women, to their acceptance into management or professional training courses, and to the very possibility of equality of opportunity or real choice, for all but a few women. Above all, we reject the assumption that these problems are the unique responsibility of each individual woman, rather than a basic social dilemma which society must solve. (NOW Statement of Purpose (1966), reprinted by permission of the National Organization for Women)

Can women reasonably expect to reach the highest rungs of the ladder of success with men if they take time away from their careers to raise families? Just how difficult is a comeback?

Confirming Men's Worst Expectations—Quitting

Abandoning a profession for a period of time to raise children, or indeed for any reason, raises many new concerns for the woman lawyer. First is the appearance of giving in to men's innermost expectations that a law school education and training is wasted on a woman. In the 1950s and 1960s when women began entering law school in small numbers, they were often openly accused of taking the place of more deserving men who had families to feed. Proving men wrong was the best revenge. No matter how many men leave the law to work in family businesses or some other profession, their training is never viewed as wasted. For women, it is.

When women in the 1950s and 1960s applied to law schools, one reason for the resistance they received was the assumption that they would marry and abandon their profession to raise children. It was argued that putting a woman through law school was a colossal waste of resources. Indeed, in 1980, when I was just starting in the job market, I was questioned on my sincerity and stick-to-itiveness. I was actually asked, "Aren't you going to get married and quit?" It was very difficult to convince prospective employers to invest time and effort in paying me and training me when, in their view, I was likely to marry and leave to raise a family. My standard reply was that at the moment I was single and would have to find time to date, meet someone I liked (loved), get married, and then have children. In the meantime, I figured I had several years ahead of me when I would have to pay my own rent. I needed a job. The question in the minds of my would-be employers was whether the job I had in mind was simply to tide me over until the big event occurred—marriage and then children. Never mind that men were not subject to the same oath of loyalty, and might leave for better opportunities that came their way down the line. Apparently, the assumption also goes, I would not have to support anyone and would never get divorced. Well into the 1980s, at the very least, a young woman lawyer was not viewed as a good investment for an employer.

Loss of Career Equals Loss of Status

A woman who leaves her job for full-time motherhood loses more than just her job. She loses her status as a "professional working woman." Her business suits hang in the closet, replaced by clothes that get sorted and dumped in the washing machine rather than taken to the dry cleaner and returned on hangers. Her identity is no longer defined by her profession, but through her children or her husband.

John Tierney of the *New York Times* reported in his column that only half the mothers in America work full-time outside the home.[1] When he originally reported this statistic in his article entitled, "Take Your Daughter to Work Day," he couched it in a tongue-in-cheek framework, saying, "Take Our Wives to Work." He caught hell from his readers and, as a result, took a trip to his son's daycare center where previously his normal duties were simply to drop him off in the morning. Mingling with the mothers, he discovered accomplished women with a variety of professional degrees and experiences who had dropped out of the workforce to be full-time parents for a few years. They expressed worry and concern about their reentry, and the complete lack of social status they formerly enjoyed. They also resented that their husbands got to have it all: well-adjusted children, good careers, and homes. Yet these women were clear about what they traded for, and would not do anything differently. In their estimation, they traded "up" for a once-in-a-lifetime chance to be around their children more and to be the beneficiaries of spontaneous hugs and smiles.

At a recent seminar, I met one woman who clearly felt she suffered a personal loss of status by changing law careers to accommodate having a family. She had previously been a full-time litigator and now worked for a nonprofit organization in a much less demanding role. She confessed that she felt as though she was not a "real lawyer" anymore. For her, a bargain with domesticity meant a loss of status and pride.

Reentry—The Fear of Falling Behind

Many say that reentry into the workforce is significantly more difficult than original entry, particularly in the field of law. One Los Angeles lawyer writes:

> I stayed home to raise my family for fifteen years. I have never recovered. I cannot seem to get anybody to consider my skills.

In some occupations it may be so difficult as to be impossible to return to the same job. Employees who "drop out," like those in the Philadelphia district attorney's office, must reapply for admission if they wish to return. The work of the office goes on, according to the district attorney; caseloads are assigned and reassigned when a lawyer leaves, and any lawyer—female or male—who leaves a job will find that the job has not been "held" for her or him, particularly after a hiatus longer than six months. As people in business for themselves know, a clientele is cultivated over a long period of time and requires constant tending. It is unrealistic to expect to return to a financially successful, independent law practice after years of being away. Clients quickly go elsewhere to lawyers who are able to meet their needs on a consistent day-to-day basis. The absent lawyer is forgotten. Indeed, it is reasonable to assume that lawyers' skills erode over time if not constantly used and honed, to say nothing of the difficulty in keeping up with the constant changes in the law. Clearly, ten or fifteen hours of continuing legal education will not do it.

The nagging and realistic fear of women looking for the right solutions to raising children is that by withdrawing from the workforce, they "fall behind," perhaps irreparably. Not all careers are irreparably damaged by stepping out for a time or by delaying the start of work. It is possible to make a comeback after a number of years' absence from the profession, but not without a plan. Following are some personal accounts from women who stepped back from the practice of law and resumed satisfying careers. Each woman engineered a way to accommodate the competing passions in her life, sometimes less perfectly than at other times. But largely this was done without a road map or role model. For some women, the demands of family meant putting careers "on hold" or beginning them after children were grown. For others, a "time out" allowed for opportunities to pursue alternative career interests.

Eastern District Court Senior Judge Norma Shapiro
Time Out: Nine Years

Taking time out to raise a family was the choice of Eastern District Court Judge Norma Shapiro. She left the workforce for nine years when her children were young.

I met with Judge Shapiro and asked her about this period in her life. I learned that she and her husband made the decision to adjust their work and lives to be home to raise their young children. Her husband adjusted his work from a private practice to less time-demanding work at a hospital. She took a leave of absence from the law, attended playgroups, and mothered on a full-time basis. But Judge Shapiro did something else. In her view, in *their* view, her withdrawal from working in a firm was temporary and one day she would return to her field of practice. Knowing that, she confides, she remained very active in outside organizations where people in various circles came to know her. She became a member of the Lower Merion School Board, Home and School Association, and Jewish Publication Society. Her contacts with men and women were extensive, so when it came time to return to work, it was not as if she had dropped off the face of the earth for nine years. Many of the men she encountered in these community activities were downtown lawyers. The contacts she maintained were invaluable. Indeed, Judge Shapiro widened her circle by being elected to the Philadelphia Bar Association Board of Governors and engaging in other bar association activities. Judge Shapiro graciously shared with me the details of her life choices, for my benefit and for the benefit of young women today facing these kinds of decisions. She advises any young woman who is raising children but plans to return to the workforce to engage in community and bar-related activities that will make her reentry less traumatic.

Philadelphia Common Pleas Court Judge Carolyn Engel Temin
Time Out: Three Years

As a young adult in the 1950s, Judge Carolyn Engel Temin initially dreamed of pursuing a dancing career, but her parents balked at her desire to move to New York on her own to pursue dance on a Juilliard scholarship. Judge Temin explains that in the decade of becoming a young woman, she, like others of her generation, was expected to pursue more traditional fields, like teaching. Under no circumstance would it ever be acceptable to move away to live on her own while still single. And so, on a lark, she decided to go to law school. Because she was to live at home, she went to the University of Pennsylvania Law School.

In retrospect, Judge Temin's decision to go to law school may have been less of a "lark" and more like destiny. While at Akiba High School, she was administered a career aptitude test, and the results predicted that Carolyn Ruth Engel would make a great lawyer. While he may have meant to be encouraging, her school principal excitedly told her that although she would never be permitted in court, she could hope to find work in the back room of a local law firm. Judge Temin says she immediately crossed off a law career in her mind.

Judge Temin married while in law school and was pregnant with her first child during her third year. Her second child came a year later. At the urging of her mother-in-law, Judge Temin made a commitment to stay home for three years while the children were young. During that time, she remained involved in the legal community by volunteering with the Volunteer Public Defenders. On Fridays she would go to the prisons and interview women prisoners in their cells.

Going back to work on a more regular basis, she began as an editor with the *Practical Lawyer*. She met a classmate on the street who asked her to join the defenders' office that was expanding in response to the Supreme Court's opinion in *Gideon*. Her classmate informed her that they were going to hire one woman. In her interview, Judge Temin was asked about her personal life. She had to swear she was not going to have any more children and had to disclose her arrangements for childcare. Later she was told she was hired partly because she was married and therefore, it was surmised, could get along with men.

Throughout her working life, Judge Temin has been the beneficiary of supportive men: her first husband who shared domestic duties and caring for their children, her father-in-law who became her preceptor and trusted her to appear in court on his firm's behalf, and a law school friend who enlisted her to come to work with him in the Philadelphia defender's association as its first woman employee.

Judge Temin coped with a young family and career by having full-time help that arrived early, stayed all day, and left after cooking dinner. Her husband's schedule had the flexibility to allow him to leave when necessary to attend school functions. In 2004, Philadelphia Common Pleas Court Judge Temin will serve as the elected president of the National Association of Women Judges.

Taylor Williams, Counsel to the Pennsylvania Supreme Court
Late Start

Taylor experienced an interim of nine years between undergraduate school at Penn State University and law school. She married ("improvidently as it later turned out"), had a daughter, and discovered that her pregnancy prevented her from working as a schoolteacher. She writes, "I was discharged from the hospital on Saturday after giving birth, and went to work the following Monday as a schoolteacher. I needed the money—I had not been permitted to teach school in a pregnant posture." In addition to working in social services, Taylor held a job with the Peoples Natural Gas Company as a public-relations representative. She writes, "I worked there for two years, driving a white car with decals depicting natural gas's 'clean blue flame' on each door panel, along with the flame logo and the unfortunate name of my employer, 'Peoples Gas.' " What followed for Taylor she recounts in her own words:

> My first job post-law school was as an attorney for the Central Legal Staff of the Pennsylvania Superior Court, and was secured through Marjorie Broderick, head of placement at the law school. Getting that job was blind luck, because it turned out to be such a nice job—like a clerkship in many ways, but with the advantages of higher pay and permanency of position. Mrs. Broderick told me about it, I sent a résumé, did the interview, and Judge Greenberg, who was in charge of the hiring, picked me. (He also picked Chuck Schliefer, also in our class.) I worked there for three years and decided I should be a "real lawyer." With the help of some of the superior court judges, I interviewed with some firms and took an offer from Abrahams & Lowenstein, a midsize firm for that time, [with forty] lawyers. I did commercial litigation, employment litigation, and transportation law. Generally I liked the firm and the people. One snafu was that the firm had no anti-nepotism policy and I was an associate at the same level as the sons of two powerful partners in the firm. I felt I was not given the golden assignments, the perks, or the pay, probably because of nepotism—or was it because I am female?

The firm fell on hard times when the most prestigious partners moved to other, larger firms. When it became apparent, after five years as a slaving associate, that partnership was not in the cards at this now-flailing firm, I moved to a "boutique" employment litigation firm with a nationwide practice. For this job, I responded to an advertisement in the *Legal*, and had the experience they were looking for. This was a very high-pressure job—much of the pressure generated by the lead partner. My experience as a mother and teacher came in handy in dealing with his childish tantrums. I stayed there for just two relatively unhappy years, before spotting another *Legal Intelligencer* advertisement, which landed me where I am now. I work for the Pennsylvania Supreme Court, litigating cases on behalf of Pennsylvania justices, judges, and the judicial system.

Paula Szortyka, Berks County Assistant District Attorney
Late Start

Paula M. Szortyka is an assistant district attorney with the Berks County District Attorney's office in Reading, Pennsylvania. She has been an able prosecutor of misdemeanors and felonies for twenty years. Paula had been out of the working world for many years when she entered law school at the age of forty-seven, when her daughter was seventeen and her son was twenty and married. She commuted to Temple Law School daily from the town of Reading by train, tearing covers off books to lighten her load. She is now seventy-two and still working in the district attorney's office. Paula takes pride in reminding a local judge to include the reference to "ladies" as well as "gentlemen" in his remarks and in challenging stereotypes along the way.

Kathryn Carlson
Late Start

Kathryn Carlson was similarly out of the job world for several years before attending law school. The mother of two preschool children and married, Kathryn sought a career that would complement her bachelor degrees in history and political science and her master's degrees in modern American history and political science. Kathryn was among the first to be able to take advantage of a newly instituted part-time day program at Temple Law School. Only by having this flexibility could she go to school by day on a less intensive schedule and be home with her children at night.

Kathryn works as a sole practitioner in a firm bearing her name in Bucks County, Pennsylvania. She employs one associate and concentrates in the areas of family law, probate, and Orphan's Court matters. Kathryn was, in her estimation, a latecomer to law school. She was thirty-five when she graduated, already married, and with children just entering school full-time. Initially Kathryn obtained a judicial clerkship with the Honorable Harriet M. Mims of the Court of Common Pleas of Bucks County. In 1986, she entered private practice in the area of family law with another 1980 classmate, Susan Devlin Scott. Kathryn and Susan continued in practice together until Susan was elected to the Bucks County Court of Common Pleas.

Grace Kennedy
Time Out: Thirteen Years

Not every career move is planned. Some moves are compromises. Grace Kennedy "retired" for a time because she had reached a dead-end in her career. A native of Albany, New York, Grace attended Fordham Law School in 1937, one of the few law schools to accept women applicants at that time. She lived in Brooklyn in the home of an aunt, ten minutes by subway from the Woolworth building that was the home of Fordham Law School. In a class of one hundred, Grace was one of two women.

Over Christmas break, a friend of the family encouraged her to go to work while attending school and, through his Albany and legislative connections, arranged for her to be interviewed at the Wall Street firm of Breed, Abbott, and Morgan. The firm had fifty men and was considered a large firm in its time. Grace thought to herself, "Am I nuts?" She was all of twenty years old when she interviewed with a partner she found "so pompous" and intimidating, who called her "Miss Coran" in a condescending voice. Grace worked each afternoon after classes throughout law school, primarily in a department supervised by a nonlawyer and concerned with tracking legislative changes for clients. She earned ten dollars a week and got her foot in the door. Upon graduating from law school, she was offered a full-time position, which Grace is convinced was because of a family friend in Albany. She advises, "Make friends with people who have a lot of pull."

Grace began working at thirty dollars a week and quickly discovered that the seven inexperienced young men hired at the same time were earning double that. "I was really burned up," she told me. She went to her supervising partner and complained about the unequal pay, only to be told, "Miss Coran, after all, you will get married and have someone to support you and they will get married and have a family to support." Never mind that they were not married and had no families to support, and never mind that they repeatedly looked to Grace for advice on how the firm worked because she was far more experienced than they. To complain further was futile and Grace consoled herself with the thought that she was working, and in a prestigious firm, at that, and that others were envious of her position. Yet, after some time, Grace realized she would not get very far in the firm because of her gender. Her employers insisted she continue working with a nonlawyer, tracking statewide legislation on behalf of clients. She never was permitted to meet clients, sign letters, claim authorship of her work, or go to court. She was always kept behind the scenes. As evidence of the firm's belief that her career was only a temporary preoccupation before marriage, they refused to put her name on her office door.

After seven years on Wall Street, Grace married Bob Kennedy and moved to Philadelphia where he took a job at Sun Company, eventually rising to become the Director of Research and Development. Grace became the mother of two boys and, thirteen years later, a girl.

Grace's legal career took a backseat to her work as mother and civic organizer in Newtown Square. But, as Grace would say, God's plan led to connections that led to the Villanova Law School where, under the direction of then Professor Lisa Richette, and future Philadelphia Bar Chancellor Jerome Bogutz, a new program for third-year law students was instituted where they would appear in court on a limited basis, supervised by an already practicing lawyer. Grace was able to get a job at Villanova supervising third-year law students and, in the process, formed a lifelong friendship with the future Judge Richette. Her work allowed her to gain admittance to the Pennsylvania bar on motion, rather than having to take another bar exam. At that time, Sun Company was starting an in-house legal department. Her work in New York navigating the Wheeler/Lay Act for clients perfectly suited her for antitrust work on behalf of the company. Grace continued her work at Sun for thirteen years. After retiring from Sun, Grace was contacted by a former Villanova law student, Amy Sosnov, Esq. She has worked with Amy and her husband, Steve, for the past six or seven years until her most recent retirement. Grace expressed a sense of relaxed surprise and pleasure with the way her life has unfolded since that time. As she expressed it to me, "God has plans for women."

Cherie Fuchs
Time Out: Ten Years

Upon graduating from Temple Law School, Cherie Fuchs joined the U.S. Army Judge Advocate General (JAG). Cherie practiced law with the army for eight years, traveling to Korea, Germany, and northern Virginia. She married a fellow active-duty JAG officer, and had one child with a second on the way before stepping down to the U.S. Army Reserves. After a third child, Cherie spent the next ten years as a stay-at-home mother, reporting for reserve duty once a month and for two weeks each year. During this period, Cherie and her family moved seven times. After resigning from active army duty, Cherie remained with the reserves and continued to practice law as a criminal defense lawyer, a prosecutor, a legal assistance lawyer, and an administrative law lawyer.

While in the reserves, Cherie was involved on the home front in Operation Desert Shield/Storm. She worked part-time for a local trust and estates lawyer in northern Virginia and full-time as a government contracts lawyer. She is currently employed with the Armed Services Board of Contract Appeals. Cherie is now a colonel in the U.S. Army Reserves, assigned to the Uniformed Services University for the Health Sciences. Her children are now fifteen, almost fourteen, and twelve. In her free moments, Cherie founded the Fayette County, Georgia, chapter of CHADD, a national nonprofit organization (with two hundred affiliates) that lends support networks to parents of children diagnosed with attention-deficit/hyperactivity disorder (AD/HD).

Geraldine Ferraro, Congresswoman and Vice-Presidential Candidate
Time Out: Fourteen Years

After graduating from law school, Geraldine Ferraro took a hiatus of nearly fourteen years to stay at home and raise three children. During that time, she remained connected to her vocation by volunteering her services for women in family court and by becoming politically active with the Forest Hills Gardens Corporation. On occasion, she did real estate work in her husband's office and, in 1970, four years after her youngest was born, was elected president of the New York Women's Bar Association. Her initial full-time job out of the home was with the Queens District Attorney's office. Geraldine Ferraro was elected to Congress in 1978, representing the ninth district of Queens, New York. On July 19, 1984, she accepted the Democratic Party's nomination as vice-president with running mate Walter Mondale. By accepting the nomination for vice-president, Geraldine Ferraro opened the eyes of the nation to the possibility of a woman leader and energized the legal profession for young women.

Susan Schulman
Time Out: Three Years

Just changing the way you work can be a kind of "dropping out." Take, for example, my classmate Susan Schulman. Susan is a successful trial lawyer in Philadelphia, specializing in plaintiffs' medical malpractice and products liability. Before attending Temple Law School, she spent a year in a Vista program during college at the University of Rhode Island, and worked at the Rhode Island Public Defender's office. Susan had this to say about her life's journey:

> Although I have had successes . . . very early in my career, I continue to feel that there is more to experience professionally than practicing law allows. I quit practicing law for three years to run two nonprofit organizations, which was professionally satisfying but financially difficult. When I returned to practicing law, I did so as an independent contractor and kept my hand in some nonprofit administration. I also ran for election to become a judge and lost, but will continue to pursue election. Most recently, I was appointed by the mayor to serve as Special Counsel to the City in an effort to lower auto insurance rates. Although I felt initially that this would be an interesting and productive job, the politics of the situation have severely limited my ability to be successful. I will probably leave this position and return to trial practice.

Since writing to me, Susan did as she predicted. She returned to her trial practice, this time with the law firm of Weber, Gallagher, Simpson, Stapleton, Fires & Newby. She and a legal team from her firm recently spent four months away from home, living out of a hotel suite, to pursue a plaintiff's commercial litigation matter. The case was brought on behalf of a prominent national bank that suffered the loss of all its East Coast records in a storage warehouse fire because the sprinkler system was never connected. The verdict for the bank was $20.7 million plus $6 million for delay damages. Susan Schulman is today a partner with her law firm and the mother of a three-and-a-half-year-old girl.

Pennsylvania Superior Court Judge Phyllis Beck
Late Start

Pennsylvania Superior Court Judge Phyllis Beck came to the law later in life, after undergraduate school, marriage, and four young children. Out of the workforce for ten years, Judge Beck confides that she became "intellectually restless." In 1961, she went to Bryn Mawr College to study psychology and child development, but says the study was not a good fit. In speaking with Judge Beck about her search, a friend asked, "What would you do if you were a man?" Judge Beck said she thought about the career choices made by her male classmates and recalled that many went to law school. Without role models and without even knowing any lawyers, she began applying to law schools. With four children at home, she decided to attend Temple School of Law, because it was the only school that had a part-time program. At that time, Dean Peter Liacouras had instituted a night program that would take eight years to complete. Judge Beck finished in five years by taking courses whenever given: summer, night, day, and weekends. She graduated in 1967. On the first day of law school, Judge Beck sat in a contracts class and realized that she was finally a round peg in a round hole—it was, to her, a perfect fit. To this day, she says the law is "endlessly interesting."

In Pennsylvania, the custom was to require each graduating law student to team with a preceptor for six months to learn the practical aspects of being a lawyer. A friend in surrounding Delaware County agreed to sign for Judge Beck as preceptor, but offered little practical advice. After six months, each new lawyer was required to undergo an ethics interview. Judge Beck said the examiner flunked her the first time because he thought there was something wrong with her—something unethical about being a mother and a lawyer. A second interviewer passed her.

Before reaching the superior court, Judge Beck worked for a time in private practice in a small firm, and then for the large firm of Duane Morris and as a professor at Temple Law School. She held the position of vice dean at the law school of the University of Pennsylvania for five years. In 1981, the legislature expanded the Pennsylvania Superior Court to fifteen members from its original seven. Judge Beck was initially appointed to the court and, in 1983, was elected and retained. In 1987, Governor Casey appointed her to chair a twenty-three-person committee on judicial reform, from which emanated the "Beck Report" that recommended major judicial structural reforms.

Conclusion

As the stories of these women demonstrate, it is certainly possible to step back from a law career for a period of time—to raise children, move from one city to another, or try a new career tack—and then make a comeback. Women have done it and gone on to satisfying and incredible careers. But not everyone makes the transition. It is difficult to start a career in the law, and doubly difficult to do it later in life or after a substantial sabbatical. The best advice from these success stories is to plan your reentry, if possible, and to stay active in the profession and in the community. Keep your contacts. When it comes time to look for work, a former classmate or employer might give you the chance you need. Develop new contacts within the community. Being known might lead to a new opportunity that reaches you by word of mouth. Remember your goals and, when opportunity allows you to shift priorities back into your work, be ready! We all know the "time out" signal, using both hands to form a "T." A football team uses a time out to plan its next play or tactic. Lawyers are no different. Sometimes a time out is what we need to plan our future moves.

ENDNOTE

1. John Tierney, *Take Our Wives to Work*, N.Y. TIMES, Apr. 30, 2002, at B-1.

"A DAY IN THE LIFE"
ELIZABETH BEST, A PLAINTIFF'S TRIAL LAWYER FROM MONTANA

I don't think I can accurately describe a day in my life, because each day is different. However, this is probably representative, and I don't think I am necessarily representative of other women lawyers.

I am a trial lawyer. I work with my husband in a two-attorney office in Montana. I get up at about 4:45 a.m. I take my dog for a run, and feed horses, chickens, a dog and cats. I do a load of laundry, unload the dishwasher, fix lunch for the kids, and take a shower. By 6:00 a.m., I am waking up kids.

By 7:15, I am out the door and get to the office at about 7:45. Today, I checked e-mail, responded to some telephone messages and e-mails, and prepared for depositions, which will last from 9:00 to 5:00. I will go home, fix dinner, tidy up the house, help kids with homework, and hit the hay by around 9:00 p.m. Pretty exciting. My husband does fill in a lot of gaps, and has maintenance duties at home and at the office, which we own, so this is not all one-sided. By Friday, the whole family is pretty beat, and we both do work on evenings and weekends as cases require.

While there are challenges to being one's own boss, primarily the worries about meeting overhead, the reduction of stress associated with not having to meet another person's demands or schedules is worth it. I also serve on a local school board, which fills any gaps in time not otherwise filled.

I think a good example of judges not giving as much weight to a woman as to a man might be in the area of discovery abuse. Defense counsel in civil cases, male and female, thrive on avoiding discovery and abusing the process. If I bring a motion for sanctions or to compel discovery, especially if the lawyer on the other side is female, it will not be unusual to be admonished for being "contentious." I have seen the same tactics used against a male trial lawyer dealt with by issuing substantial sanctions.

Chapter Thirteen

Balancing

In discussing the sphere of man we do not decide his rights as an individual, as a citizen, as a man, by his duties as father, a husband, a brother, or a son, some of which he may never undertake. Moreover he would be better fitted for these very relations, and whatever special work he might choose to do to earn his bread, by the complete development of all his faculties as an individual. Just so with woman. The education which will fit her to discharge the duties in the largest sphere of human usefulness, will best fit her for whatever special work she may be compelled to do.

Feminist leader, Elizabeth Cady Stanton,
from 1892 address to House Judiciary Committee,
for purpose of advocating suffrage for women

What Are We Balancing?

You do not have to be a Renaissance man or woman to require more than work to complete your life. There was a moment in my life when this became crystal clear. I needed major surgery and was hospitalized for nearly two weeks with all sorts of tubes running in and out of me. A critical mishap brought on more tubes and complications, and I skirted a near-death catastrophe. It was awful. During this time, when just getting out of bed was a colossal challenge, the well-intentioned medical staff would urge me on by saying that if I really tried, I could get better and go back to work. These were hardly the words of encouragement I was looking for at the time. Get better to go back to work?! I wanted something more than that. If I was going to get better faster, I wanted it to be for a life that went beyond work. I wanted time to be with people I loved, and to do the things that made me happy, in addition to work. That is not to say I wasn't happy with my work. But work is work, and although I care about what happens to my clients, I cannot say that every moment of every day is unmitigated joy or even intellectually satisfying.

I do not think that we all need major surgery to reach this type of epiphany. So many men and women today recognize that "all work" does not make a life. Each of us needs time for other things, like friends, family, working out, softball leagues (of our own, not just the kids'), pro bono activities, personal interests, volunteer work, or just a good book. I think women lawyers are on the vanguard with this approach. New approaches to work are being debated and tried at the behest of working mothers who do not want to be told they must choose between vocation and family commitments. Part-time policies and off-partner tracking at larger law firms are some of these new approaches. The controversy, I believe, that comes with accommodating mothers, is, in its most raw and underlying self, sexist.

When I began practicing law in the 1980s, it was not uncommon to find men sauntering down the hall at 3:30 or 4:00 in the afternoon in cleats, T-shirts, and sweats, on the way to a softball game in the "lawyers' league." Not only was it acceptable, there was a certain bravado to it. Ample telephone time was spent by the guys, rehashing the game, gathering teammates, and coordinating playing fields. This was all a very acceptable departure from the day's work. I compare it with a woman's need to leave the office once a week at 3:00 to carry her share of carpool duties. Somehow the softball league is acceptable and carpooling is not.

Philadelphia lawyer Barbara Vetri began her career in the 1960s and found herself on the defensive about her few weeks out of work after giving birth. She held her ground by countering that the older workaholic men took off weeks from work when their overworked hearts gave out. I have come to believe that it is the *reason* for the absence, not the typical few hours' absence itself, that is at the heart of this problem.

Regardless of whether law is practiced solo, in a small firm, in a large firm, in a corporation, in government, or as a judge, compromises and life adjustments will always be a requirement for women, more so than men. Women's insistence upon flexibility in the workplace will, I hope, result in a more liberated atmosphere for women and men. Eventually, women and men will take time, when able, to be in other places, to be with family, to write poetry, or to help an aging parent, without the scorn of their peers. In the meantime, women who balance multifaceted lives can benefit from sharing their experiences with one another. We can learn how another working woman managed, and at what cost.

Methods of Coping

A SUPERWOMAN NEVER DOES IT ALONE

The "superwoman" who could do it all was a concept born in the 1980s as women entered the workforce in full-time, high-powered careers while carrying full-time responsibility for the domestic sphere. In the opinion of Joan Williams, in her treatise entitled *Unbending Gender,* the "term deflected attention away from the fact that women were forced to do it all because men would not give up their traditional entitlement to women's household work."[1] When we speak of "family responsibilities" borne disproportionately by women and the balancing that they do, it is not just the responsibility of children to which we refer. Family responsibilities include cooking, caring for the home, laundry, shopping, caring for aging parents, maintaining social contacts, and sharing family celebrations. In her recent book, *Creating a Life: Professional Women and the Quest for Children*, Sylvia Hewlett points out that "[h]igh-achieving women continue to carry the lion's share of domestic responsibilities."[2] In fact, she reports that "43 percent of older, high-achieving women, and 37 percent of younger, high-achieving women in general feel that their husbands create more work for them around the house than they contribute."[3]

Doreen Davis, Philadelphia's second woman to be chancellor of the bar association, is a devoted mother and labor lawyer in a large firm. In her husband's words:

> Not only has Doreen done a remarkable job of leading the bar association, building a law practice, running our household, and raising our daughter, but she also has done it all backwards and in high heels![4]

Is this the ultimate "superwoman"? Picture this scenario described further by her husband:

> Whether it is a parent-teacher conference, "Take Your Daughter to Work Day," or a gymnastics team performance, Doreen tries never to miss one of Samantha's special events. For example, on one occasion after two days in Toronto at an American Bar Association meeting, Doreen flew home for one evening to join us at a family affair. The next morning she flew back to Toronto for an afternoon vote on a controversial issue affecting Philadelphia lawyers, then proceeded directly to Los Angeles for several days of hearings before the National Labor Relations Board for one of her clients. Of course, as soon as the hearings were over, she was on the red-eye back to Philadelphia in order to attend an important early morning partnership meeting. Indeed, finding the balance among our family, her firm, her practice, and the bar is Doreen's quest.

And then the secret came out. There are times, he intimates, when all she has time for is a "bedtime cuddle" with their daughter, and when cooking dinner for the family is an opportunity to "unwind." Clearly, someone else is covering the daily domestic grind of everyday dinner, homework, and domestic necessities. In my talk with Doreen, I pressed her for her secret. I probed. Does she have messy closets? Yes, she admits. When does she get home at night? One parent tries to be home by 7:00 p.m., she explained. But she often travels and is out of state four or five days each month. When does she arrive at the office? On days when she is not out among clients, she gets to the office no later than 8:30 if she chooses to exercise, otherwise much earlier. Mostly she ignores her own needs and skips exercising. Every day, a woman arrives at her home at 7:00 in the morning, gets her daughter ready and out to school, picks up her daughter from school around 2:30 in the afternoon, supervises after-school activities, carpools when necessary, supervises home-work, and departs around 7:00 in the evening when either Doreen or her husband comes home. Doreen makes every effort, she says, to be at "special events" and is thankful that her daughter's all-girl private school supplies her in advance with a detailed schedule of activities for the year, complete with play schedules and performances. She makes every attempt to arrange her schedule around these moments.

Doreen is an equity partner in a large firm and was Philadelphia Bar Association Chancellor. Behind her is a husband with a flexible career, as well as a terrific hired assistant—almost a third parent—covering the chores of motherhood. The lesson for the rest of us is all too clear. It is impossible to do everything 100 percent of the time, or be everywhere for everyone without fail. You set goals and priorities, and get help from others.

HUSBANDS WHO HELP

I do not think there is a working married woman in America who can be the best parent, cook, or housekeeper without the partnership of her mate. Frankly, some men are just better in the kitchen. U.S. Supreme Court Justice Ruth Bader Ginsburg responded to my inquiries about her life by forwarding to me her remarks appearing in the University of Tulsa Law Journal in 1997, dedicated to the U.S. Supreme Court. She reflects that a man's attention to home chores and family care "no longer mark[s] a man as strange."[5] As for her own life, she adds this:

> To the abiding appreciation of my daughter, son, and now grandchildren, meals at our house, some seventeen years ago, were taken completely off Mommy's track—she has no talent for the job—and switched to Daddy's—he has indeed mastered the art.

A lot of husbands do their fair share of family work. Cheryl Kritz, Chief Deputy City Solicitor for the Philadelphia Commercial Law Unit in Philadelphia, feels fortunate that her husband, also a lawyer, is in private practice in a two-partner firm, so he has the flexibility she lacks to balance work and caregiving. On days when school is on holiday, he brings their daughter to his office. He is home earlier than she can ever be, prepares dinner, and reviews homework. On Saturdays he shops for the week. To cover all the bases, Cheryl may call upon loyal long-term sitters, in-laws, and generous friends who carpool to school without the expectation of an equal quid pro quo.

Naomi Norwood, a Los Angeles lawyer who specializes in business litigation in a small firm, shares these sentiments:

> Of course, having a saint for a husband isn't a bad idea, either! He makes dinner during the week, I make dinner on weekends. He does regular grocery shopping and I do it for entertaining. He does all the dry cleaning dropping off and picking up. He takes the kids to the doctor and orthodontist.

A personal injury lawyer from Great Falls shares the following about her husband:

> My husband is a trial lawyer, too. We simply schedule around our kids. I burn the candle at both ends. I do laundry, get kids up, make breakfast in the a.m. We go to work. I cook and clean up in p.m. If I am busy or in trial, my husband does the above. We share all duties, although I may do more in the house, because he has to take care of mechanical stuff. We get to our kids' games. We get to their concerts. We make our

work wait, if necessary. We use the phone at home, and the computer at home. We are more mobile with those conveniences.

Some couples have undergone role reversals so the husband is the traditional stay-at-home parent. Alexis works in the trusts and estates department of a large Los Angeles firm, and she describes her relationship with her husband as one of complete role reversal:

> My husband stays at home with our children. Nevertheless, I still find that I work much less than my male colleagues and most of my female colleagues because I am just not willing to be away from my family in the evenings or on the weekends on a regular basis. I do attend a few evening programs or seminars occasionally, but I'm very rarely working in the evenings or on the weekends. I'd rather come in extremely early in the morning when my family is sleeping than stay late. By 5:30 p.m. my husband really needs me to be home and give him a break from the daily grind of raising children.

As this working parent states so well, many women who get help from their husbands and elsewhere still feel the pull to be with their children and families, not just out of duty, but out of desire. In that regard, many devise ways to find a satisfying balance that makes room for both. For some women, this requires that husbands share the cost of placing careers on hold and forgo sedate evenings at home for chores and childcare.

BABYSITTERS AND OTHER HELP AT HOME

I agree with Montgomery County Common Pleas Court Judge Dickman's assertion that starting a family concurrently with starting a practice can be almost impossible, given the time demands of both. Judge Dickman's own achievements as a law firm partner and judge have compelled her to spend enormous amounts of time networking and building connections. She echoes what many others feel: that the job of childcare primarily falls upon women, and that women's careers are first to suffer during this time. Although many husbands may be willing to share in the responsibilities of children and home, they are typically helpers rather than initiators. They will do anything asked or told, but never envision exactly what it is that must be done. They might get the eggs and milk, but only after being asked to do so.

Judge Dickman reminded me of an incident that happened to me not long after my son was born. I was back at work when a young male lawyer came to do business with one of my partners in the office, and, being a new father, boasted proudly of his new child. "Of course," he declared, "I don't get up at night with the baby. I have to be rested for work." I had one of those moments when, in a rush, the world stands silent around me and my inner voice gives out a good, long, loud scream. I was juggling work with the tugs of motherhood that had come yanking at me extra hard as a latecomer to it. I was juggling the late nights, lost nights, and sleeplessness that come with mothering. I had not been rested and fresh for weeks. I cannot say I was satisfied, but at least I felt validated, to read in the ABA's *Balanced Lives* the following: "Most male attorneys have spouses who assume the bulk of family responsibilities; most female attorneys do not."[6]

When my son was young, I paid for all-day sitters and preschool. What I earned in those years went right back out for caretaking expenses. The benefit to me was the ability to keep a career afloat, and, for part of the day, do something intellectually stimulating. It permitted me to stay in the workforce rather than drop out altogether and then later try to make a comeback—something extremely difficult to do in the legal field. Finding sitters and making the choice to have my son home rather than in daycare was one of the more harrowing decisions to make. Before my son was born, I visited several daycare centers in center city, believing I could drop in on my son during the day. Having my son quickly disabused me of the notion that I would be able to take leave of him so nonchalantly. I never imagined the wrenching scenes of our departures—he screaming and me crying. Finding the right person to be home with my baby was so difficult, because obviously he cannot report if he had a good day, if the sitter smoked or talked on the telephone, or if he wandered out the door that morning and visited the neighbors on his own (a true story of mine). I managed to be home after the after-noon nap and stay there. Those days are a blur, but I remember some particularly difficult episodes, like frantically pleading with my sitter to come to work in spite of the ice storm outside, or feeling terribly jealous of very lovely people who were enjoying my child while I worked. I interviewed all sorts of people and I tried hard not to be forced into a desperate choice. There was the woman with the jeep without windows who otherwise seemed too good to be true. She could drive to work and promised to cook sumptuous meals that she described in mouth-watering terms, but then she never appeared for work on day one. There was the sitter who stubbornly refused to put the milk away if it was left out in the morning because it was not her job; and the pre-med student who brought her books; and the sitter who quit and then ran away from home to have her own baby; and the woman who had her own baby and offered to come to my house each day. Her baby's favorite expression was to shriek. It scared the wits out of my son. It is very easy to say, "Oh, I'll get a sitter when the baby's born." In truth, it is one of the most difficult arrange-ments to find.

By the time I was able to enroll my son in preschool, I breathed a sigh of relief, knowing that he was in a safe place, with many good people around and other children to play with, as well as more hours of coverage if I needed them. The teary departure scenes continued for years. It was an awful way to start any day.

Some choose live-in nannies from foreign countries in the years their children are infants. These arrangements can be the best and the worst. Ideally, you have someone on-call, in your house, to cover those extra hours when you just cannot get home or need to get out early. But these young women (they are usually female) often have minimal childcare experience, and often do not speak English. And they live with you for better or worse. They are not, by any stretch of the imagination, Mary Poppins impersonators.

The army of backup assistants can include live-ins and live-outs, cleaning people, lawn service providers, and others. They can keep you afloat in your career and quickly empty your pocketbook.

TECHNOLOGY—MOMMY ON A BEEPER

When Christine McCarthy Smith, of Manchester, New Hampshire, became a medical malpractice trial lawyer after twenty-five years as a nurse, she says she became "mommy on a beeper." She writes:

> I became mommy on a beeper. My kids knew they could page me any-time, but they saw very little of me. I have two girls and they were fif-teen and eleven when I started school.

The security of being in touch with our children through beepers and cell phones is a national phenomenon. "Family Talk"® is the plan promoted in the industry to keep families in touch. Fathers, mothers, and children are connected through the airways. My son has a cell phone (no longer unusual for middle-schoolers), and I like knowing we can be in touch if I am late picking him up somewhere. If I am not in the office, I can still be found if there is an emergency. I like being able to call the office from the courthouse to say my case has not yet been heard, so please call my mother to get my son at school. One parent I know was convinced to give her latchkey daughter a cell phone soon after her daughter was locked out of the house because she forgot her key.

There is a flip side to all this technology. We are closely con-nected not only to our loved ones, but to our work. Our technology explosion has been a blessing and a curse. With "expectations of total availability," technology makes our work harder.[7] It also makes it "harder for attorneys to *not* work while at home."[8]

I graduated from law school in 1980 and began working as a lawyer in the city of Philadelphia in what now seems like ancient times. It was a world without computers. Lawyers wrote notes by hand, and pleadings were handwritten on yellow, fourteen-inch "legal" pads. No building in the city exceeded the 510-foot height of William Penn's statue atop City Hall, and women lawyers were still rare. Times have certainly changed. Nearly all the lawyers surveyed by the Philadelphia Bar Association in 2000 reported using computers at work, and more than 75 percent continue to work at home with computers or laptops. More than 88 percent of Philadelphia's lawyers use e-mail; 80 percent are online at work and 63 percent are online at home. Nearly 60 percent of Philadelphia's lawyers report accessing the Internet "several times a day."

We can be reached anywhere—anytime—by fax, cell phone, and e-mail, and we are expected to reply immediately. Fax service of pleadings or notices of hearings and conferences can create night-mares when they arrive at 5:00 p.m. or later. Caller ID not only lets clients know you are calling from home, but also gives away your home telephone number, opening you to calls at home at all hours. Cell phones are terrific while waiting in courtroom hallways, and ter-rible in the way they can tether you to work. E-mail is helpful for transferring long documents or communicating with that hard-to-find expert witness. It also creates the expectation, among others, that you are constantly checking your messages. At least one woman with whom I spoke refuses to give out her fax number or e-mail address, and gently declines to talk business with clients when she is home. Although it is difficult to always be on-call and "tied in" by technology, Judge Dickman sensibly reminds us that, as lawyers, we offer a service, and given our fees, our clients have a right to expect us to be available. If we are not being bothered and called, then we are out of work.

All in all, I believe that technology has been liberating for work-ing mothers. Cell phones give us the security of being in touch and on-call with our children. E-mail keeps us connected to our impor-tant work no matter where we are. E-mail even keeps me abreast of my son's extracurricular activities, like scout meetings or activities announced in school newsletters. Today's law school graduates have the advantage of entering the workforce already savvy in word processing, computerized legal research, e-mail, and Internet surfing. This is all for the better.

WORKING FROM HOME

As a sole practitioner and full-time mother, my hours in the office may be reduced, but my work continues afterward at home with the aid of computers, call forwarding, e-mail, a laptop computer, and a very discreet secretary at my main office. She can field telephone calls and, when appropriate, forward them to me at home for call-backs. In truth, I believe there is no such thing as "part-time" work if you are self-employed. New technology offers the ability to do work in multiple locations. Then again, this may not be beneficial to some. It raises multitasking to an art form.

Former Philadelphia Bar Association Chancellor Doreen Davis also credits technology with making her work more flexible. She can be on vacation and communicate with clients and they will not realize she is not in the office. Technology has revolutionized the way she works with her associates. She offers an incident that occurred recently when an associate came to her and said his child was sick and it was his turn to stay home while his wife went to work. The associate owed her an opinion letter, and so asked her to review the document with him before he left to go home at 11:00 in the morning. He made the necessary adjustments from home by computer.

On a personal note, I always felt I had two full-time occupations that overlapped. Even though I arrived at work at 9:30 a.m. and left at 3:00 p.m. when my son was in elementary school, I had the workload and responsibility of full-time work. Further, my attention to my son and husband and home also required full-time effort. Technology permitted me to be tied to my office and clients so that even if I was home, I was available. When my child was an infant and I had the opportunity and luxury to choose to "work from home" on certain days, this was even harder. As any mother knows, a child does not understand that when you are on the telephone with a judge or client, he or she should be quiet and wait. A child rarely appreciates the concept that his or her needs come second, and indeed some-times they cannot come second. I remember a conference I had with a federal judge from my home; in anticipation, I had food, bottles, and a myriad of toys lined up to keep my son entertained and happy so his little voice would not be heard through the phone. I struggled to maintain the appearance that I was seriously at work in the office while fielding this important call. It was exhausting.

With the advent of caller ID, it is harder to maintain the cha-rade of being at work while standing in the kitchen. I have more than once given away my location by running water in the kitchen sink or banging a dish on the table. "Are you home?" my client asks. I am not convinced that every client appreciates the lawyer working from home, or that doing so does not somehow jeopardize the professional respect of one's peers and clients. On the other hand, many women clients may not only understand, but admire this commitment.

Too Much Multitasking Is Not a Good Thing

A busy lawyer juggles many cases at the same time, and deals in office management to some degree and office politics to a larger degree. Overlay the demands of work with the demands of family, and life gets much more interesting. Overlap a demanding workload with the intrusion of a cell phone or the impossibility of working around children, and you have now fully loaded the circuits. It is possible to be doing too much at the same time, and, at that point, nothing gets done well. Children feel slighted and the work gets half the attention it requires. The cost of doing too much was highlighted in a *Wall Street Journal* article by Sue Shellenbarger on February 27, 2003. Its title was appropriate: "Multitasking Makes You Stupid: Studies Show Pitfalls of Doing Too Much at Once." The cost is decreased efficiency, loss of short-term memory, and increased stress. The simplest example is trying to listen to two people talking to you at the same time. Impossible. Drive to work while solving a problem at the office in your mind, and you cannot remember how the car found its way to the garage. Try solving a problem while driving children in the car at the same time, and you could wind up completely lost, with no solution to your problem and a very frustrated child. Doing it all can exact an even higher price, as one Chicago lawyer tells it:

> I worked till I dropped. I achieved everything professionally I could have hoped to achieve. I also did everything at home. EVERYTHING!! When I hit fifty, my spouse and lifetime partner decided I was too serious and left me for my child's best friend's mother—an advertising executive who giggles a lot and has the morals of a concrete slab. So I guess I did not do such a great job of balancing after all, and I wonder what my future will be.

Balancing

Simply put, balancing means cutting down on work and getting help. For some, it means shaving off a few hours of each day by arriving later and leaving earlier. Others cut back on the number of days they work during the week. Some continue their work at home while others bring their children to work. Lana Sayre of Omaha, Nebraska, a sole practitioner in the fields of bankruptcy and divorce, offers:

> I have a part-time solo practice. I keep the kids with me unless I am meeting clients or have a court appearance. My children are ages five, three, and two. Some days are better than others. I can usually put in a video or let them play on the Internet, but I am not as productive when I have to stop to mediate fights or get drinks.

I am guilty of this practice on occasion, and I know from personal observation that many others are, too. When I look around my city, particularly in those weeks just between the time camp has ended and school has yet to start, there are children everywhere. I see them in banks, lobbies, offices, and elevators, and behind food counters. I feel guilty not being at the beach with my son but, truthfully, he has been outside all summer at camp. We take plenty of vacations big and small, and he is delighted to have a chance to "surf the 'net" at his own terminal uninterrupted while in our office.

Terri R. Z. Jacobs, of Houston, Texas, works in a small office specializing in criminal defense and military law. Terri also has brought her children to work:

> I am spoiled since I work for my dad. I came to his firm with the understanding that I would bring my children to work with me. In exchange I agreed to a lower-than-market-value salary. Once my children were old enough for preschool, I put them there in the mornings and now I work part-time while they are at school and after they go to bed; I spend the afternoons and evenings with the kids. It has been difficult when I want to travel or if I'm in trial but otherwise it works well. For this reason, I focus my work on appellate and writ of habeas corpus cases, which have minimal court time.

Women who have the option of bringing their children to work are usually in partnerships with family or in practice for themselves. And, as Terri Jacobs points out, they usually carefully select their environments and the types of lawyering they do.

Carmen Matos has three children and is an involved, hands-on mother. When she worked for the government, its lenient policy for maternity leave was a great benefit. "Obtaining good childcare has been a continuous challenge. Now that my children are in their teens, they still demand my time in sports." She copes by being very "organized." Going into private practice has afforded her greater flexibility, but still requires her to juggle: "Sometimes it is very difficult to keep up with the housework and the kids. My husband has learned to cook for the family since much too often I am late, especially during trials."

Taylor Williams brought her daughter to class throughout law school and yet later found that boarding school during her daughter's teens was the best arrangement for them. Taylor has had her own unique approach, setting priorities and working from home when necessary: "Rather than balance, I have always integrated the two." Her daughter frequently accompanied her to law school and then to her office. She too brought work home. "Needless to say, many a case file has graced the dining-room table at home. I found that I simply worked on the highest priority at the time—whether that was getting a case ready for trial or helping Kate fill out the college applications."

Today, Taylor uses her balancing skills to combine, balance, and integrate her work as counsel to the Pennsylvania Supreme Court with her theatrical career. Taylor is a member of Actors Equity and has performed with the Philadelphia Shakespeare Festival, most recently in the production of *Cymbeline*, and the Bar Association Theater Wing. She has been a course planner for the Pennsylvania Bar Institute, relating theater skills to trial skills. Taylor performs a "one-woman show on women's suffrage, followed by questions and answers about the status of women today."

For Nancy of Tallahassee, Florida, work as a staff lawyer for the trial judges in state court has helped her maintain a satisfying balance in her life:

> Balancing has been the biggest challenge of my life. I have chosen a government job with relatively flexible hours and a large measure of autonomy, but with a lower income than I might make elsewhere. I have chosen to live in the same town as my parents so that they could help me with the children. I have relied on my parents for assistance with childcare, child transport, etc., but this resource is diminishing as my mother has recently passed away and my father is less able as he ages. My husband has managed to find suitable employment in our area despite the political (and therefore unstable) nature of certain positions. We have pursued our dreams as much as feasibly possible in this location. Family life comes first, before work. I have been fortunate enough to find a position I love that fits in with my family goals.

Being organized and setting priorities, and then changing them as the circumstances change, is a common suggestion from those who do a daily balancing act. Sometimes sleep is the last priority, as Alice Nelson of Tampa, Florida, now an executive director of a nonprofit organization, tells of those early years when the children were very young:

> This has been a tough one. One balance was lack of sleep [due to] studying after the kids went to bed. There have been many challenges. We used to say when we were in D.C. from 1976 until 1978 that my husband worked in the District, I worked in Baltimore, and the kids lived in the suburbs.

Some cut back on bar association activities. Naomi Norwood, a litigator from Los Angeles, offers:

> Before my daughter was born, I was involved in a lot of bar activities, and I know busy litigators who are mothers who still do that, but I don't know how. Perhaps they tend to be in larger firms without as many administrative tasks as I have.

Sometimes the house suffers, as Marilyn Hochman, a small-firm lawyer specializing in family, bankruptcy, criminal, and personal injury law, reports:

> We have the messiest house in town. I have a husband who cooks most nights. I don't do many nightly activities. I don't work for a big firm. I am a partner in a firm of four people. I take off for most school holidays and breaks. I go to soccer and take kids to the doctor, physical therapy, etc. My husband works for the state and he has a lot of sick leave to help out.

Sometimes a special family occasion is missed. Says Christine McCarthy Smith:

> I try to keep the weekends for my family. They understand that if there is a trial, then I will not be home for a while. I try to take comp time on school vacations. I also make sure I leave the office by 6:00 p.m. I may have to do work at home, but I am home. My first trial was about 200 miles from home. I missed my daughter's sixteenth birthday. She was very upset. I sent her flowers and we had a small family party when I got home.

And, in truth, it does not always come together for everyone. One New Hampshire lawyer writes:

> I am finding the balance very difficult, and almost insurmountable as I begin to think about having children. I'm beginning to think that being a lawyer is not a good way for anyone to make money, especially not for women who want to have children. I have all of these debts from law school and a husband who makes less money than I do and commutes a great distance to work every day. So now I'm trying to find a job that actually pays decently and is flexible enough with a regular enough schedule so that I could take care of a child and still pay my bills. It sucks.

Those without children still struggle to find the perfect balance in life, where work does not overwhelm all else. Moi Vienneau of Hamilton, Ontario, Canada, is a sole practitioner in personal injury and medical negligence. She relates:

> I think that I am now starting to really make efforts and working on ways to balance my life. Having a husband who is also a lawyer, and one who is also extremely focused on his goals, makes it difficult for us to take time off for family life. I should add that we have no children yet, and this allows us to concentrate on our work. Once children join us, this will absolutely change. I think we both look at this pre-children time as our way to do what we will not be able to do once we have children. The reason why I think it makes it difficult to find that balance, or at least that it has, is because neither one of us has that other person who is not in law, who is not as focused, and so we continue on our merry way, enjoying our work, and not feeling the "need" to step away from it for the other person. It is not a selfish thing, but rather, because we both are of the same mind, both are more concentrated on what we're so used to doing, as opposed to concentrating on what we're not used to doing (i.e., vacations). We have started to work at home on weekends; we're hooked up to our offices by wireless connection, which makes a big, big difference. Most people think that we lead very abnormal lives. I don't think so. I think that what works for us is "odd" to others, but then again, their desire to take five weeks of leisure is odd to us.

Another self-diagnosed "workaholic" from Sacramento, California, working in a midsize products liability firm, shared her recent efforts to bring her life into balance:

> For the first five years of my practice, I did not balance them at all. I was a workaholic and traveled more weeks than I care to admit. For that, my family life suffered quite a bit. My husband and I decided to postpone having a family—now we are still debating it. It is too easy to get settled into a work routine that leaves no room for family time or a family. Recently, however, I took back my life and have been so happy. I stopped working six to seven days a week, fifteen hours a day. I leave at a decent hour each day, rarely come in on the weekends, and hired a personal trainer to get me into shape. I spend more time on the hobbies I loved before the law that got lost in the bustle of everyday life. But it took some therapy and a lot of time to reach this point.

With family being an overwhelming priority, women recognize that compromise is inevitable. Lyle Griffin Warshauer of Atlanta, Georgia, is a small-firm personal injury lawyer, specializing primarily in medical malpractice. She voices a common sentiment:

> I have had to cut back on the hours I am in the office in order to accommodate children's activities, and to be able to spend more time on family matters. It is exceedingly difficult to "balance" the two, and I think the only way to do that is to compromise on the work aspect, but family is the most important in my view.

Adelina Martorelli finds the balancing act one of her "biggest challenges":

> I have to succeed in everything I do; that is in my nature. With this, however, I have learned the fine art of compromising. It is truly a balancing act. Accepting the fact that I can't do it all in one day and that some things won't get done until later has been hard for me. After twenty years, I am still working at it. The one thing I will not compromise on is the time I spend with my children. I don't see them during the day because they are at school and active with after-school events. But they know that at night and on weekends the family is key. They also know that if they ever need me during the day, all they have to do

is call. Likewise, work knows that if one of my children calls, they will let me know immediately.

While some blend work and family, others keep them strictly separate. Naomi Norwood, from Los Angeles, offers her method of balancing:

> I keep work and home totally separate. I do not talk on the phone to my family while at work unless it is absolutely necessary, [such as to discuss] who is picking up [my daughter] and where. My daughter does not call me at the office. When I get home, I am home. I do not work at home. I do not talk on the phone about work at home. I do not work on the weekends unless it is absolutely necessary (trial, etc.), even if it means I miss a dinner or two during the week. If I work late in the evening, I get home before my daughter goes to bed. Even at fourteen, we have an inviolate nighttime ritual.

Many women rarely find time for themselves in all this balancing. The needs of clients, employers, children, husbands, and family sometimes fill all the waking hours, leaving none for the woman in charge. Personal pleasures—even simple, short ones, like a manicure, tickets to the ballet, or a new tape for the car—should never be factored out. Naomi Norwood takes this approach:

> On mornings that I am not in court, I exercise, which helps keep me sane. I think it also helps that most of my friends are not lawyers. Our social friends we made through neighborhood, kids, and schools. I don't talk much about work on the weekends and try not to think about it much.

A single Wyoming lawyer enjoys the independence of a solo practice, where she can be her own "boss." She writes:

> My situation is very flexible because I can take [fewer] cases if I want to have more time for my personal life. I can take vacations when I want to and leave early and only answer to myself. The drawback is I don't have a set salary and I don't have a pension or 401(k) with a large company. I probably would make more money if I worked for a large,

private firm. In the summers I change clothes at my office and mountain bike phenomenal trails right from my office, or go kayaking on a famously beautiful river. In the winter I backcountry ski in the mornings before coming into work and every weekend, and sometimes ski at the resort. I have a group of friends who are all professionals and small-business owners. Most of us don't have kids yet.

A multifaceted life is not a bad thing. I find it immensely satisfying to have interesting work, a fabulous child, a garden to plant, and family dinners to give and go to. My survival technique is to set priorities for the day or the hour and do what needs to be done first. At 3:00, my son gets picked up by me from school unless I am in court. My clients can be called back at 3:30. My cases are prioritized the same way. Filing deadlines are first, and all other tasks of the day fall into place. To the extent I can accommodate bar association activities I do, but, truthfully, they have fallen to the bottom of the list lately. Writing this book became a passion for me, but this task also had to fit into its place in the day—usually after my son went to bed. Jennifer A. Lemire of Portsmouth, New Hampshire, a litigator in a small firm, is similarly upbeat:

> As a mother of an almost-four-year-old daughter, it is difficult to keep the hours I keep, but I don't have much of a choice as a litigator in a small, busy firm. And not only do I have a very busy practice, but I am active in the community as much as possible. It's who I am and I wouldn't have it any other way, except perhaps to have more time with my daughter!

Conclusion

In 2000, the ABA Commission on Women in the Profession reported that the "number of women who doubt the possibility of successfully combining work and family has almost tripled over the past two decades."[9] No one can be everything to everyone at the same time. It is impossible to be the superlawyer, supermother, supercleaner, supervolunteer, and best daughter, wife, and friend, all at once or all the time. And it does not have to be that way. At different stages of life, priorities change and sometimes more energies are required in one area and not another. Infants grow up to become independent children, and so what is needed of you changes. Carpools and homework are a precious passing phase and will not always pull you away from other activities. The house will get clean one way or another, the laundry will get done, and no one will starve. Throughout life, set your priorities and be prepared to have them change as you change and as the life you lead changes. Keep your goals in front of you and remember along the way to fit in time for yourself.

No one can expect to be all things to all persons or pursuits, all of the time. Life is a matter of choices and compromises. But here is a little secret: you do not have to be a superwoman. The truth is, none of us are. Set your priorities for today and now, and change them as your needs and the needs of your family change. Do not worry about what others may have chosen for their priorities and do not second-guess yourself about your personal choices.

"We are at our best when work and life present us with their most difficult challenges." Sharing lunch at the Pyramid Club and watching the clouds whisk by, I snatch this pearl of wisdom from the air. Lila Roomberg, my dining partner, has been associated with the law firm of Ballard Spahr Andrew & Ingersoll for fifty years. The emergence of women in the legal field parallels the narrative of her life from paralegal/librarian to senior partner in tax-exempt financing. When confronted with overwhelming professional challenges that summoned all her legal and personal talents, Lila confesses she nearly buckled. Looking back, with the perspective of years, Lila throws me a lifeline. When I am feeling the most overwhelmed, I know that I am at my best.

I am going to borrow from Deborah Willig (who borrowed it from her mother who borrowed it from Shakespeare) this pearl of wisdom:

To thine own self be true.[10]

The women in these pages who are the most content are pursuing careers that make them happy and are willingly making necessary trade-offs in other areas of their lives. Though career opportunities abound for women, many have made sacrifices unwittingly that they now question. Women must do, and be, what is right for them. If you want to work for others in a large firm, work twelve hours a day, and curtail family involvement or outside interests, do it. If you prefer to work for yourself or part-time, and curtail financial rewards, do it. Be involved in your choices and, once made, do not look back or second-guess yourself because of what someone else thinks or says.

In the words of Judge Beck, women should "not be overly influenced by their environment. That is," she says, "women buy whatever is being sold to them at the time. In the fifties, women were told they would be happiest at home, looking right and making perfect meals. That was wrong. Then the message changed to climb the male ladder of success. That was wrong. Women have to listen to their inner voices to know what is right for them."

Personal interests, outer and inner lives not dependent upon work, and involvement with friends, family, and avocations—these are the things that are important to most of the people I interviewed. Enrich yourself and the rest will follow. Do women still have to work harder? Absolutely. In the words of Judge Norma Shapiro:

> The day will come when observations about women lawyers will be obsolete. Until then, unfortunately, the successful woman advocate must be more able than her male counterpart. Fortunately, for many of them, it's not too difficult.[11]

ENDNOTES

1. JOAN WILLIAMS, UNBENDING GENDER, WHY FAMILY AND WORK CONFLICT AND WHAT TO DO ABOUT IT 46 (2000).

2. SYLVIA ANN HEWLETT, CREATING A LIFE, PROFESSIONAL WOMEN AND THE QUEST FOR CHILDREN 106 (2002).

3. *Id.* at 107.

4. Robert J. Simmons, *Love Notes from a Spouse: The First Working Mother to Lead the Nation's Oldest Organized Bar Finds Her Balance "Backwards and in High Heels"* (2000), *available at* www.philabar.org/member/pubs/phl=_lawyer/notes.asp.

5. Justice Ruth Bader Ginsburg, *Remarks on Women's Progress in the Legal Profession in the United States*, 33 U. TULSA L.J. 13, 19 (1997).

6. ABA COMM'N ON WOMEN IN THE PROFESSION, BALANCED LIVES, CHANGING THE CULTURE OF LEGAL PRACTICE 17 (2001) (prepared by Deborah L. Rhode).

7. *Id.* at 11.

8. ABA COMM'N ON WOMEN IN THE PROFESSION, THE UNFINISHED AGENDA, WOMEN AND THE LEGAL PROFESSION 17 (2001) (prepared by Deborah L. Rhode).

9. ABA COMM'N ON WOMEN IN THE PROFESSION, *supra* note 6, at 11.

10. *Hamlet*, I, iii (Polonius offers Laertes the following advice: "This above all, to thine own self be true, And it must follow as the night the day Thou canst not then be false to any man").

11. Norma Shapiro, *Bench with a Point of View: How to Create Confidence in the Courtroom, in* THE WOMAN ADVOCATE 215, 221 (Jean Maclean Snyder & Andra Barmash Greene eds., ABA 1996).

"A Day in the Life"
Kathleen D. Wilkinson, partner with Wilson, Elser, Moskowitz, Edelman & Dicker, LLP

When I was asked to write a few paragraphs about how I spend an average day balancing the responsibilities of being a partner at a large law firm with raising children, I concluded that there is no such thing as an "average day"; each day poses its own unique challenges. However, I can give a few insights in balancing as a partner in a law firm with children and on how I at least "appear" to be balancing everything. I have three children: a girl, age fourteen, in ninth grade; another girl, age twelve, in sixth grade; and a boy, age five in prekindergarten. I also have a very busy caseload, have clients who refer me business, hold leadership positions within the Pennsylvania and Philadelphia Bar Associations, and serve on a few firm committees as well. I also am somewhat involved in my community—I am president of one civic association and first vice president of another.

First, having a sense of humor and a place to escape is key. I made the wise decision to have full-time au pairs since my oldest was born fourteen years ago. As babies, my children stayed home in their warm house. When they reached the age of two, each child was enrolled in a Montessori program. By the age of four, each child was enrolled in prekindergarten. The first two years of childhood were the most difficult to cover, as au pairs can only work so many hours pursuant to the governmental program they come to the United States under. Somehow, between my husband, and my parents, we managed to make the hours work.

Once each child was enrolled in a Montessori program, there were no longer issues with the amount of hours the au pair could cover, as that gave me greater flexibility in scheduling the au pair's hours around the children's school day. As each child started school, the au pair hours became less and less, leaving more time for the au pair to assist in straightening the children's rooms and doing the children's laundry, errands, and other chores. Driving is a key au pair responsibility, with many after-school activities to attend to.

Having an au pair for me is like having an insurance policy. If a child needs to be dropped off early, or I need to go out of town, the au pair assumes immediate responsibility for getting tasks done. If a child is sick, the au pair is home and childcare is instantly taken care of. If my husband, who is also a lawyer, also has to go out of town, the au pair is there. For my children, who are not inanimate objects to be balanced in the air, having au pairs for them has resulted in them forming lasting friendships. Last summer, we traveled to Scotland to go to one of our au pair's weddings. We just received a holiday card from another au pair and it looks like a wedding in Sweden is in the works. We have enjoyed learning the cultures of England, Australia, and South Africa as well.

Now, the above assumes a perfect world where the au pair is fabulous and is liked by the children, and there are no unforeseen consequences, such as the au pair not returning home one night and my having a deposition the following day, with a ten-month-old baby to attend to. I have resorted to actually having taken one of my children, then less than a year old, to a deposition when such an emergency occurred. She obediently sat in her car seat, not uttering a sound, while I asked all types of complex questions of an insurance broker in a sophisticated lawsuit. At one point, opposing counsel whispered to me to look at the baby, who had by this point managed to slide down to the bottom of her car seat, with her head resting on the seat and her legs dangling on the rug. I interrupted the deposition and very professionally rearranged the baby in her car seat. Upon smelling something necessitating a diaper change, I rushed off to the ladies' room to attend to a very messy diaper and no changing table in sight!! She returned to the deposition newly freshened and the deposition proceeded. Opposing counsel and I arranged with the court reporter to have her appearance noted in the official deposition transcript as "present."

Short of this particular deposition, I have been fortunate to arrange for last-minute coverage in many crisis situations when we were between au pairs. This has included leaving my office early to get my youngest and either return to the office with him in a real emergency situation or work the remainder of the day from home. Today, with the Internet, BlackBerries®, cell phones, and voice mail, it has been possible for me to cover a family crisis and still be able to handle a normal day's worth of legal work. The key is to maintain composure and a sense of humor, have flexibility, and know how to escape from the craziness. The last time I had a serious childcare crisis was shortly after my youngest was born when the new au pair, who had just arrived, announced she was extremely homesick and returning to Australia the next day. I could not get a replacement for seven weeks and my maternity leave was nearing an end. Fortunately, one of the mothers of my oldest daughter's girlfriends covered for me for a few weeks while I waited for the new au pair to arrive. Without her help, I probably would have been able to use the Lipton Center, which my husband's law firm subscribes to. (The Lipton Center provides emergency childcare on a temporary basis.) I have used this center for days here and there, when an au pair needed off for one reason or another. For escape, which is essential in order to remain in balance, I either go to the shore, or to my room at home, so I can mellow out and recover from the hectic lifestyle.

As a lawyer for twenty-two years, and a mother for over fourteen of these years, I doubt my firm can appreciate the juggling that goes on behind the scenes. Statistically, there are not that many women equity partners with children at my level of experience. I hope my brief insights help others to realize that the balancing act can be done to at least make it "appear" everything is just fine!

Chapter Fourteen

Thinking About Going to Law School?

If women were admitted to the Columbia Law School, . . . then the choicer, more manly and red-blooded graduates of our universities would go to the Harvard Law School!

The Nation, Feb. 18, 1925, p. 173
Quoted by the *United States Supreme Court in United States v. Virginia*, 518 U.S. 515, 543 116 S. Ct. 2264, 2281 (1996)

Some Advice on Beginning the Endeavor

As with most graduate programs, entrance to law school is confined to students with excellent undergraduate grade-point averages and good performance on the Law School Admission Test (LSAT), a standardized test reminiscent of the Scholastic Aptitude Test (SAT) for undergraduate school. Most schools post their admission requirements on the Web or in printed materials. Some take into consideration an individual's highest LSAT score, while others average all scores taken within the preceding three years. It is important to know this about the schools to which you plan to apply *before* you take the LSAT. Schools give different amounts of weight and emphasis to LSAT scores, grades, and life experiences. Harvard's admission materials claim that Harvard does not apply a "cut-off" score when looking at an application, but its profile of students admitted gives some indication of what is required. Harvard, Yale, Columbia, Stanford, and Temple posted the following admission scores for their student bodies:

	LSAT 25/75 percentile	GPA 25/75 percentile	Year reporting
Harvard	167/173	3.76/3.94	2002
Yale	168/174	3.77/3.93	2002
Columbia	167/173	3.52/3.82	class of 2006
Stanford	upper 5% of LSAT pool	upper 5% of class	class of 2005
Temple	median 160	median 3.39	2002

Many undergraduate schools have instituted prelaw curricula, usually consisting of business and government courses. Many, if not most, law schools do not require an undergraduate prelaw major, and express a preference for a well-rounded background in the liberal arts and sciences. Academic excellence in undergraduate school, coupled with life experiences, work, and/or graduate education, contribute to the overall package most frequently sought by law schools.

Choosing a School

When choosing a law school, it is good to have some idea about where you hope to practice and how you want to practice. A number of law schools in the country (such as Harvard, Yale, Columbia, and Stanford) are nationally well known and will open doors for you, regardless of where you intend to live and work. Other schools have solid regional reputations. Assuming you wish to work in a certain city, you can find in that city alumnae from various law schools who will welcome you with open arms.

There can also be fine distinctions to consider that may be a bit difficult to uncover. For example, my niece Abigail was recently admitted to law school at both Harvard and Yale. Most of us would consider these schools among the top in prestige and excellence and the choice between the two hard to make. Yet, there is a real difference in philosophy in each of these institutions. For example, Yale, unlike Harvard, has no class ranking and no graded tests. Yale's student-friendly approach is based upon the feeling that anyone admitted has earned the right to graduate. At Yale, the culling process took place when the students were considered for admission. Harvard, on the other hand, has a reputation for graduating Wall Street corporate lawyers, and students vie for class rank. Abigail has aspirations of public service, so she chose Yale.

You should try to learn about the philosophies of the schools to which you apply, to determine whether they further your prospective professional goals. Temple University, a Pennsylvania state-sponsored school located in Philadelphia, has a strong regional base and emphasizes the opportunity for practical law experience in conjunction with local firms, government, and financial institutions. For someone from Philadelphia who knows he or she wants to remain in the area after school, the opportunities to enhance local contacts and learn practical skills can make Temple University a very attractive choice.

Cost

Most of us check the price tag before buying a toaster. Law school should not be any different. The cost of one year of law school at Harvard, Yale, Columbia, Stanford, and Temple—for tuition alone—appears in the following table (with figures taken from those posted by the institutions):

	Full-time day	Year posted
Harvard	$29,500	2002–2003
Yale	$31,400	2002–2003
Columbia	$34,580	2003–2004
Stanford	$32,424	2003–2004
Temple	$12,078 (resident)	2003–2004
	$21,028 (nonresident)	2003–2004

It is not uncommon for a law student to graduate owing $100,000, and perhaps more, especially if borrowing was necessary to complete undergraduate school. More than one large-firm lawyer complained of being stuck in her job to repay the money borrowed for tuition. Some schools have financial aid packages available. Others, like Temple University, offer part-time or night-school programs to accommodate students who continue to work while in school.

The Socratic Method

It is said that Socrates taught by answering a question with a question. In short, this is the traditional method of law school instruction and has become known as the "Socratic method." The teacher explains a set of facts and then poses a question. A student is called upon to give his or her thoughts. The teacher responds with more questions, sometimes changing the facts, to teach certain legal principles by eliciting reasoning of those principles, rather than by straightforward lecturing. Although the Socratic method is justified on the theory that it prepares a student for standing before a difficult judge and defending a legal theory or position, it can cruelly victimize an individual student who is entangled in a series of challenging questions with a teacher who knows all the answers. Often, at the end of the day, students leave without ever fully gleaning those important legal principles. Women, more so than men, suffer under

Socratic-method teaching. Temple Law Professor Marina Angel shares a dim view of the Socratic method:

> If Socrates really used this method, he wasn't given the hemlock soon enough. The "Socratic method" is based on several premises. First, the teacher is "God = Socrates." Second, there is truth, and "God = Socrates" knows what it is. Third, the students are blithering idiots, who wouldn't recognize the truth if they fell over it, and who, therefore, must be dragged, through total ridicule, to the truth as "God = Socrates" sees it.[1]

I personally witnessed one student (a woman) reduced to tears due to the Socratic method of instruction in the first year of law school. It is not, or was not, unusual for a teacher to persist for fifteen or twenty minutes with one student, questioning his or her reasoning skills before the entire class. Who does not remember Professor Kingsfield in *The Paper Chase*, handing a student a dime in front of the entire class and instructing him to call home to tell his parents he would never be a lawyer? More than one study reports than women suffer more than men from the humiliation inflicted by the often abusive application of the Socratic method. The entire experience has been found to cause otherwise intelligent, confident women to doubt their abilities completely and undermine their self-confidence.[2]

There is also a downside for women who brave the classroom by speaking out and voicing opinions. Cynthia Mason, a recent law school graduate, writes:

> I think the professors at Temple were pretty fair, though, in terms of treating men and women similarly. Peers, though, were brutal. Assertive, outspoken, female law students are considered to be bitches.

Speaking out with confidence is a trait not typically associated with feminine behavior and many women are uncomfortable, or at least unfamiliar, with arguing their views, particularly to someone in authority. As a society, we are still uncomfortable with women who, like Susan B. Anthony in 1876, charge the public podium and speak out in loud voices. The law school experience, for most women, presents not only an academic challenge, but also a soul-searching, identity-shaking upheaval.

Law school also presents students with a new way of thinking. Being a lawyer means being an advocate of a client's position, even if you can see and sympathize with the other side. It means being neutral to events and forceful in argument. It means being combative at times, and removed personally from the conflict at hand. Women, more so than men, find this shift in perspective a radical departure from their previous ways of thinking.[3] Michele Lellouche of Tampa advises: "I always tell women law students, if you can make it through the first year, it's just an endurance test to get through school." I think it is an endurance test and an experience that changes forever the way you see the world.

ENDNOTES

1. Marina Angel, *Women in Legal Education: What It's Like to Be Part of a Perpetual First Wave or the Case of the Disappearing Women*, 61 TEMP. L. REV. 799, 810 (1988).

2. Torrey Morrison, Jennifer Ries, & Elaine Spiliopoulos, *What Every First-Year Female Law Student Should Know*, 7 COLUM. J. GENDER & L. 267 (1998).

3. Sandra Janoff, *The Influence of Legal Education on Moral Reasoning*, 76 MINN. L. REV. 193 (1991).

"A DAY IN THE LIFE"
PHYLLIS HORN EPSTEIN, A LAWYER FROM PHILADELPHIA, PENNSYLVANIA, AND THE AUTHOR

I work in a Philadelphia center city firm in partnership with my husband, Earl Epstein. I have been a lawyer for nearly twenty-five years, most of those in practice at the same location and with the same partner. My practice varies depending upon the work and clients that present themselves, which to me is the attraction of working in a small firm. I have a tax advice and litigation practice, supplemented by corporate transactions, estate planning, and family law. My husband and I often overlap our work, each pitching in to help the other when it is needed.

My day starts at 7:00 in the morning when my middle-school-age son has to be roused from bed. Breakfast is served, lunch is packed, the backpack is readied, the newspaper is retrieved from the end of the driveway, and clean clothes are grabbed from the dryer, all before 7:45 when we leave the house for school. I am (usually) ready for work by this time and, after dropping him with his gear, I head straight for the office.

My day consists of answering telephone calls, responding to e-mail or other correspondence, and preparing legal pleadings or other documents. Some days I am in court or at hearings in Philadelphia or the surrounding counties. I work at a frantic pace to complete whatever needs to be done that day, with one eye always on the clock. By 2:30, I fly out of the office to pick up my son from school, supervise homework, shop, and cook dinner, while simultaneously continuing to work by telephone, e-mail, and fax machine. Some days are just worse than others. The other day, two years' worth of negotiations on a deal were coming to fruition. Drafts and redrafts of a final agreement were flying back and forth while half the telephone lines in my office building were down, including the line to my fax machine (my opposing counsel was unable to exchange documents by e-mail), and . . . the fax machine in my house just died. I had to be in my office and have documents hand-delivered. I threw my son in the car and we raced back into town to complete this transaction, hand-delivering final documents before day's end at 5:00 p.m. Dinner is usually at 6:30 or 7:00. Afterward there is time for school projects, my son's violin practice, laundry, food shopping, and getting my son off to bed. By 10:00 p.m. the house has usually settled down and I sit at the computer to write for two hours. At midnight, my husband drags me from my desk so that I can pass out in bed.

Conclusion

Finding Our Own Voice

In writing this book, I have been struck by the forces that whipsaw a woman in the legal profession. I am amazed at how long these forces have been battering our psyches, even when we are not conscious of their incessant gale-force winds.

Women lawyers cannot simply do their jobs. They must monitor their demeanor and balance their femininity with the toughness required to be advocates. They must examine their hemlines, their pantyhose, their pantsuits, their jewelry, and their hairstyles to suit the occasion, the client, and the profession. They must choose new names if they marry and sever ties to their old sources of identity, or choose to keep their names and spend their lifetimes explaining their family ties to the likes of Blue Cross clerks and hotel concierges. And, if they do keep their names, they must be concerned about the statement that this "act of rebellion" makes to the ones they love, or to the clients from an older generation who may be offended.

While writing a legal brief or researching an obscure local county rule of procedure that can sideline a case, a woman lawyer must question the value of time spent begging county clerks for local forms with time spent away from children, family, and loved ones. A woman lawyer feels like a poor lawyer when tending to a child's homework, and a poor mother when working overtime, to say nothing of the level of disorder that can be imposed upon the family home when work outside the home takes precedence. The constant guilt of that drags a girl down.

And, instead of just doing her job, a woman lawyer constantly gauges her "success" by unrealistic standards that are masculine. Her life rarely is single-dimensional, with a climb up the ladder starting from day one out of law school. She must worry about her aging ovaries and her attractiveness to men. She must be prepared to have her career take a backseat to family for a period of time without feeling that she is missing out or destroying her future career and wasting her degree, thereby confirming what many men have accused her of doing in the first place: depriving a man of the opportunity to make a living as a lawyer, an opportunity that he needs more than she, so he can support his wife and children.

These winds have blown for nearly two hundred years, sapping women of their energies and calling upon them to summon all the courage and all the gumption they have to claim what is rightfully theirs. A career in the law is within a woman's "sphere," within her nature, and part of her mission and destiny, if she wants it, in the way she wants it. If a woman in this profession remains true to her original motivations for entering the law, and accepts the cornucopia of opportunities as a gift, then a career in the law can be eminently satisfying.

I believe there are more sisters than queen bees in this profession. I myself have been the beneficiary of the open hand of fellow women lawyers from a variety of backgrounds. Some have held positions of authority in government or in their own law firms, but not all. Each woman who participated in this book shared her personal thoughts with me as if we were old friends. I consider it my privilege to know each of them and to share this journey with such wonderful companions.

In my research for this book, I came upon these words by Susan B. Anthony:

> We shall some day be heeded, and . . . everybody will think it was always so, just exactly as many young people think that all the privi-

leges, all the freedom, all the enjoyments which woman now possesses always were hers. They have no idea of how every single inch of ground that she stands upon today has been gained by the hard work of some little handful of women of the past.

Younger women who fill half the vacancies in law school classes, who are spared the barbs and hassles of overt discrimination, and who have numerous female role models in positions of authority may, hopefully, in reading these pages, come to understand the history of women in their profession and the struggles that preceded their smoother entry.

I believe the first women lawyers of the nineteenth and twentieth centuries made it possible for women to gain acceptance by our society as professionals, and successfully challenged their subservient roles and "mission." Nevertheless, even with the increased presence of women in the field, I was impressed at how many of the same battles exist with little change. The early pioneers in women's lawyering struggled to find work and then balance work with family. They had great difficulty breaking into the business world where businesses were run by men who employed male lawyers. They struggled with what to wear in court. Judges debated their role in society and whether their gender specially qualified them for certain fields of law. Women lawyers still experience turmoil about their responsibilities as good lawyers and their desires to be good mothers.

Our perceptions of who we could or should be were rocked by the sixties. Finishing three grueling years of law school was just the beginning of our learning curves. As difficult as the law work was, it was nothing compared with the monumental work of compromise and balance that my classmates have struggled with these twenty-five years to achieve happiness at work and at home. It is not that each of us has felt outside the norms of society by becoming lawyers and pursuing male-dominated careers, or, for some, even withdrawing from law careers altogether. It is the inner struggle for self-acceptance and self-esteem that has been so enormous, and the struggle for respect among our colleagues and clients.

The lives of my classmates reflect the increased opportunities for women in the legal world over the past two decades. They also reflect ingeniousness, creativity, and a sense of humor in balancing work and personal life and gaining respect for abilities in what was predominantly a male world when we started. We may not feel compelled to choose between families and work, but we still do struggle with arranging it. We may not feel arbitrarily restricted to practice in certain fields of law, and yet we still struggle to sustain ourselves in traditionally male fields of law where male networking predominates.

By sharing our experiences with one another, we can mentor one another and hopefully make greater advancements in our practices and feel less alone. Twenty-five years later, we have learned life lessons to impart to each other and to the women of the next classes of law school graduates. My perception is that in the next twenty-five years (maybe fifty), men will join us in seeking broader opportunities in the legal profession to accommodate desires to lead more balanced lives. Many who secretly wish to do so now may feel liberated by our examples. Indeed, we are trailblazers for men, leading them toward more humanistic lives that will not cut them off from family and relegate them to their offices.

Professor Maleson reminded me again of the days in law school when nothing seemed clear. There were only questions followed by more questions. One day a student approached her in frustration. His notes had been neat and orderly until that day, when she raised a differing perspective in class. Now, nothing was neat and orderly about his notes. She advised him that the study of law would require him to be less tidy. But my room is tidy, he protested. "No," she answered. "The law requires you to be accepting of nuance. There are many ways to look at the same thing. The end result is not always wrapped up in a neat bow." That is exactly how I feel when I conclude this book. There are so many issues and very few absolute answers. No one can tell a woman how to balance her life with family or even whether to make that choice. No one can tell a woman how she should name herself. No one can dictate the parameters of "success" for women or for men. I am comfortable with not having all the answers. I hope that by raising issues, I have contributed in a meaningful way to the dialogue.

I believe that the real revolution will come when men in larger numbers begin to question the restraints of *their* lives, so the next book will be about family, career, and success, identifying men and women interchangeably. It is my hope that these pearls of wisdom will be picked up by men as well as women, so that in my legal lifetime, changes will occur. Men who confide that they would love to work part-time will do so. Women who need to work part-time can still achieve rewarding careers. Men and women will "have it all" without one sacrificing for the other or going without, unless they want to; without children sacrificing for their parents; and without individuals sacrificing themselves for a model of success they picked up somewhere secondhand, that never really fit at all.

I am probably completely utopian in my thinking but, in my defense, I submit that I am on the fading edge of the baby-boomer generation. I was touched by the sixties and, although too young for a personal appearance at Woodstock, I grew up playing Joni Mitchell and hearing her plea to get us back to the Garden of Eden—maybe because I grew up with friendly brothers and no sisters, or maybe because I grew up with an adoring father, uncles, and male cousins. I do not know all the reasons why. I do know that men have been my friends and allies my whole life, and I would love to liberate the men as well as the women to get us all back to the Garden.

Appendix A

Philadelphia Bar Association
1999 Model Employer Policies for Parenting Lawyers
Preamble

In 1989, the Philadelphia Bar Association developed the Model Employer Policies of Family Responsibility to provide guidance to law firms and legal departments in their efforts to assist lawyers in achieving a rewarding balance of commitment to the profession and commitment to their families. The aspirations of the original Model Policies remain the same today.

In the years since the Model Policies were first introduced, parenting lawyers in the City of Philadelphia have entered into alternative work arrangements with their employers with increasing frequency. It is now clear that there is no single "ideal" model for such arrangements. Rather, the circumstances of each lawyer and employer are unique, and the lawyer and employer must work together to create a satisfactory alternative arrangement. This is especially true of any successful alternative work arrangement in a smaller firm, in which the lawyers may find themselves particularly interdependent.

Thus, any successful arrangement must accommodate not only the parenting needs of the lawyer, but also the responsibilities of the lawyers affected by the arrangement. Of course, the needs of the clients serviced by the lawyer, as well as the economic and practical realities of the practice of law, must be taken into consideration. Simply put, no alternative work arrangement will succeed unless it retains flexibility and is implemented in a way that eases the burdens of all concerned, and assures that all professional obligations are handled satisfactorily.

Even with these challenges, in 1999 parenting lawyers are thriving throughout Philadelphia under a variety of creative alternative work arrangements. Such arrangements vary from reduced schedules to telecommuting, flextime and even job-sharing.

These 1999 revised Model Policies are intended to provide a framework for the development of individualized firm policies. The Model Policies reflect the experiences of Philadelphia lawyers over the past ten years and are intended to encourage both parenting lawyers and their employers to continue to work together to build creative solutions to meet the professional and family commitments of the parenting lawyer. Without a doubt, we as a profession and a community will all benefit from this effort.

Appendix B

Philadelphia Bar Association Model Policy for Parenting Lawyers
Disability as a Result of Pregnancy, Childbirth, and Related Medical Conditions

A. Eligibility for Disability Benefits

An attorney disabled due to pregnancy, childbirth and/or any complications arising from those conditions is treated in the same manner as attorneys who are disabled for any other medical reason and is eligible to receive disability benefits according to the terms of the disability income benefits program of the firm.

[Alternative A (For Firms with Limited or No Disability Benefits): Eligibility for Disability Leave. An attorney disabled due to pregnancy, childbirth and/or any complications arising from those conditions is entitled to a paid leave during the period of the disability.]

B. Commencement Date and Presumptive Time Period

Given the demands of the job and the high expectations for performance placed on all attorneys, the firm presumes disability for a period of twelve weeks following the birth of a child, and grants paid disability leave for this period, without the need for independent medical verification of disability.

In addition, a pregnant attorney may elect to leave work up to two weeks prior to the anticipated date of birth without medical certification of disability. These two weeks are in addition to the regular disability leave outlined above.

In either instance, the attorney must notify the firm's benefits coordinator of the date of commencement of her disability leave and the date of the birth of her child, so that adequate records can be maintained.

C. Disability Before or After the Presumptive Time Period

Regardless of when the attorney elects to commence her presumptive disability period, disability leave in excess of the allotted number of weeks is granted only in the event that the employee provides the firm's benefits coordinator with the appropriate medical certification as required for other disabilities covered under the disability policy.

D. Effect on Partnership or Salary Increase

The use of disability leave as a result of pregnancy, childbirth and related medical conditions shall not be a factor in or affect a partnership (or other promotional decision) or salary increase determination. Pregnancy, childbirth and related medical conditions are an integral part of human existence; they are not to be considered as voluntary and optional undertakings by the affected lawyers.

The use of disability leave as a result of pregnancy, childbirth and related medical conditions may affect the timing of the partnership (or other promotional decision) or salary increase determination only to the extent that other medical disabilities affect the timing of the partnership or salary increase determination. For example, if the use of medical leave to recover from gall bladder surgery would not affect the timing of the determination, neither can the use of medical leave for pregnancy or childbirth.

E. Leave Options

At the attorney's option, the attorney may also apply for a leave of absence under the firm's childcare leave policy as set forth in Policy 2 below.

COMMENTS

1. Definition and Eligibility (Section A)

This policy was originally developed to comply with the requirements of Title VII of the Civil Rights Acts of 1964. It is applicable to the medical conditions experienced as a result of being pregnant, of bearing a child, and of recovering from childbirth. This type of leave is sometimes referred to as maternity leave, but it should not be confused with leave to parents (male and female) for the purpose of caring for an infant or child after its birth. Those leaves are covered under Model Policy 2: Childcare Leave.

The Pregnancy Discrimination Act of 1978 requires employers who are covered by Title VII to treat women affected by pregnancy, childbirth and related medical conditions the same as non-pregnant persons who are "similar in their ability or inability to work. . . . for all employment-related purposes, including receipt of benefits under fringe benefit programs."

This policy therefore simply restates the effect of that law. Thus, if the law firm has a disability benefit program which permits paid or unpaid leaves to persons with non-pregnancy disabilities, it must offer the same paid or unpaid leaves to women affected by pregnancy, childbirth or related medical conditions.

2. [Alternative Section A]: Firms and Organizations without Disability Benefits or with Limited Disability Benefits

If a firm does not have a general disability benefits program as assumed in section A, such a firm may nevertheless wish to consider offering a paid or unpaid leave for pregnancy, childbirth or related medical conditions, to the extent this is economically feasible. Alternative A has been drafted to serve that purpose.

The Supreme Court has held in *California Federal Savings and Loan Association v. Guerra*, 479 U.S. 272, 107 S. Ct. 683, 93 L.Ed.2d 613 (1987) that the Pregnancy Discrimination Act was intended by Congress to be "a floor beneath which pregnancy disability benefits may not drop—not a ceiling above which they may not rise" 107 S. Ct. at 692 (approving the language of the Court of Appeals at 758 F.2d 390, 396 (9th Cir. 1985)). In that case a California statute which required employers to provide leave and reinstatement to employees disabled by pregnancy, but not by other conditions, was found not to be a violation of Title VII because of its provisions favoring pregnant workers above other disabled workers.

3. Commencement Date and Presumptive Period (Section B)

Because the period of disability for a normal, uncomplicated pregnancy and delivery can be generally approximated, many firms prefer to establish a presumptive period of disability for which the disabled attorney need furnish no medical verification. Such a presumptive period eases the administrative burden on both the firm and the affected attorney.

This policy uses the presumptive period of 12 weeks for all childbirth under the assumption that the work of an attorney may be so demanding in terms of time, commitment, stamina and potential stress that optimal physical fitness is necessary for performance of the job. Some firms may opt for a shorter presumptive period.

The firm may wish to require the attorney to prepare, when practicable, a "departure memorandum," which outlines the attorney's ongoing responsibilities and a plan for meeting those responsibilities during the attorney's leave.

4. Resignation or Termination

This policy does not include any provision regarding the effect of the employee's resignation or termination of employment upon the use of disability leave. Resignation or termination of employment at the end of the disability period in no way affects the use of the disability benefits since the employee has earned the right to those benefits by her work preceding the disability period.

Some organizations specify that the right to take childbirth disability leave is contingent upon the attorney advising the firm in advance that she intends to return to work on some basis at the end of the leave period. Such a provision is not permitted, however, unless such a requirement is also imposed on the use of other types of medical disability leave.

5. Reinstatement

This policy has no provision about reinstatement upon completion of the leave. The lawyer, however, must be reinstated when the leave is completed. Some organizations, especially those with highly structured departments, may prefer to include a provision indicating whether the attorney, upon return to work, will be placed in the same or an equivalent position.

6. Application to Attorneys With Alternative Work Schedules

Attorneys working on a reduced or flextime schedule or using a telecommuting arrangement who are affected by pregnancy, childbirth and related medical conditions receive the same disability benefits that such attorneys with non-pregnancy disabilities receive under the general disability policy.

Where attorneys with reduced work schedules are not covered by a disability leave program, the firm or organization may nevertheless opt to institute such a leave for personnel affected by pregnancy, childbirth or related medical conditions.

Appendix C

Philadelphia Bar Association Model Policy for Parenting Lawyers
Childcare Leave

A. Paid Childcare Leave

1. *Eligibility:* Childcare leave is provided to allow attorneys, male and female, to care for children newly arrived in their families. Every attorney is entitled to a two-week paid leave for the following childcare purposes:

   (a) the birth of a child of the attorney;

   (b) the adoption of a child by the attorney;

   (c) the placement of a child for foster care in the family of the attorney.

2. *Special Provision for Adoptive Parents:* In addition to the leave in sub-paragraph A.1 above, an attorney who has adopted a child is entitled to six weeks of paid leave immediately prior to or following the adoption.

3. *Application:* The two-week paid childcare leave is not in addition to the disability leave as a result of pregnancy, childbirth and related medical conditions during the first year following the arrival of the same child.

B. Extended Unpaid Childcare Leave

1. *Eligibility:* In addition to any paid leave (including paid childcare leave and disability leave as a result of pregnancy, childbirth and related medical conditions described above), every attorney may request an unpaid leave of absence for a period of up to nine months for the following childcare purposes:

(a) the birth of a child of the attorney;

(b) the adoption of a child by the attorney;

(c) the placement of a child for foster care in the family of the attorney.

2. *Criteria for Granting Request:* This leave is available to attorneys who are in good standing with the firm regardless of the attorney's seniority, upon request to the appropriate department chair or firm decision maker. Approval will be given unless the leave would unduly disadvantage the firm as a whole, or the work of the department or practice group directly affected.

3. *Reduced Work Schedule*: An attorney may work on a reduced work schedule during the period when he or she otherwise could be totally absent from work pursuant to this Child Care Leave Policy, provided that the attorney's department has work for the attorney on this basis. The nature of the arrangement, including the attorney's schedule of hours, workload, compensation, and benefits, will be determined by [insert appropriate person] together with the attorney. Approval will be given unless the reduced schedule would unduly disadvantage the work of the firm as a whole or the department or practice group directly affected.

C. Effect on Benefits

1. *Paid Childcare Leave:* During the paid childcare leave, the attorney will receive the same benefits she or he would have received had that attorney been working full-time.

2. *Extended Unpaid Childcare Leave:* The firm or organization shall maintain health insurance benefits during the unpaid extended family care leave, regardless of the attorney's level of seniority. Other benefits will be maintained during the unpaid extended family care leave at the discretion of and in the circumstances determined by the firm. All benefits shall be restored after the leave has ended.

D. Effect on Partnership or Salary Increases

1. *Paid Childcare Leave:* The use of paid childcare leave shall affect neither a partnership determination nor its timing, nor shall paid childcare leave affect any salary increase an attorney might receive.

2. Extended Unpaid Childcare Leave: Use of extended unpaid childcare leave shall not be a factor in any partnership or salary increase decision. Use of extended leave may affect the timing of the determination if:

(a) any other unpaid leave affects the timing of the partnership or salary increase determination; and,

(b) the extended leave is used i) for more than a period of one year during the time preceding the partnership or salary increase decision; or ii) for a substantial amount of time during the last year before the decision is made.

COMMENTS

1. The Family Medical Leave Act

The Family Medical Leave Act, 28 U.S.C.S. § 2601 et seq. (the "FMLA") entitles covered employees to 12 work weeks of leave (either unpaid or paid) during any 12 month period (1) because of the birth of a child of the employee and in order to care for the child and (2) because of the adoption or foster care placement of a child. Under the FMLA, the leave may be unpaid. The FMLA applies to employers who employ 50 or more employees.

The protections of the FMLA will be referenced where applicable. However, it sets forth a "bottom level" of safeguards that is, or should be, exceeded by law firms.

2. Eligibility

Childcare leaves are available to all men and women attorneys. They are available not only to biological parents, but also to adoptive parents and to attorneys who are providing foster care to a child. The model policy provides a presumption that the request will be granted, but also allows for consideration of the working needs of the law firm in granting the request.

The FMLA requirements apply only to an employee with one year and 1250 hours of service. Such a limitation is not recommended in the model policy. Some firms may nonetheless opt to use a minimum employment period before an attorney becomes eligible for childcare leave. Those firms may want to leave it flexible. For example, one organization with a leave of absence policy provides that "normally" employees with less than one year of service are not eligible for extended leaves. Such phrasing of the policy allows the firm to extend the leave to employees with less than one year of service in appropriate circumstances.

3. Paid Childcare Leave

The policy provides for two weeks of paid leave. Some firms may opt to provide paid leave for longer periods of time, particularly since it is not in addition to childbirth disability leave.

Recognizing that adoption of a child can be an expensive and time-consuming process, that adoptive parents have physical and emotional stresses and bonding needs just as biological parents do, and that paid disability benefits typically will not be available, the policy provides an additional six weeks of paid leave to adoptive parents.

4. Extended Unpaid Childcare Leave

The extended unpaid childcare leave provides for a leave of absence of up to nine months for childcare purposes. The most common use of this extension probably will be for the care of a newborn infant.

5. Effect on Benefits

It is crucial to the welfare of families that health insurance benefits be in effect at all times. This policy provides for their continuation during all childcare leaves. Some firms may find it necessary to require employee payment of the required premiums if the extended leave is for a long period of time. If this is necessary the firm should take all reasonable measures to insure that no lapse of coverage occurs.

The FMLA requires the employer to maintain eligibility for coverage under any "group health plan" during the employee's FMLA leave. The taking of leave shall not result in the loss of any employment benefit accrued prior to the leave. 29 U.S.C.S. § 2614(a)(2) and (c)(1).

6. Notice

Some firms may choose to add a requirement that employees give advance notice of a leave. The FMLA requires that at least 30 days notice shall be given for leave which is foreseeable based on an expected birth or placement or "such notice as is practicable." 29 U.S.C.S. § 2612(e).

The firm may wish to require the attorney to prepare, when practicable, a "departure memorandum," which outlines the attorney's ongoing responsibilities and a plan for meeting those responsibilities during the attorney's leave.

7. Return to Work and Reinstatement

The policy contains no provision regarding the circumstances of the return to work of the attorney. It assumes reinstatement to former position upon return to work. The FMLA requires that employees returning from FMLA leave be restored to their position, or its equivalent, upon return from leave. 29 U.S.C.S. § 2614(a). Such "restoration" may be denied under certain economic circumstances, and as to employees who are among the highest-paid 10 percent of employees. 29 U.S.C.S. § 2614(b).

Some firms may opt to make the right to take leave contingent upon the attorney's advising the firm in advance that she or he intends to return to work on a full or reduced basis upon the completion of the leave. If so, the firm should include that requirement in its written policy and the requirement should be discussed with the attorney before the leave is begun.

Some organizations, especially those with highly structured departments, may also prefer to include a provision stating whether the attorney, upon return to work, will be placed in the same or an equivalent position. In no circumstances, however, may the use of the leave be the basis for demotion or other retaliatory work action.

8. Application to Attorneys with Alternative Work Arrangements

A firm may opt to include a provision indicating the circumstances in which child care leave applies to attorneys with pre-existing alternative work arrangements. The FMLA does not provide for a "reduced leave schedule" for family leave unless the employee and the employer so agree. 28 U.S.C.S. § 2612(b).

Appendix D

Philadelphia Bar Association Model Policy for Parenting Lawyers
Family Care Leave

A. Definition

Every attorney may request an unpaid leave of absence for a period of up to twelve weeks to care for the attorney's own health, or to care for the attorney's child, spouse, domestic partner, parent or member of the household who is ill or experiencing a serious health condition. The leave period need not be continuous, but may be taken in shorter occasional segments as needed.

B. Criteria for Granting Request

This leave will be granted to attorneys who are in good standing with the firm upon request to the appropriate department chair or firm decision-maker.

C. Effect on Benefits

The attorney will receive the same benefits she or he would have received if working full-time.

D. Discretionary Extension

1. *Time:* The length of the unpaid family care leave may be extended beyond twelve weeks at the discretion of the managing committee [or other appropriate decision-maker] of the firm.

2. *Reason:* Unpaid family care leave may also be granted for other difficult family situations needing the attention of the attorney at the discretion of the managing committee [or other appropriate decision-maker] of the firm.

E. *Effect on Partnership or Promotion*

The use of one twelve-week family care leave shall have no effect on the partnership or other promotional determination or its timing.

COMMENTS

1. *Eligibility*

Unpaid family care leaves are available to all men and women attorneys. This provision recognizes that newborn infant care is not the only family responsibility that attorneys have. An older child may be ill or handicapped. A seriously ill parent or spouse may require the care of the attorney, as may other family emergencies and difficulties. The attorney may have a serious health problem that requires an extended leave. Attorneys need the flexibility to be able to handle these family problems.

The Family Medical Leave Act, 29 U.S.C.S. § 2601 *et seq.* (the "FMLA") requires employers with more than 50 employees to grant 12 weeks of leave in any 12-month period to an employee (1) to care for a spouse, son, daughter or parent with a serious health condition, or (2) because of a serious health condition of the employee.

The FMLA requirements apply only to an employee with one year and 1250 hours of service. Such a limitation is not recommended in the model policy. Firms that do opt to use a minimum employment period may want to leave it flexible. For example, one organization with a leave of absence policy provides that "normally" employees with less than one year of service are not eligible for family care leaves. Such phrasing of the policy allows the firm to extend the leave to employees with less than one year of service in appropriate circumstances.

2. *Effect on Benefits*

It is crucial to the welfare of families that health insurance benefits be in effect at all times. This policy provides that all benefits continue in effect during a twelve-week (or less) leave. If the firm in its discretion allows a longer leave, health insurance benefits should remain in effect at all times. Some firms may find it necessary to require employee payment of the required premiums if the extended leave is for a long period of time. If this is necessary the firm should take all reasonable measures to insure that no lapse of coverage occurs.

The FMLA requires the employer to maintain eligibility for coverage under any "group health plan" during the employee's FMLA leave. The taking of leave shall not result in the loss of any employment benefit accrued prior to the leave. 29 U.S.C.S. § 2614(a)(2) and (c)(1).

3. Notice

Some firms may choose to add a requirement that employees give advance notice of a leave. The FMLA requires that at least 30 days notice shall be given for leave which is foreseeable based on an expected birth or placement or "such notice as is practicable." 29 U.S.C.S. § 2612(e).

The firm may wish to require the attorney to prepare, when practicable, a "departure memorandum," which outlines the attorney's ongoing responsibilities and a plan for meeting those responsibilities during the attorney's leave.

4. Return to Work and Reinstatement

The policy contains no provision regarding the circumstances of the return to work of the attorney. It assumes reinstatement to former position upon return to work. The FMLA requires that employees returning from FMLA leave be restored to their position, or its equivalent, upon return from leave. 29 U.S.C.S. § 2614(a). Such "restoration" may be denied under certain economic circumstances, and as to employees who are among the highest-paid 10 percent of employees. 29 U.S.C.S. § 2614(b).

Some firms may opt to make the right to take leave contingent upon the attorney's advising the firm in advance that she or he intends to return to work on a full or part-time basis upon the completion of the leave. If so, the firm should include that requirement in its written policy and the requirement should be discussed with the attorney before the leave is begun.

Some organizations, especially those with highly structured departments, may also prefer to include a provision stating whether the attorney, upon return to work, will be placed in the same or an equivalent position. In no circumstances, however, may the use of the leave be the basis for demotion or other retaliatory work action.

5. Application to Attorneys with Alternative Work Arrangements

A firm may opt to include a provision indicating the circumstances in which family care leave applies to attorneys with pre-existing alternative work arrangements. The FMLA does not provide for a "reduced leave schedule" for family leave unless the employee and the employer so agree. 28 U.S.C.S. § 2612(b).

Appendix E

Philadelphia Bar Association Model Policy for Parenting Lawyers
Alternative Work Arrangements

I. REDUCED WORK SCHEDULES

A. Definition

An attorney who is in good standing with the firm [organization] is entitled to be considered for a reduced work schedule. A reduced work schedule is defined as an arrangement in which the attorney receives reduced compensation in return for reduced work hours.

B. Requests for Reduced Work

An attorney desiring a reduced work schedule should submit a proposal to the appropriate department chair or supervisor as far in advance of the proposed commencement of the arrangement as possible. The firm [organization] shall respond to the request as soon as possible. Approval will be given if the proposal is practical and can be accommodated by the law firm as a whole and the practice group or groups which will be directly affected.

If the firm [organization] promulgates guidelines governing reduced work schedules, those guidelines will be made public to all attorneys within the firm [organization].

C. Effect Upon Content and Quantity of Work Assignments

The firm will expect that an attorney with a reduced work schedule, like all attorneys, will provide quality and timely service to clients. The firm, in turn, will respect and support the decision to work a reduced schedule and make every effort possible to ensure that the quantity of work given the attorney is consistent with the arrangement. In addition, the firm will make reasonable efforts, within the constraints of the attorney's schedule, to provide the type of work assignments, experiences and opportunities that are valuable or necessary to achieve partnership or promotion.

D. Effect on Compensation and Benefits

1. *Compensation:* Compensation for attorneys with reduced work schedules shall be adjusted according to the anticipated hours to be worked by the attorney as compared to the expectation of hours worked by others with full schedules.

Aside from that adjustment, the standards used to determine compensation for attorneys with reduced work schedules shall be the same as those used to determine compensation for attorneys with full schedules. An attorney working on a reduced schedule is eligible for salary increases and bonuses in the same manner as those working a full schedule.

2. *Benefits:* Full health insurance benefits will be made available, to the extent feasible, to all attorneys, regardless of their schedules. Attorneys with reduced work schedules shall be entitled to the same amount of paid vacation as other attorneys, but that vacation shall be paid at the attorney's reduced salary. Attorneys with reduced work schedules shall, to the extent feasible, be entitled to all other benefits (such as retirement benefits) on an adjusted basis.

E. Effect on Partnership or Promotion

Employment on a reduced schedule in and of itself shall not preclude or otherwise affect employment advancement such as eligibility for partnership or promotion. The firm may consider the amount, duration and quality of work experience of an attorney with a reduced schedule in the same way that it would consider the amount, duration and quality of work experience of an attorney with a full schedule in making the partnership or promotion decision.

F. Review

The approval of the reduced schedule work plan can be reviewed by the appropriate firm decision-maker at any time, but in any event will be reviewed annually. The attorney with the reduced schedule will participate in the review. The review will ascertain the effectiveness of the plan for the attorney's and the firm's purposes and will determine whether an appropriate percentage of the workload has been chosen.

II. JOB-SHARING

In practice settings where it is feasible, the firm encourages the sharing of one position between two attorneys. The firm welcomes proposals from attorneys in regard to the sharing of offices, secretaries, salary, workload, benefits and any other applicable arrangements. Such proposals will be seriously considered and accepted where appropriate.

III. FULL-TIME OPTIONS

A. Flextime.

"Flextime" is a rearrangement in, but not a reduction of, office hours. It includes "compressed time," in which an attorney handles a full workload in fewer, longer workdays. It also includes arrangements whereby an attorney works, for example, from 7:00 a.m. to 4:00 p.m. instead of from 9:00 a.m. to 6:00 p.m.

B. Telecommuting

"Telecommuting" refers to the location where work is performed, rather than the amount of work produced. For example, an attorney who works from home two days per week has a telecommuting arrangement.

C. Compensation and Benefits

An attorney using a flextime or telecommuting arrangement is responsible for a full workload and is entitled to full compensation and benefits. If a flextime or telecommuting arrangement is combined with a reduced work schedule, see I.D. above.

D. Requests for Flextime or Telecommuting

The firm recognizes that attorneys may need to work unusual hours on occasion. The firm also recognizes that many attorneys work at home on occasion. Firm approval generally is not necessary for these circumstances.

An attorney desiring to work on an unusual schedule on a long-term basis, however, or an attorney desiring to work outside the office on a regular basis during one or more weekdays, should submit a proposal for the schedule to the appropriate department chair or supervisor. Approval will be given if the proposal is practical and can be accommodated by the practice group or groups that will be directly affected.

COMMENTS

1. Reason for Policy

It is critically important that the legal profession support and encourage active participation by lawyer parents—male and female alike—in nurturing and childcare. Accordingly, employers should grant requests for alternative work arrangements for purposes of child care whenever possible. Such accommodation of the needs of working parents is plainly in the best interests of the profession because it will enable employers to attract and retain talented lawyers.

In addition to childcare, there are a variety of personal circumstances—such as an ill spouse or the need to provide elder care—which may make an alternative work arrangement desirable to an attorney. Therefore, the policy does not set forth any requirement that the reduced work schedule be for childcare purposes. Some employers may want to add a sentence providing that a reduced schedule is not available (without express permission) to attorneys who wish to engage in outside employment.

2. Structure of Alternative Work Arrangements

This policy states that an attorney desiring an alternative work schedule should submit a proposal, but it does not state how many hours the attorney should work or how the proposal should be structured. Different practice settings have different needs and different parents have different childcare needs. Numerous creative and flexible work schedules can be developed to meet these varied requirements. Attorneys and firms should feel free to create the most advantageous arrangement possible.

3. *Length of Service*

Some firms may opt to use a minimum employment period before an attorney becomes eligible for childcare leave. Those firms may want to leave it flexible. For example, the policy might provide that "normally" employees with less than one year of service are not eligible for alternative work arrangements. Such phrasing of the policy allows the firm to permit such arrangements for employees with less than one year of service in appropriate circumstances.

Another alternative is to permit lateral hires with at least one (or two) year(s) of legal experience elsewhere to work on a reduced schedule immediately upon joining the firm.

4. *Effect on Compensation and Benefits*

Compensation should be offered on an appropriate, adjusted basis. The policy as drafted does not set forth a formula for calculating compensation. Some firms may choose to offer an adjusted salary. For example, if an attorney works 80% of the hours that a similarly situated full-time attorney works, the attorney on the reduced schedule would receive 80% of the compensation that the full-time attorney would make. Other firms calculate compensation based on an hourly rate. All formulas must compensate the attorney for the same necessary—but potentially unbillable—time, such as that spent on administrative matters and continuing legal education.

It is strongly recommended that full medical benefits be offered to attorneys on reduced work schedules, whose need for insurance is no different from that of other attorneys. In the alternative, benefits can be offered on an appropriate adjusted basis. If, for example, in the case of health insurance, the employer pays for 100% of the cost of such insurance for full-time associate attorneys, then the employer should at minimum pay for 80% of the cost of the insurance for any attorney working 80% of full-time. The attorney would be responsible for the remainder of the cost. If the employer's health insurance carrier will not cover workers on a reduced schedule, the cost to the employee of obtaining private insurance should be partially reimbursed by the employer.

It is also strongly recommended that attorneys with reduced work schedules be permitted the same amount of paid vacation as full-time attorneys, but at their reduced salary.

5. Effect on Status with the Firm and on Future Advancement

Once the decision to allow a reduced work schedule is made, the employer should support and respect the arrangement. Moreover, every effort must be made to avoid making the attorney a "second class citizen" within the firm. To the extent possible, work assignments should be similar in quality and opportunity to those given to full-time lawyers. The attorney who works on a reduced schedule in turn will be expected to produce work of the same quality as attorneys who work full-time. The objective criteria for promotion or partnership should remain the same for all attorneys, regardless of whether or not they have worked on a reduced schedule.

There may be some instances in which long-term employment on a reduced schedule results in a longer period of time in which to accumulate the experience level necessary for partnership or promotion. In those cases, partnership or promotion may be delayed to allow the proper experience level to be achieved. If the firm chooses to develop specific formulas delineating the impact of reduced schedules on the timing of advancement decisions, it is strongly recommended that such guidelines be disclosed to all attorneys. For example, a firm might state that work on a reduced schedule for a cumulative period of two years or less will have no impact upon the timing of partnership, while a reduced schedule for more than two years will delay partnership for one year.

6. Partners with Reduced Work Schedules

Although the policy does not specifically mention partners with reduced work schedules, similar accommodations should be considered for both associates and partners.

7. Job Sharing

Job sharing means the sharing of one position between two attorneys. The attorneys might share an office, a secretary, a workload, a salary and some benefits. (Both attorneys would have to have health insurance, but arrangements may be possible where the firm's contribution to that insurance would not increase.)

For employers reluctant to support a reduced work schedule because of a fear that a part-time worker requires a full-time overhead expense, the institution of job-sharing, where feasible, would alleviate that concern.

8. *Telecommuting*

Some employers may want to limit the amount of time that an attorney may work outside the office, stating, for example, that an attorney must be in the office for at least three days per week. Some employers may want to require that an employee arrange for childcare during the hours that he or she intends to work at home.

Appendix F

Philadelphia Bar Association
Statement of Goals of Philadelphia Law Firms and Legal Departments for the Retention and Promotion of Women

I. Introduction

Even though women have entered the legal profession in increasing numbers over the past two decades, women lawyers continue to be underrepresented at the higher levels of the profession. It is difficult to account for all of the discrepancy between the number of men and women entering the profession and those achieving full participation in the profession. To the extent that women encounter obstacles based upon stereotypes and gender-based considerations, correction is essential, not only because it is professionally responsible, but also because discrimination is illegal. As leaders of the Philadelphia legal community, the signatories can and will use their best efforts to ensure that the attitudes and practices at law firms and legal departments promote the full representation and participation of women at all ranks of the profession.

Therefore, each *signatory* to the Statement of Goals of Philadelphia Law Firms and Legal Departments for the Retention and Promotion of Women (the "Statement of Goals") agrees to engage in critical self-evaluation to identify and correct any attitudinal barriers or organizational bias impeding women's progress within the signatory's law firm or legal departments.

II. Statement of Goals for Retaining and Promoting Women to All Levels in Law Firms and Legal Departments

EACH SIGNATORY PLEDGES TO PURSUE THE FOLLOWING GOALS:

(a) Full and Equal Participation of Women: To remove any barriers to full and equal participation of women in all levels of the work, responsibilities and rewards of the law firm or legal departments.

(b) Retention: To improve the rate of retention of women attorneys employed by the law firm or legal departments.

(c) Promotion: To improve the rate at which women are promoted or invited to partnership in each law firm and to senior counsel status in each legal department.

We believe that these goals are interrelated and mutually dependent because, if women are full participants and assured of equal opportunity to achieve their potential, women will become vested in furthering the success of their law firm or legal departments and, over the long term, attain equal representation.

III. Guidelines for Pursuing the Goals of the Retention and Promotion of Women Lawyers to Partnership and Management Positions

EACH SIGNATORY PLEDGES TO PURSUE THE GOALS OF INCREASING RETENTION AND PROMOTION RATES FOR WOMEN LAWYERS BY CRITICALLY EXAMINING AND, WHERE NECESSARY, MODIFYING THE FOLLOWING COMPONENTS OF EMPLOYMENT FOR LAWYERS:

(a) Interviews: Avoiding inappropriate inquiries about personal lives, child-bearing plans and physical appearance.

(b) Attitudes: According women lawyers the same presumption of competence, commitment and ultimate success as is accorded men lawyers.

(c) Opportunities: Ensuring that the opportunities for women lawyers are equivalent to those provided to men lawyers in the assignment of work necessary to develop skills and acquire experience for success and achievement; access to training, guidance and mentoring; opportunity to develop formal and informal relationships with partners, senior counsel and clients; and participation in firm governance and management of legal departments.

(d) Work Environment: Exercising diligence and sensitivity to ensure that the work environment is as hospitable to women lawyers as to their male colleagues by according high priority to principles of equality and anti-discrimination; prohibiting office functions at clubs that discriminate on the basis of gender; eliminating obstacles based upon stereotypical and gender-based views of women; and adopting a policy on sexual harassment.

(e) Compensation and Other Privileges of Employment: Awarding compensation and other privileges of employment to women lawyers without regard to gender.

(f) Standards for Retention and Promotion: Employing consistent and publicized standards for promotion that accurately and fairly assess the candidate's ability to practice at the level of partner or senior counsel, by: emphasizing observable past performance as well as the attorney's capacity to obtain and retain clients; being respectful of diverse, successful practice styles which complement the law firm and legal departments; and adopting a long-term perspective that balances attorneys' family and other societal/social responsibilities with the responsibilities and objectives of the law firm or legal departments.

(g) Process for Retention and Promotion: Conducting written evaluations in a candid manner and on a sufficiently frequent basis to allow for both growth and improvement and for early notice to candidates who are not expected to progress within the practice.

(h) Monitoring: Monitoring whether women are retained and promoted at rates comparable to the rates at which men are retained and promoted and whether the goals committed to herein are met. To the extent law firms or legal departments find that there is a discrepancy between the rates at which women and men are retained or promoted or that talented lawyers are choosing to leave, law firms or legal departments should honestly and sensitively consider whether the criteria employed to measure progress within the practice are positively related to successful practice; and whether discriminatory bias, no matter how subtle, has affected the evaluation process.

Appendix G

Philadelphia Bar Association
Statement of Goals of Philadelphia Law Firms and Legal Departments for Increasing Minority Representation and Retention*

I. Introduction

(a) The number of African-American, Hispanic-American and Asian-American (collectively *Minority*) lawyers practicing in law firms and corporate and institutional legal departments in the City of Philadelphia has long been small in relation to the total number of lawyers employed by such law firms and legal departments and in relation to the total number of practicing Minority attorneys in the City of Philadelphia (approximately 1200).

(b) In a profession that has prided itself in leading the fight for equal opportunity under the law, it is essential that we make further progress in achieving greater representation of Minority lawyers at all levels in our own firms and legal departments.

(c) The increased enrollment of Minorities in law school, which now averages 18% of the total enrollment in the Philadelphia area law schools alone and 15% of the total enrollment in law schools nationwide, affords an opportunity for increasing the representation of Minority lawyers in firms and legal departments,

*The Statement of Goals was originally developed by the Association's Committee on Minorities in the Profession and endorsed by the Board of Governors in 1993. Since then, more than fifty law firms, corporations, and other legal employers have adopted the Statement of Goals.

provided there is the will to do so and that concrete steps such as those enumerated below continue or are taken.

II. Statement of Goals for Increasing Minority Representation at All Levels of Law Firms and Legal Departments

EACH SIGNATORY PLEDGES TO PURSUE THE FOLLOWING GOALS:

Full and Equal Participation of Minorities

To achieve participation of Minority lawyers at all professional levels in its law firm or legal department.

Minority Hiring

To achieve the goal of hiring, during the period of 1993 through 1997, a substantial number of Minority lawyers. A desirable goal (not a quota) to be achieved would be at least 10% of the total number of all lawyers hired by such firm or legal department during the period 1993-1997. We believe that this goal is realistically attainable if the steps recommended in Section III are continued or are taken.

Retention

To improve the rate of retention of minority attorneys employed by law firms and institutional legal departments.

Minority Partners and Senior Legal Department Counsel

To promote or invite to partnership in each law firm and to senior counsel status in each corporate and institutional legal department Minority lawyers who meet the firm's or legal department's criteria for partnership or senior counsel status. We believe that this goal and the hiring and retention goals set forth in the preceding paragraphs are related and mutually dependent in that, if recruitment and retention programs are successful, then, over time, the number of Minority partners and senior counsel will correspond more closely to the percentage of Minority lawyers hired by the firm or legal department. Firms and legal departments that have Minority lawyers at the senior level are better able to recruit Minority law graduates. The more successful a firm or legal department is in recruiting, the more likely it is that more Minority lawyers will achieve partnership or senior counsel status.

III. Steps to Be Taken by Firms and Legal Departments in the Recruitment Process

EACH SIGNATORY PLEDGES TO PURSUE THE GOAL OF INCREASING THE NUMBER OF MINORITY LAWYERS HIRED BY TAKING ALL OR SOME OF THE FOLLOWING STEPS:

A. Continuing to utilize hiring criteria for all lawyers (Minority and non-Minority) that include academic grades, public service, communication skills, leadership, integrity, resourcefulness and other factors which indicate potential for success in the law firm or legal department.

B. Utilizing summer programs and student internship programs.

C. Increasing the pool of Minority law student applicants who meet the firm's or legal department's hiring criteria by:

    i.   interviewing at law schools having significant numbers of Minority law students; and

    ii. identifying Minority students through placement administrators, faculty members, former summer associates and Minority law student organizations at law schools and by job forums, receptions and other activities for law students.

D. To the extent that a law firm or legal department engages in lateral hiring, increasing the lateral Minority attorney applicant pool by:

    i.   communicating with law school placement administrators and faculty members for referrals to practicing Minority lawyers;

    ii.   requesting professional recruiters, when used, to include Minority candidates in their searches;

    iii. requesting Minority bar associations for referrals; and

    iv.   requesting Minority partners or law firms for referrals.

E. Recruiting Minority applicants by involving partners and senior counsel in the recruitment process.

F.   Communicating to all lawyers the firm's or legal department's commitment to the goals set forth in this statement.

IV. Steps to Be Taken by Firms and Legal Departments for Retention and Promotion of Minority Lawyers to Partnership and Management Positions

EACH SIGNATORY PLEDGES TO CONTINUE TO PURSUE THE GOAL OF INCREASING RETENTION AND PROMOTION RATES FOR MINORITY LAWYERS BY DOING THE FOLLOWING:

A.   Exercising diligence and sensitivity to ensure that the opportunities for Minority lawyers are equivalent to those provided to non-Minority lawyers in the assignment of work on a consistent basis of the type necessary to develop skills and acquire experience for success and advancement;

B.   Initiating or enhancing efforts aimed at increasing retention rates for Minority attorneys, focusing on allocation or interesting work, training and guidance, relationships with partners and senior counsel, client contacts, feedback and pro bono opportunities;

C.   Exercising diligence and sensitivity further to ensure that the work environment is as hospitable for Minority lawyers as it is for non-Minority lawyers by providing that:

- Minority lawyers receive equal opportunity to perform significant work assignments for important clients and partners;
- Minority lawyers receive equal training, mentoring, guidance, feedback and opportunities to grow and succeed;
- Minority lawyers are included in work-related social activities with other lawyers and clients;
- Programs are adopted for all new lawyers that enhance their understanding of business concepts, client relations, client development and their confidence in dealing with such matters;
- Policies are adopted that prohibit law firm or legal department sponsored functions at private clubs that discriminate on the basis of race, creed, religion or gender;

○ Implementing a formal mechanism through which Minority attorneys may voice concerns as they arise and through which feedback is solicited from all attorneys regarding the quality of their professional experiences, including work assignments, training, office atmosphere and relationships with colleagues and clients;

○ Ensuring equal opportunities for Minority lawyers to achieve partnership or senior counsel status by:

▪ Using the same criteria for Minority and non-Minority lawyers in evaluating lawyers for promotion to partnership or senior counsel status;

▪ Guiding the development of Minority lawyers in the same manner as non-Minority lawyers;

▪ As Minority lawyers near consideration for partnership or senior counsel status, assigning responsibility for important client matters to senior Minority lawyers in the same manner and extent that such matters are assigned to senior non-Minority lawyers.

Appendix H

Biographical Materials
Written and Personal Interviews Conducted by the Author

FELLOW LAW SCHOOL GRADUATES

I graduated from the Temple University Beasley School of Law in May of 1980. Many of the women I initially interviewed either in person or by written questionnaire were my fellow law school graduates.

KATHRYN G. CARLSON

Ms. Carlson is a sole practitioner in Bucks County, Pennsylvania, specializing in family law.

THE HONORABLE TOBY LYNN DICKMAN

When the Honorable Toby Lynn Dickman was elected to the Court of Common Pleas of Montgomery County, Pennsylvania, in 2002, the number of women judges in the common pleas courts doubled. Judge Dickman's time on the bench was preceded by a long partnership with Rubin, Glickman and Steinberg, where she specialized in the practice of family law. Judge Dickman balances her work on the bench with being the mother of a ten year old.

CHERIE FUCHS

Ms. Fuchs has practiced law with the military since graduating from law school. She is currently a member of the Judge Advocate General, holding the distinguished position of colonel in the U.S. Army Reserves.

CHERYL KRITZ GOLD

Cheryl Kritz Gold began her career as a law clerk to Philadelphia Court of Common Pleas Judge Klein, then joined the city solicitor's office, first in housing and then in the law department. She has since been promoted from an assistant city solicitor to the position she now holds, Deputy Assistant City Solicitor, which places her in charge of her unit directly under the city's top lawyer, the city solicitor. She is responsible for reviewing and negotiating city contracts and meets frequently with the mayor and city council members. She is the mother of a ten year old, and is the only person I know who actually attended Woodstock.

SUSAN HOLMES

Ms. Holmes, a resident of New York, is the owner of Accessories by Susan, a jewelry-design enterprise that she established after law school. A mother, wife, and businesswoman, Susan balances a number of roles with success.

JOSY W. INGERSOLL

Josy W. Ingersoll is currently a partner with Young Conway Stargatt & Taylor, LLP, a law firm of more than seventy-five lawyers in Wilmington, Delaware, concentrating in intellectual property and corporate litigation. She became the firm's first woman partner in 1986 and was elected to its management committee, also as the first woman, in 2000. She is the mother of two grown children.

BERNICE KOPLIN

Bernice Koplin is currently a partner with Schachtel, Gerstley, Levine & Koplin, PC, where she specializes in tax-related matters. Bernice began law school with me in 1977, but immediately transferred into a four-year day program, as opposed to a three-year day program, to accommodate her schedule as mother of a six-month-old baby and three-and-a-half-year-old toddler. Before entering law school, Bernice had successfully pursued a career as a law librarian. Bernice is a tax lawyer and has been an active member of the ABA Tax Section, where our paths often cross.

ADELINA GERACE MARTORELLI

Adelina Gerace Martorelli is currently employed as a trust officer with Nationwide Trust Company in Newark, Delaware. In her position, she advises clients in matters of trusts and financial planning.

CARMEN L. RIVERA MATOS

Inspired by the civil rights movement, Carmen L. Rivera Matos has spent the past years litigating matters of employment and civil rights on behalf of individuals seeking redress of grievances. Much of that time was spent as a trial lawyer for the Equal Employment Opportunity Commission. Between 1995 and 1997, she worked for a small firm and became a named partner. Carmen is currently a sole practitioner in Doylestown, Pennsylvania, and a mother of three. She continues to concentrate in the field of employment law and is active presenting seminars and training in matters of equal employment opportunity law and civil rights. Her work has provided her with a myriad of satisfying moments. She provides this one:

> In 1981, when I filed my first pregnancy case, the defense lawyer asked me why . . . my client wanted[ed] to work during pregnancy. I responded,

"Because Title VII of the Civil Rights Act as amended by the Pregnancy Discrimination Act says [she] can!"

KAREN W. McDONIE

Ms. McDonie was formerly a corporate lawyer with the firm of Rohm & Haas. She is currently a resident of the state of Texas, where she and her husband raise cattle and Irish Draught and Irish Sporthorses.

JACQUELINE M. ROBERTS

After a six-month position as clerk to a judge in one of Philadelphia's courts of common pleas, Jacqueline M. Roberts became a sole practitioner in Philadelphia and has remained self-employed all these years. She began her own title insurance agency in 1983 and was the first licensed minority title agent in the Commonwealth of Pennsylvania.

SUSAN SCHULMAN

After taking time away from her work as a civil litigator to work for the city of Philadelphia, Susan recently returned to her trial practice, this time with the law firm of Weber, Galagher, Simpson, Stapleton, Fires & Newby. After a four-month trial, Susan and her colleagues obtained a $26.7 million verdict for one of their clients. Susan balances her busy work schedule with being the mother of a young toddler.

JAYNE SPANGLER-WEISS

Jayne Spangler-Weiss is currently employed as counsel for Amtrak Railways, after having worked part-time for the law firm of Ballard

Spahr. She balances her work with being the mother of a fourteen-year-old daughter.

PAULA M. SZORTYKA

Ms. Szortyka is currently an assistant district attorney with the Berks County district attorney offices in Reading, Pennsylvania. Ms. Szortyka started law school at the age of forty-seven, and now, at the age of seventy-two, she is "still practicing."

A. TAYLOR WILLIAMS

Taylor Williams currently works as counsel to the Pennsylvania Supreme Court. Her experiences leading to her present position include a judicial clerkship in a Philadelphia common pleas court, and several years as a litigation associate in a midsize Philadelphia firm. Taylor is a member of Actors Equity and has performed with the Philadelphia Shakespeare Festival. She is the mother of Kate, who frequently attended law school with her mother, doing homework in the back of the classroom. Today, Kate is a corporate lawyer.

THE WOMEN OF 2002

Nearly 50 percent of law school students today are women. What are their motivations? Not having grown up with the feminist thinkers of the 1960s, what were their reasons for enrolling? And what are their aspirations? How do they imagine their lives in the next five years? Ten years? Twenty years? Do they think about having families, and, if so, what do they expect will happen to their careers? Do they envision employing nannies? Taking time off from work? Do they have any good ideas that escaped us over these past twenty years? I went off to talk to the following graduating women of the Temple Law School class of 2002.

ARLYN KATZEN LANDAU

Arlyn Katzen Landau is a 2002 graduate of Temple University School of Law. She is married and beginning her career as a law clerk with Pennsylvania Superior Court Judge Phyllis Beck. Arlyn has wanted to be a lawyer, she says, "as far back as [she] can remember." Arlyn grew up in the Washington D.C. area and attended an all-girl private school from third through twelfth grade, a school that she claims "breeds motivated women." Her undergraduate work was done at the University of Pennsylvania, where she concentrated in the sociology subjects of law and deviance, none of which, she charges, were helpful in law school. Arlyn has already, even before finishing law school, interned with the district attorney's offices in Philadelphia, a law firm in New Jersey, and a judge in a Philadelphia court of common pleas.

CYNTHIA MASON

Cynthia Mason is a recent Temple Law School graduate. She received her B.A. in cultural anthropology at the University of Pennsylvania, and worked for three years after college before beginning law school, for Philadelphia's Balch Institute for Ethnic Studies, the Free Library Foundation, and Culture Quest Tours. Cynthia received honors from the law school for outstanding oral advocacy in the spring of 2000. At school, she was active in the *Political and Civil Rights Law Review* and the Student Public Interest Network. Cynthia is currently involved with the Holocaust Victims Assets Litigation Settlement Project, where she reviews questionnaires to identify potential account holders.

SARA SHUBERT

Sara Shubert graduated from Temple Law School in 2002, at the age of twenty-four. She attended law school directly after graduating from Vassar College in New York as an English major. Sara claims she was drawn to the law because of her love of reading and writing.

AMANDA TURNER[1]

Amanda Turner is also a 2002 graduate of Temple Law School. Amanda asked that I not identify her by her real name, without giving me specific reasons. I am impressed by the level of anxiety Amanda must feel in gaining acceptance into the legal world by her insistence upon anonymity. One can only surmise about where those pressures are greatest: friends, family, potential employers, or peers. Amanda received her undergraduate degree in criminal justice from Temple University and proceeded to law school without a break. Like many others in her class and in other years, Amanda found little time to develop a social network while in law school, let alone keep up with old friends, although she did meet her current boyfriend during her first year of law school. She reports that even her "parents complained regularly about [her] lack of attendance at family events."

FOUR LAW PROFESSORS

Under the deanship of Peter J. Liacouras[2], Temple Law School actively recruited women as professors and as students. Four remarkable women professors of law at Temple agreed to reflect with me upon the journey they have taken in the past twenty-five years and the changes for women in the law that they have observed from their special vantage.

PROFESSOR ALICE ABREU

I first met Professor Alice Abreu when I was matriculating at night in the Master in Taxation program at Temple Law School. Professor Abreu taught in the graduate tax program and joined the faculty of Temple Law School on a full-time basis. Before joining Temple, Professor Abreu clerked for U.S. Eastern District Court Judge Edward N. Cahn in Pennsylvania. Professor Abreu had also been an associate at the Philadelphia law firm, Dechert, Price & Rhoads, concentrating in the field of federal income taxation. Professor Abreu has written and published extensively in her field. She is an active member of the ABA Section of Taxation, where our paths often cross. At the Temple Law School, she chaired the faculty selection committee from 1995 to 1997, held the Charles Klein Chair of Law and Government from 1993 to 1996, and was the 1992 nominee of Temple Law School for the University Lindback Award for Excellence in Teaching. She is a frequent speaker on tax issues, and was chair of the 47th Annual Penn State Tax Conference in 1993 and chair of the AALS Tax Section in 1997.

Alice Abreu was born in Cuba and arrived in this country in 1960 at the age of nine. Her family left Cuba after the Castro regime nationalized the Esso refinery where her father was employed as the manager. In the fourth grade in Miami, Alice excelled in math, as she had yet to learn to read, write, or speak English. Alice graduated from Cornell undergraduate school with a major in psychology, and later from Cornell Law School.

PROFESSOR MARINA ANGEL

A native of New York, Professor Marina Angel grew up in the days of anti-Tammany Hall politics, where politicians were all lawyers. Inspired by her city and "a good teacher in high school," Professor Angel has garnered a lifetime of awards and honors throughout her professional career, including the Philadelphia Bar Association's Sandra Day O'Connor Award and the Pennsylvania Bar Association's Anne X. Alpern Award, both in recognition of her efforts on behalf of women lawyers. In 2004, Professor Angel received the ABA's prestigious Margaret Brent Award.

Professor Angel graduated magna cum laude from Columbia Law School in 1969, where she received numerous awards, including the Jane Marks Murphy Prize for the Outstanding Woman Graduate. Her activism can be traced back to the days when she chaired the

Student Search Committee for the president of Columbia University. Professor Angel made Philadelphia her home when she attended the University of Pennsylvania Law School to attain an LLM degree in 1977. In January of 1979, she arrived at Temple University Law School as a professor in the areas of labor and employment, criminal justice, juvenile law, and violence against women. She has since been active at the law school as Associate Dean for Graduate Legal Studies, and Director of the Summer Program in Greece. She has served on and chaired numerous committees, and was adviser to the Women's Law Caucus. Her activism extends to the university at large, and she is currently a representative to the University Faculty Senate. She has been a prolific writer and active member of a number of bar associations, including the Pennsylvania and Philadelphia Bar Associations. Today she practically "single-handedly" puts together the Annual Report Card on Women for the Pennsylvania Bar Association. She has frequently been a guest professor at other law schools in the United States and abroad. In 1989, she was the Temple Law Review Faculty Honoree and the Women's Law Caucus Honoree, and was voted the George P. Williams Memorial Award for Outstanding Professor of the Year.

PROFESSOR LAURA LITTLE

Professor Laura Little is a newer addition to the Temple Law School faculty. She began teaching at Temple University School of Law in 1990, five years after having graduated summa cum laude and clerking for Supreme Court Chief Justice Rehnquist. Professor Little earned her undergraduate degree from the University of Pennsylvania in 1979. After graduating from Temple Law School, Professor Little clerked for Chief Justice William H. Rehnquist (October Term 1986) and for Judge James Hunter, III, of the U.S. Court of Appeals for the Third Circuit (1985–1986). Before joining the faculty at Temple Law School, Professor Little worked from 1987 to 1990 as a lawyer in Philadelphia, representing large media clients (*Philadelphia Inquirer* and *Philadelphia Daily News*) on First Amendment issues.

PROFESSOR DIANE MALESON

Professor Diane Maleson received her undergraduate degree from Bryn Mawr College and her law degree from Temple University. She has been associated with the law school for eighteen years in the positions of professor, vice dean, associate dean, and acting law librarian. She is currently chair of the Law School Administrative Committee and editor of the *American Journal of Legal History*. Professor Maleson is a law review author, secretary of the American Association of Law Schools' Section on Torts, and participant in the Arthur Levitt Public Policy forum "concerning the nominating process for Supreme Court Justices."[3] Diane Maleson was my first-year torts professor and the first woman lawyer and law professor I ever laid eyes upon.

THREE CHANCELLORS OF THE PHILADELPHIA BAR ASSOCIATION

The Philadelphia Bar Association celebrated its 200th anniversary in March 2002. As an institution, the association traces its roots to an organization formed by seventy-one lawyers paying $2.00 annual membership fees and called the Law Library Company of the City of Philadelphia. It was indeed just that, an actual library club dedicated as a resource for Philadelphia's practitioners. In the beginning, the library was located at Independence Hall, until it moved in 1819 to the second floor of Congress Hall.[4] A second lawyers' organization was formed in 1821 under the name of Associated Members of the Bar of Philadelphia, with a hierarchy and structure resembling the current bar. There were two standing committees, and leaders bore the titles of chancellor and vice chancellor.

In 1827, the two organizations merged and the surviving entity was renamed the Law Association of Philadelphia. Its first chancellor was William Rawle, and first vice chancellor, Horace Binney. William Rawle was the first of a long dynasty of Philadelphia lawyers, ever-present as the firm of Rawle and Henderson. Horace Binney likewise was a prominent lawyer of his day, well known nationally for representing the first and second banks of the United States and well known locally for representing the city of Philadelphia in the matter of the Stephen Girard trust. In that case, he successfully represented the city before the U.S. Supreme Court in a decision that ultimately resulted in the creation of Philadelphia's Girard College and the city's control over the multimillion-dollar Stephen Girard estate.[5]

Today, women's representation among Philadelphia's lawyers has increased to 34 percent; still a minority, but one with an increasingly high profile. In 1992, after 180 years, Philadelphia lawyers elected their first woman chancellor of the bar association, Deborah Willig, a labor lawyer representing workers. They repeated this feat in 2000 by electing Doreen Davis, also a labor lawyer, but on the side of management. The chancellor of the Philadelphia Bar Association for 2003, Audrey Talley, is an African-American woman from the law firm of Drinker, Biddle & Reath, LLP.

DEBORAH R. WILLIG

Deborah R. Willig was the first woman to be elected as chancellor of the Philadelphia Bar Association. She is currently the managing partner of the Philadelphia law firm Willig, Williams & Davidson. Hers is a midsize firm engaged in the practice of labor-relations law on the side of labor unions, and plaintiffs in matters of employment discrimination. Her work has gained her the respect of mayors, union leaders, and other veteran labor negotiators. The city's chief negotiator, Joseph Bloom, describes her this way:

> She knows how to negotiate. She knows how to settle, when to settle. She knows when there's a deal. She is as tough an advocate as you would meet, but she's reasonable. And she's a person of her word.[6]

Her opponents in management agree. Labor lawyer Thomas Felix has said that she "is one of the most accomplished labor lawyers in Philadelphia."[7]

Deborah Willig graduated from Temple Law School in 1975. In undergraduate school at the University of Pennsylvania and in law school, Deborah garnered awards and honors, including being the first woman president of the law school's Student Bar Association. Upon graduating, she was fortunate to clerk for Philadelphia Common Pleas Court Judge Lisa A. Richette, one of Philadelphia's diamonds, who also agreed to participate in this book. In addition to her exhausting list of professional activities, Deborah has published in her field and given numerous speeches and lectures. She has also been a tireless advocate of women's issues and has been honored on numerous occasions for her leadership. In 2002, she was awarded the Temple Law Alumni Association Founder's Day Award, and the Agent of Change Award from Women's Way. In the same year, the Pennsylvania Bar Association's Women in the Profession Committee awarded her firm the award for Promotion of Women to Leadership Positions. Other personal honors include the Sandra Day O'Connor Award of the Philadelphia Bar Association and Labor Human Rights Award of the Jewish Labor Committee.

DOREEN DAVIS

Doreen Davis became the seventy-third chancellor of the Philadelphia Bar Association in 2000. She was the second woman to hold the job. Doreen is currently a partner with the law firm Morgan Lewis, in the labor and employment law practice group. Doreen moved to Morgan Lewis in May of 2001, after a time at the firm of Montgomery, McCracken, Walker & Rhoads, LLP, where she served for four years as chair of the labor and employment law department. Commenting on her transition, she spoke of the needs of her clients and also said this: "As important, Morgan Lewis provides an excellent supportive environment for working professionals who, like me, are committed to leading full professional and personal lives. I look forward to continuing to build my practice there."

Doreen Davis was an undergraduate student at Penn State University, where she majored in labor studies. Her J.D. was earned from Temple University School of Law in 1978, where she graduated magna cum laude. Doreen's practice in employment litigation is focused upon management labor law on a nationwide basis. Before becoming chancellor, Doreen was active in the Philadelphia Bar Association, serving on many committees and as chair of the Young Lawyers Section. She was elected twice to the Bar Association's Board of Governors and was eventually its chair.

Doreen's rocky childhood and rise to success has been chronicled in an article authored by her husband, Robert Simmons, also a lawyer. He writes that "Doreen had to overcome a childhood of extreme poverty and an abusive father who tried to stifle her dream of attending law school." Doreen is from a small town northwest of Wilkes Barre, Pennsylvania, where jobs were scarce. Her father worked in the coal mines and her mother worked in a local textile factory while raising six children. At the age of twelve, Doreen found a job in a local bingo hall, to provide herself with pocket money. By high school, she rose to the position of bingo caller. Her love of books and her ambition propelled her to college and then law school, the first in her school district to achieve that accomplishment, so her husband writes. Doreen is a devoted mother to their teenage daughter.

AUDREY TALLEY

Audrey Talley was chancellor of the Philadelphia Bar Association in 2003. She is a woman and she is African-American. She is making history as the third woman and the first African-American chancellor of the Philadelphia Bar Association. Audrey's enthusiasm for my exploration into Philadelphia's women lawyers came early in my project. I called her to discuss the work she had done in 1997 with the Philadelphia Bar Association, surveying the "trailblazing" women lawyers in Philadelphia (graduates before 1960) about their early experiences. She encouraged me to continue the work begun and looked forward to sharing our stories.

Audrey Talley is currently a partner at the Philadelphia law firm of Drinker, Biddle & Reath, LLP, where her practice concentrates in federal and state securities laws and compliance, public and private offerings, general corporate finance and corporate law matters, as well as compliance matters related to the financial services industry. Audrey has written and lectured in the areas of money management and investment companies.

Audrey Talley attained her bachelor's degree from Vanderbilt University in 1973. She received a master's degree from the University of Southern California in 1978, and her J.D. from Boston University School of Law in 1981. She has been named as one of "Pennsylvania's Best 50 Women in Business" by the business journals of Pennsylvania and the Pennsylvania Department of Community and Economic Development. Audrey has lent her time to professional associations in her field and on behalf of her community. She has participated in the position of chair on many committees, most notably as co-chair of the Pennsylvania Bar Association's Commission on Women in the Profession and chair of the Philadelphia Bar Association's Business Law Section and Board of Governors. During her service with the Philadelphia Bar Association Committee on Women, Audrey launched the "Statement of Goals of Philadelphia Law Firms and Legal Departments for the Retention and Promotion of Women Lawyers." A copy appears as Appendix F to this book.

Audrey has been recognized with the 2002 Community Women's Education Project Woman of Distinction Award, the 2001 NBA Women Lawyers Division Doris Mae Harris Award, and the 1999 Philadelphia Congress of the National Political Congress of Black Women-Chisolm Award.

WOMEN OF EXCELLENCE

I had the good fortune to interview a number of accomplished women who have demonstrated excellence in their fields and activism in their communities. If I had never written a book, I would have considered the opportunity to speak with these women sufficient reward. They are enormously busy and yet graciously gave of their time for the benefit of all women who share this profession.

LESLIE ANNE MILLER
First Woman President of the Pennsylvania Bar Association

The Pennsylvania Bar Association was founded in 1895.[8] One hundred and three years later, in 1998, it had its first woman president: Leslie Anne Miller. Before serving as president of the Pennsylvania Bar Association, Ms. Miller became the first chair of its Commission on Women in the Profession.

Leslie Anne Miller's illustrious career in the law was sparked by an early interest in politics, refined by a master's degree from Rutgers University in 1974, where she matriculated as a Fellow at the Eagleton Institute of Politics. Her degree in law was earned in 1977 at the Dickinson School of Law. In 1994, Leslie obtained an LLM in Trial Advocacy, with honors, from Temple University Law School. Leslie has been a shareholder and partner with the law firm of McKissock and Hoffman, PC (from which she is now on leave), for most of her professional career, specializing in insurance defense litigation and mediation.

In addition to becoming president of the Pennsylvania Bar Association, Leslie Miller has held a number of offices within the association, including the first woman chair of the House of Delegates, first chair of the Commission on Women in the Profession, and first woman chair of the Young Lawyers Division. She has been active with the Philadelphia Bar Association and has volunteered her efforts as a board member for a number of nonprofit entities. Leslie has been a teacher over these past years in a variety of forums, including Temple Law School, and has served the Philadelphia Court of Common Pleas as Judge Pro Tempore. Most recently, she was appointed general counsel to Pennsylvania's Governor Rendell.

As president of the Pennsylvania Bar Association, Leslie created the Council on Judicial Independence for the purpose of promoting an independent judiciary. To bring quality legal services to all of

Pennsylvania's citizens, she advocated increased pro bono activity for Pennsylvania's lawyers and supported increased funding of community legal services.

In recognition of her untiring efforts on behalf of women in the law and in business, Leslie Anne Miller has been the recipient of many honors and awards throughout her career. To name just a few, Leslie received the Anne X. Alpern Award from the Pennsylvania Bar Association, Commission on Women, and the Sandra Day O'Connor Award from the Philadelphia Bar Association, both in 1999. In 1998, she was granted the Star Award from the Forum of Executive Women in Philadelphia, and in 1996 was added to the Pennsylvania Honor Roll of Women. Upon receiving the Anne X. Alpern Award, Leslie Miller was recognized by her peers for her persistent efforts on behalf of women in the law. In the words of Pennsylvania Superior Court Judge Phyllis Beck:

> Throughout her tenure as president of the PBA, Leslie has been a tireless advocate for women in the legal profession. . . . Her efforts to enhance the role of women and create a balanced playing field for male and female lawyers is just one example of Leslie's extraordinary leadership.[9]

THE HONORABLE LYNNE ABRAHAM
Philadelphia's District Attorney

The Honorable Lynne Abraham, Philadelphia District Attorney, is truly one of the city's diamonds. Born and raised in Philadelphia, District Attorney Lynne Abraham became a graduate of Temple University in 1962 and Temple University School of Law in 1965. I met with Lynne Abraham in her office for the purpose of interviewing her for this book and, I must admit, had no idea what to expect. Everyone in the city knows of her and the notorious cases that swirl around her and her offices: Allen Iverson, Mumia, Ira Einhorn. Before being admitted, I was asked if I was allergic to cats. I found Lynne Abraham to be honest, intelligent, friendly, and interesting.

For a while during our talk, one of her cats in residence perched on my shoulder and purred.

Lynne Abraham truly enjoys her work, and it is evident. It is evident in the numerous public service activities to which she belongs and gives her time, in the way the district attorney offices function, and in the innovative programs she has introduced, such as Operation Cease Fire (to bring in unlawful guns off the streets), the Public Nuisance Task Force, the drug treatment court, the Cyber Crime Unit, and more. The city, in turn, reelected her in 2001 for an additional ten years. Many recognize her strengths and popularity as the Philadelphia District Attorney, and beg her to concede her superior influence over her predecessors, the Honorable (now supreme court justice) Ron Castille and former Mayor Ed Rendell, to which she replies in typical manner:

> I'm here to do a job, I love what I do, I work hard, I love this city, I want to serve again, and I'll leave it to history to decide who was the most influential. When I'm dead and buried it won't make a dime's worth of difference.

District Attorney Lynne Abraham measures success on the job by winning cases ethically and professionally. She will remind you that "today's victim is tomorrow's defendant."

The district attorney began her career in the regional counsel's office of the U.S. Department of Housing and Urban Development, where she prepared federal loans, grants, and contracts for urban renewal projects. In 1967, she became an assistant district attorney, which she interrupted in 1972 to serve as executive director of the Philadelphia Redevelopment Authority. In 1974, she served as legislative consultant to the city council, where she assisted in conducting investigations, drafting legislation, and revising portions of the Philadelphia Home Rule Charter. Also in 1974, District Attorney Lynne Abraham served as a research assistant to the Honorable Alexander F. Barbieri, a judge of the Philadelphia Court of Common Pleas, and court administrator of Pennsylvania, where she assisted in the production of a three-volume work on workers' compensation.

In 1976, she became a judge in the municipal court of Philadelphia, presiding primarily over misdemeanor criminal matters. In 1980, she became a judge of the Philadelphia Court of Common Pleas, presiding over homicide and major felony trials.

In 1991, Lynne Abraham was elected to the office of Philadelphia District Attorney, the city's chief law enforcement office, which has responsibility for prosecuting more than 70,000 criminal cases yearly and overseeing a professional staff of 300 assistant district attorneys and 275 support staff. In 2001, she won reelection for an additional ten-year term.

District Attorney Lynne Abraham's devotion to her work and to the people of Philadelphia is evident in the many organizations to which she lends her energies and the many institutions that seek her as a speaker and educator. It would be impossible to list each and every such institution or organization, but mention of a few is in order. District Attorney Lynne Abraham has been a frequent lecturer at a number of city universities, including Temple University Law School. She has participated in numerous seminars, panel discussions, and conferences, at times as keynote speaker at meetings of a long list of professional and nonprofit organizations, including the American Bar Association, Anti-Defamation League of B'nai Brith, Pennsylvania Bar Association, University of Pennsylvania, Children's Literary Initiative, Organization for Security and Cooperation in Europe, and Pennsylvania Psychiatric Society Committee on Women.

District Attorney Abraham is a member of, and active participant in, numerous organizations. She is a board member and the founder of Urban Genesis, a nonprofit organization that funds after-school programs for children, summer camp for inner-city children, and Thanksgiving dinners for more than 250 families each year. She is a board member of I-LEAD (of which she is also a founder), the American Red Cross, Big Brothers/Big Sisters, and the Police Athletic League. She is the vice president of the National District Attorneys Association and legislative chair for the Pennsylvania District Attorneys Association, and serves on the executive committee of the Anti-Defamation League of the B'nai Brith.

District Attorney Lynne Abraham declines to list her awards and honors, and many have been bestowed upon her. For District Attorney Abraham, it seems that her reward is when people come to her and declare, "You've changed my life."[10]

CHARISSE LILLIE
Former Philadelphia City Solicitor

Charisse Lillie was born and raised in segregated Houston, Texas, in a conclave she calls an "African village," where she attended a segregated elementary school. It would be wrong to assume that under these circumstances Charisse grew up deprived of the American dream. At home, Charisse was surrounded by the art world. Her father was a jazz musician. Her mother was involved with the theater, and today teaches English at the University of Pittsburgh. Her extended family included a cousin who was a criminal defense trial lawyer and a number of "brilliant" schoolteachers. Her parents sent her to Catholic junior high and high schools, where she was among the first of her race to attend as a result of the changes compelled by the Supreme Court's desegregation ruling in *Brown v. Board of Education*. By her own account, Charisse Lillie was "born with a lot of confidence." When she attended Wesleyan University in 1970, her sense of being an outsider was as a non-New Yorker from the outreaches of Texas, and not on account of her race. She took this in stride, with humor.

Charisse Lillie obtained her law degree from Temple University School of Law in 1976, as a member of the dean's honor list, and a master's degree from Yale Law School in 1982. She is currently a partner and chair of the litigation department of Ballard Spahr Andrews & Ingersoll, LLP. From 1990 to 1992, she served as Philadelphia City Solicitor, the first woman of color to hold that position. Her earlier legal career included positions as Philadelphia Redevelopment Authority General Counsel, Assistant U.S. Attorney for the Eastern District of Pennsylvania, professor at Villanova University School of Law, Community Legal Services Deputy Director, and trial attorney with the U.S. Department of Justice. She has clerked for the Honorable Clifford Scott Green of the U.S. District Court for the Eastern District of Pennsylvania, and served on a number of Philadelphia's government commissions. Along with her numerous awards and honors in recognition of her efforts on behalf of women and on behalf of civil rights, Charisse Lillie has served as chair of the Philadelphia Bar Association Board of Governors and chair of the American Bar Association Commission on Racial and Ethnic Diversity in the Profession, and is a member of the Standing Committee of Federal Judiciary. She has been mentioned as one of the city's best lawyers by *Philadelphia Magazine* and the *Legal Intelligencer*, and as among Philadelphia's Influential African Americans in 2002 by the *Philadelphia Tribune*.

Charisse Lillie is an adviser to her clients on matters of diversity and antidiscrimination. She conducts antidiscrimination training and nudges corporations to make positive changes for diversity. Charisse enjoys her work and feels she is able to effect institutional changes that have positive impacts upon the lives of many people. Charisse is married to a criminal defense lawyer and is the mother of a sixteen-year-old daughter and two stepchildren. Reflecting upon her career and life, Charisse stated, "The stars have been lined up for me."

THE HONORABLE SANDRA SCHULZ NEWMAN
First Woman Seated on the Pennsylvania Supreme Court

Sandra Schulz Newman is the first woman to become a justice of the Pennsylvania Supreme Court. She has held that position since 1996, preceded by a judgeship with the Commonwealth Court of Pennsylvania from 1994 to 1996. Judge Newman reached the Pennsylvania Supreme Court through a tough campaign that included visits to sixty-seven counties in Pennsylvania and resulted in a 300,000-vote margin of victory. Her campaign foreshadowed her style as a hardworking, never-tiring, and gutsy supreme court justice.

It is a difficult task to provide a short summary of a distinguished life. Let me begin at the beginning. Judge Newman received her undergraduate degree from Drexel University in 1959, her master's degree from Temple University in 1969, and her law degree from Villanova University in 1972. She began her career as an assistant district attorney in Montgomery County, Pennsylvania, and then went on to private practice for twenty years as a senior partner with Astor, Weiss & Newman. Judge Newman has received many honors and awards throughout her career, in recognition of her achievements and dedication to community. To name just a few: She received the Susan B. Anthony Award from the Women's Bar Association of Western Pennsylvania, for "dedication to the elimination of gender bias in the legal system and the legal profession and for being an exemplary role model for women aspiring to the practice of law and to judicial office." She was honored by Drexel University with the Drexel 100 Award for being one of Drexel's 100 outstanding living alumni, by Villanova with the Medallion Award (only the third woman to receive that award), and by Temple University with the Legion of Honor Gold Medallion, Chapel of the Four Chaplains. She has been named as Person of the Year or Woman of the Year by numerous associations. Judge Newman is in frequent demand as a guest speaker or keynote speaker for professional conferences on women's issues, family law, and judicial events. She has been an educator and an active participant, often as chair or on the board of trustees, of many nonprofit organizations.

THE HONORABLE MARY ANN COHEN
First Woman to Be Elected Chief Judge of the U.S. Tax Court

Judge Mary Ann Cohen is the first woman to be elected Chief Judge of the U.S. Tax Court. She was appointed to the court on September 24, 1982, for a fifteen-year term, succeeding Cynthia Hall. President Clinton reappointed her to a second fifteen-year term in 1997. Judge Cohen was twice elected by her peers as chief judge of the court, first in 1996 and again in 1998.

When I first met Judge Cohen at an ABA Tax Section meeting in Washington, D.C., she was living in southern California and practicing tax law with the firm of Abbott & Cohen. She was gracious, friendly, and supportive, and, for me, a role model. Judge Cohen attained her law degree in 1967 from the University of Southern California, and was an active participant in the ABA Tax Section. She has authored numerous articles and participated in panels on the topics of tax and business litigation. I thought of her immediately when I began this book, and she again graciously gave of her time to talk about the changes she has experienced for women tax lawyers.

Judge Cohen spoke of her parents, neither of whom were college educated. Her mother was in the paint contracting business with her uncle, and her father was a traveling salesperson. She learned bookkeeping for the painting business from her uncle, and originally planned to become an actuary. She noticed that out of four hundred actuaries in the country at that time, none were women. Midway through college she changed her plans to become a certified public accountant. However, when it came time to take the exam, she opted for law school. Upon graduating from law school, Judge Cohen became associated with the prominent and well-respected tax lawyer Lee Abbott, in a firm that came to be Abbott & Cohen. With her wry sense of humor, Judge Cohen recalls that early in her career, she was turned down for employment by a prominent tax lawyer because of her gender; she was later supported by that very same man for tax court judge.

JANE BERGNER

Jane Bergner is a tax lawyer in Washington, D.C. Her law practice concentrates on tax litigation, tax collection, tax planning, estate and gift taxation, planning and administration, and local taxation. She is highly experienced, representing clients before the Internal Revenue Service for tax audits and tax appeals.

Jane is a sole practitioner alongside her husband, also a tax lawyer. Jane graduated from Vassar College in 1964 and Columbia

Law School in 1967. She is a contributing author to numerous tax reference series and has published numerous tax-related articles. She is active in the District of Columbia Bar Association, where she was the chair, from 1991 to 1993, of the Tax Audits and Litigation Committee of the Tax Section; she won an award for best Section Community Outreach Project in 1992. Jane has been an equally active member of the ABA Section of Taxation.

CATHERINE BARONE
University of Pennsylvania Class of 1948

Ms. Barone is currently a sole practitioner and has in her career been counsel to the Pennsylvania Railroad and assistant attorney general in the Pennsylvania Department of Revenue.

THE HONORABLE PHYLLIS BECK
Senior Judge, Pennsylvania Superior Court

In 1983, the Honorable Phyllis Beck became the first woman elected to the Pennsylvania Superior Court, having first been appointed in 1981 by then Governor Richard Thornburgh. Judge Beck was elected to a ten-year term in 1983 and retained in 1993. Judge Beck is a 1949 graduate of Brown University. After marriage, four children, and some graduate studies in psychology at Bryn Mawr College, Judge Beck began law school at Temple University in 1962. She completed her law studies as a part-time evening student and, before joining the superior court, worked as an associate with the firm of Goodis, Greenfield, Nanin and Mann, and then Duane Morris. She served on the faculty at Temple University Law School before becoming vice dean of the University of Pennsylvania Law School. In 1987, Judge Beck was appointed by Pennsylvania's Governor Casey to chair the Governor's Judicial Reform Commission, from which emanated the "Beck Report," an influential and well-respected report that advocated recommendations for reform to Pennsylvania's judicial system. In 1990, Judge Beck received the Pennsylvania Bar Association's Judicial Award.

JANE BRODERSON
Business Entrepreneur, and Mother of Five

Jane Broderson is a 1983 graduate of Cornell Law School. She resides in Penn Valley, Pennsylvania, and, in addition to raising five sons, has started three successful businesses—an adoption agency, an executive recruiting firm, and a continuing legal education business.

NANCY CARON
In-House Counsel to Firemen's Fund Insurance Company, and Mother of Four

After ten years as a litigator, Nancy Caron became in-house counsel with the Firemen's Fund Insurance Company. A 1983 graduate of Marquette Law School, Nancy combines work in the general counsel's office with being a mother of four.

PATRICIA HIRSCH FRANKEL
University of Pennsylvania Class of 1957

Ms. Frankel is a sole practitioner in Reading, Pennsylvania.

GRACE KENNEDY
First Woman Associate in a New York Wall Street Firm

The voice on the other end of the line was strong and enthusiastic. It was Grace Kennedy. She called to talk with me about my "project." She thought it was wonderful that someone would document the lives of Philadelphia's women lawyers. She had much to tell.

I met with Grace at her home and she talked for two and a half hours straight, telling me the story of her life. I was enthralled and grateful to be the one listening. Grace is in her eighties—she thinks. She is not quite sure, except she knows that she is not yet ninety. She is remarkable for her energy and acumen. Grace only recently retired from the practice of law—again, as she describes it. She continues to serve on the Board of Legal Services in Delaware County, Pennsylvania, as she has for the past twenty years. She is still a member of the Newtown Square Zoning Commission, which she helped found. In the early years, she helped write the zoning laws for Newtown Square. She has always been involved in community affairs and, nearly thirty years ago, started a women's club in Newtown Square that is still ongoing and active.

THE HONORABLE LISA RICHETTE
Senior Judge of the Philadelphia Court of
Common Pleas, Criminal Division

Judge Lisa Aversa Richette is currently a judge in the Philadelphia Court of Common Pleas, Criminal Division, a position she has held for the past twenty years. Her official biography notes that she is the first woman of Italian origin to serve on the Pennsylvania judiciary.

In 1957, Judge Richette became Calendar Judge, Felony Jury Program, a position she held for twenty years. In 1971, she became a judge in the Philadelphia Felony Jury Program, presiding over 1,500 jury and nonjury trials from 1971 until 1982. She has been a lecturer at Temple University Law School in the years between 1972 and 1984, a clinical professor of law at the Villanova Law School, and a lecturer at Yale Law School. Earlier in her career, she worked as a Philadelphia assistant district attorney (1954 to 1964), where she served as chief of the family court division for a number of years (1956 to 1964). For a period of time between 1964 and 1971, she was engaged in the private practice of law.

Judge Richette has been a tireless advocate for those who are the most powerless in our society: adolescent mothers, abused children, and runaway youth. She has achieved numerous local and national honors, and, through her work, national stature, resulting in appearances on *Nightline* and *Good Morning America.*

A south Philadelphia native, Judge Richette received her bachelor's degree from the University of Pennsylvania and her law degree from Yale University. Her admission to practice law in Pennsylvania came in 1954. Judge Richette returned to the Philadelphia area to practice law upon the invitation of Richardson Dilworth, Philadelphia's district attorney at the time, a man who later became the city's mayor. Judge Richette worked as an assistant district attorney, predominately in matters pertaining to family court. During her career, Judge Richette was responsible for implementing the Villanova Law School clinical trial program, in which Grace Kennedy was an instructor. She has been a frequent speaker and lecturer at Temple University School of Law. She is well known in Philadelphia for her intelligence, directness, and flamboyant personal style. Judge Richette is the author of an award-winning book, published in 1969 and entitled *The Throwaway Children*, a personal and thoughtful treatise about children in the family court system. Many have commented that she was ahead of her time.

LILA ROOMBERG
Partner at Ballard Spahr Andrews & Ingersoll

A graduate of New York University Law School, Lila Roomberg began her legal career with Sylvania Electric, after which she was hired by the law firm of Ballard Spahr Andrews & Ingersoll as a paralegal/librarian. In 1971, she became the first woman partner of her firm. Ms. Roomberg has practiced primarily in the field of tax-exempt financing. She has been recognized for her untiring efforts on behalf of women in the legal profession. In 2000, the Philadelphia Bar Association awarded her the prestigious Sandra Day O'Connor Award, and, in 2002, the Pennsylvania Bar Association awarded her the Anne X. Alpern Award. Ms. Roomberg is active in the Philadelphia and Pennsylvania Bar Associations, serving on the

Pennsylvania Bar Association Women in the Profession Executive
Council and as editor of its newsletter and directory. She was the
founder of the Philadelphia Bar Association Child Care Services
Committee, and coauthor of the alternative work arrangement proposals put forth by both the Pennsylvania and Philadelphia Bar Associations. Ms. Roomberg is the author of *Turning Adversaries into Allies
in the Workplace*, which is filled with advice based upon personal
experience on engineering a legal career.

THE HONORABLE NORMA L. SHAPIRO
First Woman on the U.S. Eastern District Court of Pennsylvania

With her appointment by President Jimmy Carter in 1978, Judge
Norma L. Shapiro became the first woman to sit as judge on the Eastern District Court of Pennsylvania. After receiving a B.A. degree with
honors in political theory from the University of Michigan in 1948,
Judge Shapiro entered the University of Pennsylvania Law School as
one of eight women. She excelled and became editor of the law
review. Upon graduating magna cum laude in 1951, Judge Shapiro
served as a law clerk to Justice Horace Stern of the Supreme Court of
Pennsylvania, after which she was offered the job as law librarian at
one of Philadelphia's large law firms. Turning that prize offer down,
Judge Shapiro taught legal writing for a period of time at the University of Pennsylvania, where her presence served as a role model for a
new generation of women lawyers. Judge Shapiro entered private
practice with the law firm of Dechert Price and Rhoads, taking a hiatus of nine years to raise three children. She was the first woman at
Dechert to make partner and served on the firm's policy committee.

Judge Shapiro has served as chair of the ABA Conference of Federal Trial Judges and as its delegate in the ABA House of Delegates, as
chair of the Coordinating Council for the ABA Justice Center, and as
chair of the Judicial Division Program Committee. She is also a
member of the executive committee of the National Conference of
Federal Trial Judges. In 1997, as a representative of the Judicial Division to the Section Officers Conference, she served as chair of the

Annual Section Officers Conference. Judge Shapiro was the first woman to serve as a member of the Philadelphia Bar Association Board of Governors and later became its first female chairperson.

In August of 1999, Judge Shapiro received the prestigious ABA Margaret Brent Award. She was selected as a 1996 inductee to the Distinguished Daughters of Pennsylvania and was honored as the first recipient of the Philadelphia Bar Association Sandra Day O'Connor Award in October 1993. In 1991, Judge Shapiro received the Federal Bar Association Bill of Rights Award. Upon her appointment as chair of the ABA Judicial Division, Judge Shapiro shared the following thoughts:

> Each of us has to continue the mutual effort to form a more perfect union. Those who are privileged to be elected or appointed judges, whether state or federal, have a special obligation to protect our constitution. Acting together, through a professional association, helps us to meet our responsibilities. We can educate ourselves to manage our work better, and educate others to understand the importance of an independent judiciary. We can work with lawyers to encourage respect for the rule of law locally, nationally, and even internationally. Also, you can't underestimate the importance of the socialization, the friendships that we form, that nourish our spirit and add to the joy of judicial life.[11]

THE HONORABLE CAROLYN ENGEL TEMIN
Judge, Philadelphia Court of Common Pleas

She meant to become a dancer, but, in 1955, nice, single, Jewish girls from Philadelphia did not take off on their own and move to New York to study dance. The result was an illustrious career in the law and a lifetime dedicated to the rights of women, indigents, and justice. In 2000, Judge Carolyn Engel Temin was recognized for her professional achievements and positive impact upon women in the law by having bestowed upon her the Anne X. Alpern Award of the Pennsylvania Bar Association, Commission on Women in the Profession.

Judge Temin received a Bachelor of Fine Arts from the University of Pennsylvania in 1955, and a law degree from the University of

Pennsylvania in 1958. In 1964, she joined the Defender Association of Philadelphia as the first woman lawyer to be hired on a full-time basis. Judge Temin's years at the Defender Association of Philadelphia were highlighted by positions of division chief, ultimately leading to her next position as chief counsel, and acting secretary to the Pennsylvania Board of Probation and Parole. In her position, she "was responsible for day-to-day supervision of all parole agents in Pennsylvania. Under Judge Temin's tenure, the Parole Rules were revised to make them more relevant and fair and the hearing procedures were revised to incorporate due process concepts which were not, at that time, required by law. Judge Temin also trained parole agents in new rules and procedures." In 1971, Judge Temin became an assistant district attorney in Philadelphia, where she held the position of senior trial assistant, assigned for consecutive periods to the Appeals Division, the Homicide Division, and Chief of Election Investigations.

In 1984, Judge Temin was elected as judge on the Philadelphia Court of Common Pleas. She was retained for a second ten-year term commencing in January 1994. In the year she was elected, the number of women judges on the Philadelphia Court of Common Pleas doubled from five to ten. From 1991 to 1994, Judge Temin served in the Homicide Division of the court, and was Homicide Calendar Judge from 1994 to 1998, giving her the added responsibility of scheduling the entire homicide docket. As Chief Criminal Calendar Judge for four and a half years, she was responsible also for the major felony docket. Currently, she sits as a judge in the Civil Trial Division, overseeing trials of complex major cases. Judge Temin has been appointed to several committees by the Pennsylvania Supreme Court and the Administrative Judge of the Trial Division of the Philadelphia Court of Common Pleas, and has throughout her career written and lectured extensively on issues of criminal justice. She is the principal author of the *Pennsylvania Benchbook for Criminal Proceedings,* first issued in 1986 and the official criminal benchbook of the Pennsylvania Conference of State Trial Judges.

Judge Temin is active in many professional associations and nonprofit associations of personal interest, including the National Conference of State Trial Judges (to which she is a delegate), the Pennsylvania Conference of State Trial Judges (elected its first woman president in 1992), the National Association of Women Judges, and the Philadelphia Dance Alliance, to name just a few. In 1993, she founded the Task Force to Insure Gender Fairness in the Courts and sat as its first chair. The task force's mission "was to conduct an investigation into the existence of gender bias in the courts and document its findings and recommendations in a report to be disseminated to the bench and the bar." For all this and more, Judge Temin has been duly recognized with numerous awards and honors. Justice Temin looks forward to serving as president of the National Association of Women Judges in 2004.

DIANE UNIMAN

Diane Uniman, a Phi Beta Kappa graduate of the University of Pennsylvania, also studied French at La University de Poitiers in La Rochelle, France. She went to Temple Law School for a year and transferred to Seton Hall University School of Law, where she earned her degree. She was admitted to the New Jersey and Pennsylvania bars in 1980. Diane won a national competition for her legal writing from the American Society of Composers, Authors, and Performers (ASCAP). She practiced law for many years at a major insurance company, and was an adjunct professor of business law at Mercer County Community College. Though from time to time she still does some appellate work, Diane decided to change her focus and has written a screenplay and a musical, both of which are currently in production, and has published articles and poetry in various journals. She recently won an award for her writing from the New Jersey Dramatist Society. Diane studied opera for many years, sang in the New Jersey State Opera Chorus, and currently sings for various fundraisers. She coproduced, wrote original songs for, and performed in The New Jersey Grand Opry, a children's country-western musical review. Diane also spends time cultivating an entrepreneurial health business. She is currently on the auxiliary board of the Robert Wood Johnson University Hospital and the Academy of Muse in Princeton, and is a member of the Israeli Task Force of the Greater Middlesex County Jewish Federation. She lives with her husband, a lawyer, and two sons in North Brunswick.

BARBARA VETRI
Temple University Class of 1960

Barbara is a glamorous woman, working in private practice in the city of Philadelphia. The third in line of four siblings, Barbara recalls wanting to be a lawyer from her childhood days. Still, she was never invited to join a study group with the men. While her children were young, she partnered with other women to balance her obligations. Barbara Vetri has gained the respect and admiration of her family, friends, peers, and clients in a long and fulfilling career in private practice.

BARBARA KRON ZIMMERMAN
University of Pennsylvania Law School Class of 1956

Barbara Kron Zimmerman met me for coffee at Starbucks® and brought with her the 1956 yearbook from the University of Pennsylvania Law School. We looked at pictures of her class, which included notables such as Dolores Korman, who would become Judge Dolores Sloviter of the Eastern District Court of Pennsylvania, and Peter Liacouras, future dean of Temple University School of Law. Of her class, Barbara was one of seven women graduates. The class before her, she notes, had no women. She is most proud of her yearbook because, as its editor, she recommended a tradition at the law school of having an annual yearbook. A picture of Barbara appears in a group of fel-low—mostly male—law students, under the caption of Wilson Law Club, another first for women. On a later page, a picture of the future Judge Norma Shapiro appears as a legal writing teacher; she is surrounded by men.

Barbara Kron Zimmerman has been a Philadelphian all her life, attending Girls High School at Broad and Olney Streets, where typing was definitely not in the curriculum for the students of this all-girl, academic, public high school. She graduated from all-women Bryn Mawr College (made famous by alumnae Katherine Hepburn) in 1953 and moved straight into law school at the University of Penn-sylvania. Upon graduating in 1956, Barbara was fortunate to find a position in the office of the general counsel for General Accident Insurance Company, under general counsel Harold Scott Baile. It was there that Barbara fulfilled her obligations of preceptorship and met her first mentor. Harold Baile hired her and supported her career by giving her opportunities inside and outside the office, in a display of public support. Barbara subsequently worked part-time in the Philadelphia law firm now known as Pepper, Hamilton and Scheetz, and then as research associate for University of Pennsylvania Dean Fordham. Called back from "retirement" by the dean after her first child was born, Barbara Kron Zimmerman helped create the Penn Law Alumni Directory. After a second child and second "retirement," Barbara worked at the American College in legal editing. Barbara claims to be fully and finally "retired" since 1980.

KATHLEEN D. WILKINSON

Kathleen D. Wilkinson is a Summa Cum Laude graduate of Kean University with a Bachelor of Arts degree in political science and sec-ondary education and was elected as a member of Phi Kappa Phi National Honor Society. She received her J.D. from Villanova Law School where she was a member of the Law Review and a semifinal-ist of the Reimel Moot Court Competition. She is President of the J. Willard O'Brien Inn of Court. In her practice as a partner at Wilson,

Elser, Moskowitz, Edelman & Dicker LLP in Philadelphia, PA, she handles complex cases in products, insurance, construction, premises, brokers and professional liability.

Active in women's and bar association activities, she serves as cochair of the Philadelphia Bar Association's State Civil Committee and Ruth Bader Ginsburg Legal Writing Competition. She was cochair of the Committee on Women in the Profession, working on such issues ranging from business development to family and career. She also was elected to and served on the Board of Governors for three years. She is a delegate to the House of Delegates of the Pennsylvania Bar Association and as a member of the Judicial Candidate Evaluation Committee. She is a cochair of the Pennsylvania Bar Association's Commission on Women in the Profession and has worked on model policies for parenting lawyers and the Quality of Life Task Force. She has authored numerous articles on legal matters as well as participating as a presenter in continuing legal education seminars. Somehow, she also finds time to devote to community activities and to raise her three children.

OTHERS OF EXCELLENCE

Others mentioned throughout this book, but not interviewed, include Justice Sandra Day O'Connor, Justice Ruth Bader Ginsburg, Geraldine Ferraro, and Dolores Sloviter. Two distinguished gentlemen gave me their time and thoughtful comments.

JEROME E. BOGUTZ

Jerry Bogutz, who has served as chancellor of the Philadelphia Bar Association and as president of the Pennsylvania Bar Association, graduated from the Pennsylvania State University and Villanova Law School. An author of articles for legal publications, he has served the profession in a multitude of ways almost too numerous to mention. He served as an adjunct clinical professor of law at Villanova Law School, served as president of the Pennsylvania Bar Foundation, chairman of the American Bar Association Commission on Advertising, chairman of the ABA, JAD Lawyers Conference, chairman of the Pennsylvania Bar Trust, and president of the Pennsylvania Futures Commission on Justice in the Twenty-First Century, all combined with a busy private practice over a period of over forty years.

Somehow he has also found time to serve as a member of the advisory board of the Pennsylvania Medical Professional Liability Catastrophe Loss fund and has served as executive counsel of the National Conference of Bar Presidents, a director of the Greater Philadelphia Chamber of Commerce, a director of Jefferson Park Hospital, and a director of the American Judicature Society. He also claims to be a pretty good golfer.

GERRY L. SPENCE

Gerry Spence, born and educated in the small towns of Wyoming where he has practiced law for nearly fifty years, has become one of the most widely recognized lawyers in the United States. He has spent a lifetime representing the poor, the injured, the forgotten, and, as he describes them, "the damned," against mammoth government and mammoth corporations. He has tried and won many nationally known cases, such as the Karen Silkwood case, the defense of Randy Weaver at Ruby Ridge, the defense of Imelda Marcos and the case against *Penthouse* magazine for Miss Wyoming. He has never lost a criminal case.

Gerry is the founder of Trial Lawyers College which has established a revolutionary method of training lawyers for the people, and believes that what he has learned needs to be shared with those who will continue to strive for justice on behalf of ordinary people. The author of twelve books, including the best-seller *How to Argue and Win Every Time,* he is a frequent guest on such television programs as *Larry King Live,* where he can be recognized by his signature fringed western jacket, his droll sense of humor, and his insightful and thoughtful comments about the most newsworthy legal cases of the day. In his spare time he is also a noted photographer and poet.

INTERVIEWS CONDUCTED THROUGH ONLINE SURVEY
SPONSORED BY PSYCHDATA ONLINE SERVICES

Amber Anderson. Fort Worth, Texas. 1997 graduate of University of Texas. Amber practices law in a small firm of five lawyers, where she specializes in personal injury trial law.

Nichole Berklas. Los Angeles, California. 2001 graduate of New York University. Nichole practices law in a medium-sized firm, where she specializes in real estate law.

Carolyn J. Beyer. Cedar Rapids, Iowa. 1977 graduate of Creighton University in Omaha, Nebraska. Carolyn writes, "I have my own law firm and I am affiliated with a larger law firm as of-counsel." Carolyn has a general practice—approximately 50 percent litigation, including personal injury and medical malpractice work, and 50 percent family law.

Theile M. Branham. Columbia, South Carolina. 2000 graduate of University of South Carolina. Theile practices law in a small firm (two lawyers), where she specializes in plaintiffs' litigation (medical malpractice, products liability, personal injury, construction law, and civil rights).

Kathryn Clarke. Portland, Oregon. 1979 graduate of Northwestern School of Law at Lewis and Clark College. Kathryn has a solo practice, where she works "primarily" on matters of appellate law and constitutional litigation.

Carolyn Delizia. Fort Myers, Florida. 1999 graduate of Tulane. Carolyn practices law in a midsize law firm (fifty lawyers), where she specializes in family law.

Susan DiMaria. Somerville, New Jersey. 1987 graduate of Brooklyn Law School. Susan practices law in a medium-sized suburban firm (eight partners, four associates, five of-counsel).

Wendy Girardin. Naples, Florida. 1993 graduate of Nova Southeastern University Law School in Fort Lauderdale. Wendy left the private practice of law to open her own firm as a licensed private investigator.

Mary Gordon. Salt Lake City, Utah. 1994 graduate of S.J. Quinney College of Law, University of Utah. Mary practices law in a small firm, where she specializes in commercial law, estate planning, and ERISA matters.

Gwen Hutcheson Griggs. Jacksonville, Florida. 1993 graduate of University of Florida. Gwen has a solo practice, where she concentrates in corporate and transactional law.

Betsey Herd. Tampa, Florida. 1994 graduate of University of Memphis. Betsey practices law in a medium-sized plaintiffs' firm, where she specializes in medical malpractice and personal injury matters.

Marilyn J. Hochman. Oviedo, Florida. 1985 graduate of Nova Southeastern University Law School in Fort Lauderdale. Marilyn has a general law practice in a small Florida firm.

Terri R. Z. Jacobs. Houston, Texas. 1992 graduate of Georgetown University Law Center. Terri practices law in a small, private practice firm, where she specializes in criminal defense and military law.

Patricia M. Joyce. East Greenwich, Rhode Island. 1983 graduate of New England School of Law in Boston.

Michele Lellouche. Jacksonville, Florida. 1991 graduate of Florida State University. Michele is employed in the field of employee benefits, working with a software company that writes retirement plans and makes the software to administer them.

Jennifer A. Lemire. Portsmouth, New Hampshire. 1995 graduate of Suffolk University Law School. Jennifer practices law in a small, seven-lawyer firm, where she is primarily engaged in general civil litigation, with a heavy concentration in family law.

Christina Lewis. Austin, Texas. 1983 graduate of University of Texas School of Law. Christina is a sole practitioner, specializing in the area of plaintiffs' personal injury litigation.

Mary Alice McLarty. Dallas, Texas. 1983 graduate of Texas Tech. Mary is a sole practitioner, specializing in the area of plaintiffs' personal injury litigation.

Alice K. Nelson. Gainesville, Florida. 1976 graduate of Stetson College of Law in St. Petersburg, Florida. Alice is the executive director of a not-for-profit public interest law firm of four lawyers, specializing in the fields of civil rights, disability rights, and special education.

Naomi Norwood. Los Angeles, California. 1981 graduate of UCLA. Naomi practices law in a small firm, where she specializes in the area of business litigation.

Amy Packer. Denver, Colorado. 2000 graduate of University of Denver College of Law. Amy practices law in a small firm (two lawyers and two support staff), where she specializes in personal injury litigation.

Karen Richardson. San Fernando, California. 1978 graduate of Mid-Valley College of Law. Karen is employed with the government in the area of criminal defense.

Lana Sayre. Omaha, Nebraska. 1998 graduate of University of Nebraska College of Law. Lana is a sole practitioner, working primarily in the fields of bankruptcy and divorce.

Christine McCarthy Smith. Manchester, New Hampshire. 2000 graduate of Massachusetts School of Law. Christine works in a firm of eight lawyers, where she is a medical malpractice trial lawyer.

Rebekah E. Swan. Los Angeles, California. 1996 graduate of Whittier Law School. Rebekah is currently practicing law in a small firm of five lawyers, where she specializes in matters of probate, trust, and conservatorship litigation.

Moi Vienneau. Hamilton, Ontario, Canada. 1992 graduate of University of Windsor in Ontario, Canada. Moi is a sole practitioner, specializing in personal injury and medical negligence litigation.

Caroline Vincent. Los Angeles, California. 1978 graduate of USC Law School. Caroline is a full-time mediator/arbitrator.

Lyle Griffin Warshauer. Atlanta, Georgia. 1993 graduate of Cumberland School of Law, Samford University. Lyle practices law in a small firm, where she specializes in personal injury and medical malpractice litigation.

Tammy C. Woolley. Birmingham, Alabama. 1997 graduate of Birmingham School of Law. Tammy works in a medium-sized firm, where she specializes in employment litigation.

Alexis. Los Angeles, California. 1999 graduate of Georgetown University Law Center. Alexis practices law in a large firm, where she specializes in trusts and estates.

Emily. Durham, North Carolina. 2001 graduate of University of North Carolina Law School. Emily practices law in a small firm, working in general matters including estates, real estate, traffic, and litigation.

Jayne. Jackson Hole, Wyoming. 1996 graduate of University of Washington School of Law. Jayne is a sole practitioner, specializing in plaintiffs' personal injury, land use, and commercial litigation.

Laurel. Tampa, Florida. 1999 graduate of University of Florida. Laurel is a judicial law clerk for a federal judge in Florida.

Nancy. Tallahassee, Florida. 1986 graduate of Stetson University College of Law. Nancy is a staff attorney for the trial judges in the Florida state courts.

Anonymous. Sacramento, California. 1996 graduate of University of the Pacific, McGeorge School of Law. Products liability practice in a midsize firm.

Anonymous. Los Angeles, California. 1975 graduate of Saint Louis University School of Law. Nonprofit management and reporting.

Anonymous. Pensacola, Florida. 2001 graduate of Florida State University.

Anonymous. Naples, Florida. 1986 graduate of Western New England. Criminal prosecution/government.

Anonymous. Gary, Indiana. 1978 graduate of Valparaiso School of Law. Personal injury and family law in a small, private firm.

Anonymous. Concord, New Hampshire. 1994 graduate of Boston College. Tax and estate planning in a small law firm.

Anonymous. Columbus, Ohio. 1989 graduate of Stetson University College of Law. Business transactions and estate planning in a small firm.

Anonymous. Billings, Montana. 1986 law school graduate. Family and administrative fields, and government.

Anonymous. Gadsden, Alabama. 2000 graduate of University of Alabama. General litigation in a small firm.

Anonymous. Long Island City, New York. 1996 graduate of Benjamin N. Cardozo Law School. Personal injury litigation in a small firm.

Anonymous. Lafayette & Delphi, Indiana. 1997 graduate of Indiana University in Bloomington. General litigation in a two-partner law firm.

Anonymous. Santa Monica, California. 1989 graduate of Georgetown University Law Center. Employment and business litigation in a firm of one hundred lawyers.

Anonymous. Los Angeles, California. 1985 graduate of Hastings College of Law. Defense lawyer for medical device and pharmaceutical companies, practicing in a large firm.

Anonymous. St. Petersburg, Florida. 1990 graduate of Florida State University. Solo civil trial lawyer, in plaintiffs' first-party property and casualty insurance law.

Anonymous. Sugar Land, Texas. 1983 graduate of University of Texas School of Law. Personal injury litigator in a small firm.

Anonymous. Great Falls, Montana. 1981 graduate of University of Montana. Personal injury litigator in partnership with her husband.

Anonymous. Chicago, Illinois. 1980 graduate of Northwestern University Law School. Accident and injury litigation in solo practice.

Anonymous. Santa Monica, California. 1998 law school graduate. Currently working in a small firm of eight to ten lawyers.

Anonymous. Baltimore, Maryland. 1995 graduate of University of Maryland. Currently employed at a law school in academic administration, after eight years practicing business and intellectual property law.

Anonymous. Los Angeles, California. 1993 graduate of Southwestern University School of Law. Sole practitioner in family law.

Anonymous. Manchester, New Hampshire. 2000 graduate of Wake Forest University. Estate planning, tax, business, and probate in a small firm.

ENDNOTES

1. A pseudonym.
2. Retired chancellor of Temple University, Peter J. Liacouras was a graduate of the 1956 class of the law school of the University of Pennsylvania, along with Barbara Kron Zimmerman and Judge Dolores Sloviter. Peter J. Liacouras was Temple University School of Law Dean from 1972 to 1982.
3. Temple Law Profiles (2002), *available at* http://www2.law.temple.edu.
4. *The Beginning 1802–1852*, 64 PHILA. LAW dt. 59 (2002).
5. *Id.* at 60.
6. Edward Power, *In Labor's Corner, a Legal Eagle*, PHILA. INQUIRER, Aug. 3, 1988, at 4-B.
7. *Id.*
8. Mission Statement of the Pennsylvania Bar Association: "To enhance the science of jurisprudence; to promote the administration of justice; to see that no one, on account of poverty, is denied his or her legal right; to secure proper legislation; to encourage thorough legal education; to uphold the honor and dignity of the Bar; to cultivate cordial relations among the lawyers of Pennsylvania; and to perpetuate the history of the profession and the memory of its members."

9. Pennsylvania Bar Association's Public and General Information Section, *available at* www.pabar.org/.

10. Gwen Shaffer, *Tough Love, Part 2*, Philadelphia Citypaper.net (May 10–17, 2001), *available at* http://citypaper.net/articles/051001/cs.cover.lynne2.shtml (downloaded on July 8, 2002).

11. *An Interview with Judge Normal L. Shapiro* (September 1996), *available at* http://www.uscourts.gov/ttb/septtb96/shapiro.htm (downloaded on July 30, 2002).

About the Author

Phyllis Horn Epstein is a graduate of Temple University School of Law and also received her LLM in Taxation from Temple University at night while teaching contract law at La Salle College in the morning and practicing law in a small firm in the afternoon. She is now a partner in Epstein, Shapiro & Epstein, practicing taxation, corporate transactions, family law, and whatever else needs to be done. Phyllis has been a lecturer for continuing legal education panels on issues of taxation. She has been an author of articles for tax-related periodicals and a contributing author to the Tax Litigation chapters of a series published by CCH Federal Tax Service. Phyllis has been an active participant with the Tax Section of the American Bar Association, and at one time served as the editor of the section newsletter. In her spare time she writes books. Phyllis is married to her law partner, J. Earl Epstein, and is the mother of a thirteen-year-old son, Charles.

Bibliography

Books

Chesler, Phyllis. *Women and Madness*. Garden City: Doubleday & Company, Inc., 1972.

Drachman, Virginia. *Sisters in Law: Women Lawyers in Modern American History*. Cambridge, Massachusetts: Harvard University Press, 1998.

Evans, Susan B., and Joan P. Avis. *The Women Who Broke All the Rules: How the Choices of a Generation Changed Our Lives*. Naperville: Sourcebooks, 1999.

Ferraro, Geraldine A. *Ferraro, My Story*. New York: Bantam Books, 1985.

——. *Framing a Life*. New York: Scribner, 1998.

Greer, Germaine. *The Female Eunuch*. New York: McGraw-Hill Book Company, 1970.

Gurko, Miriam. *The Ladies of Seneca Falls, The Birth of the Women's Rights Movement*. New York: MacMillan Publishing Co., Inc., 1974.

Hellerstein, Erna Olafson, Leslie Parker Hume, and Karen M. Offen, eds. *Victorian Women*. Stanford: Stanford University Press, 1981.

Hepperle, Winifred L., and Laura Crites, eds. *Women in the Courts*. Williamsburg, Virginia: National Center for State Courts, 1978.

Hewlett, Sylvia Ann. *Creating a Life, Professional Women and the Quest for Children*. New York: Talk Miramax Books, 2002.

Jong, Erica. *How to Save Your Own Life*. New York: Signet Book, New American Library, 1977.

Kanowitz, Leo. *Women and the Law, The Unfinished Revolution*. Albuquerque: University of New Mexico Press, 1969.

McNamee, Gwen Hoerr, ed. *Bar None, 125 Years of Women Lawyers in Illinois.* Chicago: Chicago Bar Association Alliance for Women, 1998.

Morello, Karen Berger. *The Invisible Bar, The Woman Lawyer in America: 1638 to the Present.* New York: Random House, 1986.

Nash, Gary B. *First City, Philadelphia and the Forging of Historical Memory.* Philadelphia: University of Pennsylvania Press, 2002.

O'Connor, Justice Sandra Day. *The Majesty of the Law.* New York: Random House, 2003.

Roomberg, Lila G. *Turning Adversaries into Allies in the Workplace.* New York: Vantage Press, Inc., 1999.

Shakespeare, William F. *Hamlet.* Baltimore: Penguin Books, 1969.

Shapiro, Norma. "Bench with a Point of View: How to Create Confidence in the Courtroom." In *The Woman Advocate,* ed. Jean Maclean Snyder and Andra Barmash Green. Chicago: American Bar Association, 1996.

Snyder, Jean Maclean, and Andra Barmash Greene, eds. *The Woman Advocate.* Chicago: American Bar Association, 1996.

Vrato, Elizabeth. *The Counselors.* Philadelphia: Running Press, 2002.

Ward, Geoffrey C., and Ken Burns. *Not for Ourselves Alone; The Story of Elizabeth Cady Stanton and Susan B. Anthony.* New York: Alfred Knopf, 1999.

Williams, Joan. *Unbending Gender: Why Family and Work Conflict and What to Do About It.* New York: Oxford University Press, 2000.

Wymard, Ellie. *Conversations with Uncommon Women.* New York: Amacom, 1999.

Law Review Articles

Abreu, Alice G. "Lessons from LatCrit: Insiders and Outsiders, All at the Same Time." *University of Miami Law Review* 53, no. 4 (1999): 787.

Angel, Marina. "Women in Legal Education: What It's Like to Be Part of a Perpetual First Wave or the Case of the Disappearing Women." *Temple Law Review* 61 (1988): 799.

——. "The Glass Ceiling for Women in Legal Education: Contract Positions and the Death of Tenure." *Journal of Legal Education* 50, no. 1 (2000): 1.

——. "Comments in Reply: It's Becoming a Glass House." *Journal of Legal Education* 50, no. 3 (2000): 454.

Babcock, Barbara Allen. "A Real Revolution." *University of Kansas Law Review* 49, no. 4 (2001): 719.

Baker, Joe G., and Brian K Jorgensen. "Leaving the Law: Occupational and Career Mobility of Law School Graduates." *Journal of Legal Education* 50, no. 1 (2000): 16.

Blum, Vanessa. "An Inside Look at DOJ Lawyer Diversity." *Legal Times* (October 28, 2003).

Crimm, Nina J. "A Study: Law School Students' Moral Perspectives in the Context of Advocacy and Decision-Making Roles." *New England Law Review* 29 (1994): 1.

Ginsburg, Justice Ruth Bader. "Remarks on Women's Progress in the Legal Profession in the United States." *University of Tulsa Law Journal* 33, no. 1 (1999): 13.

——. "In Commemoration—The 75th Anniversary of Women at Columbia Law School." *Columbia Law Review* 102, no. 6 (2002): 1441.

Janoff, Sandra. "The Influence of Legal Education on Moral Reasoning." *Minnesota Law Review* 76 (1991): 193.

Morrison, Torrey, Jennifer Ries, and Elaine Spiliopoulos. "What Every First-Year Female Law Student Should Know." *Columbia Journal of Gender and Law* 7 (1998): 267.

Podgor, Ellen S. "Lawyer Professionalism in a Gendered Society." *South Carolina Law Review* 47 (1996): 323.

Slotkin, Jacquelyn H. "You Really Have Come a Long Way: An Analysis and Comparison of Role Conflict Experienced by Women Attorneys Today and by Educated Women Twenty Years Ago." *Women's Rights Law Reporter* 18 (1996): 17.

Subotnik, Dan. "Seeing through 'The Glass Ceiling': A Response to Professor Angel." *Journal of Legal Education* 50, no. 3 (2000): 450.

Magazine Articles

Blodgett, Nancy. "I Don't Think That Ladies Should Be Lawyers." *ABA Journal*, December 1, 1986, 48.

Fisk, Margaret Cronin. "A Two-Decade Rise to the Top." *National Law Journal*, December 21, 2001, at http://www.law.com.

Graham, Deborah. "It's Getting Better, Slowly." *ABA Journal*, December 1, 1986, 54.

Lewis, Jone Johnson. "A Soul as Free as the Air: Profile of Lucy Stone." *Women's History Guide* (June 28, 1999; updated March 16, 2000), at http://womenshistory.about.com/library/weekly/aa062899.htm.

Lyons, Jeff. "The Case for Flex-, Part-Time Attorneys." *Philadelphia Bar Reporter* 31, no. 8 (2002): 5.

Nigro, Robert. "Guideposts for New Generations." *Philadelphia Lawyer* 61, no. 4 (1998): 68.

Rottenberg, Dan. "One Shining Moment: Why Philadelphia Lawyers Are Different." *Philadelphia Lawyer* 64, no. 4 (2002): 118.

Simmons, Robert J. "Love Notes from a Spouse: The First Working Mother to Lead the Nation's Oldest Organized Bar Finds Her Balance 'Backwards and in High Heels.' " *Philadelphia Lawyer* (2000), online reporter, at www.philabar.org/member/pubs/phl_lawyer/notes.asp.

St. John, Gerard J. "This Is Our Bar!" *Philadelphia Lawyer* 64, no. 4 (2002): 52.

Talley, Audrey C. "Walking with Destiny, Women Lawyers in Philadelphia." *Philadelphia Lawyer* 64, no. 4 (2002): 72.

News Articles

Alvarez, Lizette. "Iranian Lawyer, Staunch Fighter for Human Rights Wins Nobel." *New York Times*, October 11, 2003, at A-1.

Bellafante, Ginia. "Sic Transit Ally: A '90s Feminist Is Bowing Out." *New York Times*, April 21, 2002, Sunday edition, sec. 9, at 1.

Fenner, Randee G. "Letter to the Editor." *New York Times*, April 26, 2002.

Gan, Carole F., Contact. "New from UC Davis Health System." March 21, 2003, at http://news.ucdmc.usdavis.edu/news/medicalnews/women lawyers.html.

Glater, Jonathan D. "Women Are Close to Being Majority of Law Students." *New York Times*, March 26, 2001, at A-1.

Ross, Emma. "Biological Clocks Start Ticking in Late 20s—Study." London Reuters, downloaded from AOL on May 2, 2002.

———. "Study Examines Human Fertility." London AP, downloaded from AOL on May 2, 2002.

Sciolino, Elaine. "A Prize, Laureate Says, 'Good for Democracy.' " *New York Times*, October 11, 2003, at A-6.

Sepos, Melissa. "Survey: Philadelphia Lawyers Fewer in Number." *Philadelphia Business Journal*, October 6, 2000.

Shellenbarger, Sue. "Perils of Part-Time: Flexible Work Hours Aren't Nearly as Heavenly as They Sound," *Wall Street Journal*, June 27, 2002, at D1.

Tierney, John. "Take Our Wives to Work." *New York Times*, April 30, 2002, at B-1.

"Tough Love Part 2." Philadelphia *Citypaper*, May 10–17, 2001, at http://citypaper.net/articles/051001/cs.cover.lynne2.shtml.

Surveys

ABA Commission on Women in the Profession, "A Current Glance of Women in the Law." 2002.

ABA Commission on Women in the Profession, and Deborah L. Rhode. "Balanced Lives, Changing the Culture of Legal Practice." 2001.

ABA Commission on Women in the Profession, and Deborah L. Rhode. "The Unfinished Agenda, Women and the Legal Profession." 2001.

ABA Division for Media Relations and Public Affairs. "Facts about Women and the Law." 1998.

Angel, Maria. "Our Faculty: Gender and Race." August 26, 2003.

Association of American Law Schools, and Richard A. White. "Statistical Report on Law School Faculty and Candidates for Law Faculty Positions 2000–2001." (Available at http://www.aals.org/statistics/index.html.)

Catalyst. "Women in the Law: Making the Case, Executive Summary." 2001.

Erdos & Morgan. "Philadelphia Bar Association Survey." June 2000.

Northwest Research Group, Inc., for the Glass Ceiling Task Force. "2001 Self-Audit for Gender and Racial Equity; A Survey of Washington Law Firms." 2001.

Pennsylvania Bar Association, Women in the Profession. "Ninth Annual Report Card." 2003.

Philadelphia Bar Association Board of Governors. "2000 Survey of the Profession." June 29, 2000. (Presented by Samuel H. Becker, Chair, Bar-wide Survey Committee.)

State Bar of Wisconsin. "The Economics of Law Practice in Wisconsin: 2001 Survey Reports." *Wisconsin Law Review* 74, no. 6 (2001).

U.S. Census Bureau, U.S. Department of Commerce. "Census Facts for Women's History Month." February 28, 1997. (From LaVerne Vines Collins, Chief, Public Information Office. Available at http://www. census.gov/Press-Release/fs97-02.html.)

U.S. Department of Labor, Bureau of Labor Statistics. "Occupational Outlook Handbook; Lawyers." 2004-05 edition. (Available at http://www. bls.gov./oco/ocos053.htm.)

Cases

Andrews v. City of Philadelphia, 895 F.2d 1469 (3d Cir. 1990).

Bradwell v. Illinois, 83 U.S. 130 (1873).

Burke v. Friedman, 556 F.2d 867 (7th Cir. 1977).

Delaski v. Merrill Lynch, Pierce, Fenner & Smith, Inc., 65 Fed. Appx. 368 (3d Cir. 2002).

Dubowsksi v. Stern, Lavinthal, Norgaard & Daly, 922 F. Supp. 985 (D.N.J. 1996).

EEOC v. Dowd & Dowd, Ltd., 736 F.2d 1177 (7th Cir. 1984).

Ezold v. Wolf, Block, Schorr & Solis-Cohen, 983 F.2d 509 (3d Cir. 1993).

Hishon v. King & Spalding, 467 U.S. 69 (1984).

In re Goodell, 292 Wis. 232 (1875).

In re Kilgore, 18 Am. L. Rev. 478 (1884).

In re Lockwood, Supreme Court of Virginia, October Term 1893.

In re Motion to Admit Miss Lavinia Goodell to Bar, 292 Wis. 232 (1875).

In re Petition of Leach, 34 N.E. 641 (Ind. 1893).

Lilly v. Roadway Express, 6 Fed. Appx. 358 (7th Cir. 2001).

Meritor Savings Bank v. Vinson, et al., 477 U.S. 57 (1986).

People ex rel. Rago v. Lipsky, 63 N.E.2d 642 (Ill. App. Ct. 1945)

Reed v. Reed, 404 U.S. 71 (1971).

Richette v. Ajello, 72 Pa. D. & C.2d 22 (Philadelphia Court of Common Pleas 1974).

Royster Guano Co. v. Virginia, 253 U.S. 412 (1920).

State of Ohio ex rel. Joseph Cyrill KRUPA v. Green, 177 N.E.2d 616 (Court of Appeals of Ohio, Eighth District, Cuyahoga County 1961).

United States Supreme Court in United States v. Virginia, 518 U.S. 515, 543 116 S. Ct. 2264, 2281 (1996).

White v. Crook, 251 F. Supp. 401 (M.D. Ala. 1966).

Statutes and Regulations

Equal Pay Act; 29 U.S.C. § 206(d)(1) (1963).

Fair Labor Standards Act of 1938, as amended; 29 U.S.C. § 206 *et seq.* (1963).

Family Medical Leave Act, 29 U.S.C. § 2601 *et seq.* (1993).

Pregnancy Discrimination Act of 1978, 42 U.S.C. § 2000e(k) (1978).

Title VII of the Civil Rights Act of 1964, as amended; 42 U.S.C. §§ 2000e *et seq.* (1964); 42 U.S.C. § 1981(a) (1977).

29 C.F.R. § 1620.13 (1999).

Interviews

Celebrating More Than a Century of Women Lawyers in Philadelphia 1883–1997, Philadelphia Bar Association.

Oral Legal History Project; transcript of an interview with Judge Dolores Sloviter, April 2, 1999, University of Pennsylvania, downloaded June 13, 2002, from http://www.law.upenn.edu.

I personally interviewed a number of women lawyers for this book by various means. Some chose to remain completely anonymous to me or revealed only their first names. Some requested that I use pseudonyms. The women of my law school class, the graduates of Temple University School of Law (now the Beasley School of Law), answered a questionnaire and, on occasion, followed up with more detailed responses by telephone or e-mail. Over the past two years, I was privileged to interview in person or by telephone a number of distinguished women from my area or from my field of practice, tax law. Some responded to my inquiries by handwritten letter. Over the course of the last year, I conducted an online computer survey of women lawyers through the services of Psychdata Online, to gather the experiences of women beyond my community. Responses came from a number of states, as well as

Canada. Some women hailed from big cities, others from small Midwest towns. Their profiles ranged widely in age, experience, and legal field.

Miscellaneous

AFL-CIO, The Pay Gap by Occupation (2004), at http://www.aflcio.org/yourjobeconomy/women/equalpay/ThePayGapByOccupation.cfm.

American Bar Association News Release, March 2002.

Congressional Research Service, The Library of Congress, Salaries of Federal Officials: A Fact Sheet, prepared by Sharon S. Gressle, January 24, 2004, at http://www.senate.gov/reference/resources/pdf/98-53.pdf.

Encarta® World English Dictionary (North American Edition, © 2004), Microsoft Corporation. All rights reserved. Developed for Microsoft by Bloomsbury Publishing plc.

Girl Scouts of Greater Philadelphia, March 12, 1990.

http://www.akingump.com.

http://www.ballardspahr.com.

New York Lawyers, Chart: Equity Partner Compensation at Highest 25 NY Firms, January 27, 2003, at http://www.nylawyer.com/news/03/01/012703c.html.

NOW Statement of Purpose

Seneca Falls Declaration on Women's Rights

Susan B. Anthony, The Solitude of Self

Women and Attorneys of Color, 2003 Summary Chart (2003).

Index

Selected Books from . . .
THE ABA LAW PRACTICE MANAGEMENT SECTION

Women Rainmakers' Best Marketing Tips, Second Edition
By Theda C. Snyder
If you're looking for an action-oriented and realistic approach to rainmaking that will enhance your professional and personal life, then this book should be number one on your reading list! The book contains well over a hundred tips you can put to use right away. These are ideas that have worked for other successful rainmakers and can work for you. Learn creative marketing techniques that will build your client base. Discover new action plans that fit your personal style and strengthen your rainmaking skills. The book includes sample press releases and a wealth of newly revised and accessible information that is easy to implement.

The Lawyer's Guide to Marketing Your Practice, Second Edition
Edited by James A. Durham and Deborah McMurray
This book is packed with practical ideas, innovative strategies, useful checklists, and sample marketing and action plans to help you implement a successful, multi-faceted, and profit-enhancing marketing plan for your firm. Organized into four sections, this illuminating resource covers: Developing Your Approach; Enhancing Your Image; Implementing Marketing Strategies and Maintaining Your Program. Appendix materials include an instructive primer on market research to inform you on research methodologies that support the marketing of legal services. The accompanying CD-ROM contains a wealth of checklists, plans, and other sample reports, questionnaires, and templates - all designed to make implementing your marketing strategy as easy as possible!

The Lawyer's Guide to Marketing on the Internet, Second Edition
By Gregory Siskind, Deborah McMurray, and Richard P. Klau
The Internet is a critical component of every law firm marketing strategy – no matter where you are, how large your firm is, or the areas in which you practice. Used effectively, a younger, smaller firm can present an image just as sophisticated and impressive as a larger and more established firm. You can reach potential new clients, in remote areas, at any time, for minimal cost. To help you maximize your Internet marketing capabilities, this book provides you with countless Internet marketing possibilities and shows you how to effectively and efficiently market your law practice on the Internet.

The Lawyer's Guide to Palm Powered™ Handhelds
By Margaret Spencer Dixon
The Palm-powered handheld is now an essential part of everyday life for an increasing number of lawyers. Whether you are a beginner, an advanced user, or simply deciding whether a Palm® PDA is right for you, this book will show you how a Palm Powered™ handheld can make you more efficient and effective at what you do. Written by a lawyer for lawyers, this guidebook provides helpful tips and tricks for getting the most out of Palm applications. Learn to take full advantage of your Palm Powered™ handheld to manage addresses, appointments, expenses, and time; write memos; take notes; check e-mail; read books and documents; and much more. In addition, you'll find a wealth of suggested Web sites and handy tips from top legal power users. If you're a lawyer searching for a book to get you up and running on the Palm platform and become a Palm power-user, look no further!

How to Start and Build a Law Practice, Platinum Fifth Edition
By Jay G Foonberg
This classic ABA Bestseller—now completely updated—is the primary resource for starting your own firm. This acclaimed book covers all aspects of getting started, including finding clients, determining the right location, setting fees, buying office equipment, maintaining an ethical and responsible practice, maximizing available resources, upholding your standards, and marketing your practice, just to name a few. In addition, you'll find a business plan template, forms, checklists, sample letters, and much more. A must for any lawyer just starting out—or growing a law practice.

Making Partner: A Guide for Law Firm Associates, Second Edition
By John R. Sapp
Many factors come into play in achieving the goal of making partner: the quality of your work; how you relate to your superiors, fellow associates, and staff; how you entertain your clients; your choice of outside activities; even publications you read. Do you know what you should and should not be doing? Do you really know what your chances are at your firm? This concise, straightforward book looks at all these factors and provides detailed advice on how to create your own strategic plan for success.

Flying Solo: A Survival Guide for the Solo Lawyer, Third Edition
Edited by Jeffrey R. Simmons

More and more lawyers, both new and seasoned, are opting to start their own practice. This book will give solos—as well as small firms—all the information needed to build a successful practice. This book is a must-have reference for the solo or small firm in any area of law practice. This comprehensive guide contains 55 chapters that tell you how to make the decision to go solo, determine the best kind of practice, handle money issues, choose a location for your office, work with other professionals, organize and run your business, manage billing and cash flow, choose computers and equipment, and much more. Cutting-edge issues such as Web ethics, telecommuting, and the best technology for a solo or small office are also covered.

The Lawyer's Guide to Fact Finding on the Internet, Second Edition
By Carole A. Levitt and Mark E. Rosch

Written especially for legal professionals, this revised and expanded edition is a complete, hands-on guide to the best sites, secrets, and shortcuts for conducting efficient research on the Web. Containing over 600 pages of information, with over 100 screen shots of specific Web sites, this resource is filled with practical tips and advice on using specific sites, alerting readers to quirks or hard-to-find information. What's more, user-friendly icons immediately identify free sites, free-with-registration sites, and pay sites. An accompanying CD-ROM includes the links contained in the book, indexed, so you can easily navigate to these cream-of-the-crop Web sites without typing URLs into your browser. Also, subscribe to *The Lawyer's Guide to Internet Fact Finding E-Newsletter* to stay current on the most valuable Web sites each month!

Collecting Your Fee: Getting Paid From Intake to Invoice
By Edward Poll

This practical and user-friendly guide provides you with proven strategies and sound advice that will make the process of collecting your fees simpler, easier, and more effective! This handy resource provides you with the framework around which to structure your collection efforts. You'll learn how you can streamline your billing and collection process by hiring the appropriate staff, establishing strong client relationships from the start, and issuing client-friendly invoices. In addition, you'll benefit from the strategies to use when the client fails to pay the bill on time and what you need to do to get paid when all else fails. Also included is a CD-ROM with sample forms, letters, agreements, and more for you to customize to your own practice needs.

Through the Client's Eyes: New Approaches to Get Clients to Hire You Again and Again, Second Edition
By Henry W. Ewalt

This edition covers every aspect of the lawyer-client relationship, giving sound advice and fresh ideas on how to develop and maintain excellent client relationships. Author and seasoned practitioner Henry Ewalt shares tips on building relationships and trust, uncovering some unlikely ways to make connections in addition to traditional methods. Marketing techniques, including brochures, newsletters, client dinners, and sporting events are discussed. Other topics that are covered include client intake, client meetings, follow-up, dissemination of news, fee setting and collection, and other client issues. Completely revised and updated, including information on using e-mail communications and more.

Effective Yellow Pages Advertising for Lawyers: The Complete Guide to Creating Winning Ads
By Kerry Randall

Yellow Pages advertising is very competitive, highly regulated, and sometimes complicated. Many lawyers advertise in the same arena for the same business. A poorly designed ad can spell disaster for a solo or small practice, but an effective ad can be the engine that drives your client development programs forward. This book will guide you through the process of:

- dentifying your unique place in the market
- Defining and then targeting an audience that will be influenced by your message
- Creating content that produces results
- Instilling confidence in your potential client that you are the best possible choice to call

Effective Yellow Pages Advertising for Lawyers: The Complete Guide to Creating Winning Ads is written to enable you to attract new business to your practice by creating advertising that gets attention, holds attention, and most importantly, gets potential clients to call.

The Lawyer's Guide to Balancing Life and Work: Taking the Stress Out of Success
By George W. Kaufman

Beautifully written with warmth and seasoned wisdom, The *Lawyer's Guide to Balancing Life and Work* is designed to help you achieve professional and personal satisfaction in your career. Inside, you'll find philosophical approaches, practical examples, and valuable exercises to help you reconcile your goals and expectations with the realities and demands of the legal profession.

30-Day Risk-Free Order Form
Call Today! 1-800-285-2221
Monday–Friday, 7:30 AM – 5:30 PM, Central Time

Qty	Title	LPM Price	Regular Price	Total
_____	Women Rainmakers Best Marketing Tips, Second Edition (5110492)	24.95	27.95	$_____
_____	The Lawyer's Guide to Marketing Your Practice, Second Edition (5110500)	79.95	89.95	$_____
_____	The Lawyer's Guide to Marketing on the Internet, Second Edition (5110484)	69.95	79.95	$_____
_____	The Lawyer's Guide to Palm Powered™ Handhelds (5110505)	54.95	64.95	$_____
_____	How to Start and Build a Law Practice, Platinum Fifth Edition (5110508)	57.95	69.95	$_____
_____	Making Partner: A Guide for Law Firm Associates, Second Edition (5110482)	39.95	49.95	$_____
_____	Flying Solo, Third Edition (5110463)	79.95	89.95	$_____
_____	The Lawyer's Guide to Fact Finding on the Internet, Second Edition (5110497)	69.95	79.95	$_____
_____	The Lawyer's Guide to Fact Finding on the Internet E-mail Newsletter (5110498)	37.95	44.95	$_____
_____	Collecting Your Fee (5110490)	69.95	79.95	$_____
_____	Through the Client's Eyes, Second Edition (5110480)	69.95	79.95	$_____
_____	Effective Yellow Pages Advertising (511-0478)	44.95	54.95	$_____
_____	The Lawyer's Guide to Balancing Life and Work (5110367)	$24.95	$29.95	$_____

*Postage and Handling	
$10.00 to $24.99	$5.95
$25.00 to $49.99	$9.95
$50.00 to $99.99	$12.95
$100.00 to $349.99	$17.95
$350 to $499.99	$24.95

**Tax
DC residents add 5.75%
IL residents add 8.75%
MD residents add 5%

*Postage and Handling $_____
**Tax $_____
TOTAL $_____

PAYMENT
❑ Check enclosed (to the ABA)
❑ Visa   ❑ MasterCard   ❑ American Express

_____
Account Number   Exp. Date   Signature

Name _____ Firm _____
Address _____
City _____ State _____ Zip _____
Phone Number _____ E-Mail Address _____

Note: E-Mail address is required if ordering the
The Lawyer's Guide to Fact Finding on the Internet
E-mail Newsletter (5110498)

Guarantee
If—for any reason—you are not satisfied with your purchase, you may
return it within 30 days of receipt for a complete refund of the price of the
book(s). No questions asked!

Mail: ABA Publication Orders, P.O. Box 10892, Chicago, Illinois 60610-0892
♦ Phone: 1-800-285-2221 ♦ FAX: 312-988-5568

E-Mail: abasvcctr@abanet.org ♦ Internet: http://www.lawpractice.org/catalog

CUSTOMER COMMENT FORM

Title of Book:_____

We've tried to make this publication as useful, accurate, and readable as possible. Please take 5 minutes to tell us if we succeeded. Your comments and suggestions will help us improve our publications. Thank you!

1. How did you acquire this publication:

☐ by mail order   ☐ at a meeting/convention   ☐ as a gift

☐ by phone order   ☐ at a bookstore   ☐ don't know

☐ other: (describe) _____

Please rate this publication as follows:

	Excellent	Good	Fair	Poor	Not Applicable
Readability: Was the book easy to read and understand?	☐	☐	☐	☐	☐
Examples/Cases: Were they helpful, practical? Were there enough?	☐	☐	☐	☐	☐
Content: Did the book meet your expectations? Did it cover the subject adequately?	☐	☐	☐	☐	☐
Organization and clarity: Was the sequence of text logical? Was it easy to find what you wanted to know?	☐	☐	☐	☐	☐
Illustrations/forms/checklists: Were they clear and useful? Were there enough?	☐	☐	☐	☐	☐
Physical attractiveness: What did you think of the appearance of the publication (typesetting, printing, etc.)?	☐	☐	☐	☐	☐

Would you recommend this book to another attorney/administrator? ☐ Yes ☐ No

How could this publication be improved? What else would you like to see in it?

_____

_____

_____

Do you have other comments or suggestions? _____

_____

_____

Name _____

Firm/Company _____

Address _____

City/State/Zip _____

Phone _____

Firm Size: _____ Area of specialization: _____

We appreciate your time and help.

LawPracticeManagementSection
MARKETING • MANAGEMENT • TECHNOLOGY • FINANCE

JOIN the ABA Law Practice Management Section (LPM) and receive significant discounts on future LPM book purchases! You'll also get direct access to marketing, management, technology, and finance tools that help lawyers and other professionals meet the demands of today's challenging legal environment.

Exclusive Membership Benefits Include:

Law Practice Magazine
Eight annual issues of our award-winning *Law Practice* magazine, full of insightful articles and practical tips on Marketing/Client Development, Practice Management, Legal Technology, and Finance.

ABA TECHSHOW®
Receive a $100 discount on ABA TECHSHOW, the world's largest legal technology conference!

LPM Book Discount
LPM has over eighty titles in print! Books topics cover the four core areas of law practice management – marketing, management, technology, and finance – as well as legal career issues.

Law Practice Today
LPM's unique web-based magazine in which the features change weekly! Law Practice Today covers all the hot topics in law practice management *today* – current issues, current challenges, current solutions.

Discounted CLE & Other Educational Opportunities
The Law Practice Management Section sponsors more than 100 educational sessions annually. LPM also offers other live programs, teleconferences and web cast seminars.

LawPractice.news
This monthly eUpdate brings information on Section news and activities, educational opportunities, and details on book releases and special offers.

Complete the membership application below.

Applicable Dues:
$40 for ABA members   o$5 for ABA Law Student Division members

(ABA Membership is a prerequisite to membership in the Section. To join the ABA, call the Service Center at 1-800-285-2221.)

Method of Payment:
Bill me   Charge to my: oVisa   oMasterCard   oAmerican Express
Card number _____ Exp. Date _____
Signature _____ Date _____

Applicant's Information (please print):
Name _____ ABA I.D. number _____
Firm/Organization _____
Address _____ City/State/Zip _____
Telephone _____ FAX _____ Email _____

Fax your application to 312-988-5528 or join by phone: 1-800-285-2221, TDD 312-988-5168
Join online at www.lawpractice.org.

I understand that my membership dues include $16 for a basic subscription to *Law Practice Management* magazine. This subscription charge is not deductible from the dues and additional subscriptions are not available at this rate. Membership dues in the American Bar Association and its Sections are not deductible as charitable contributions for income tax purposes but may be deductible as a business expense.

Women Lawyers—Find the Perfect Balance

Are you trying to "live a life" in addition to being a lawyer? Managing your career, money, family, business, time . . . and everything in between can be a daunting task! The ABA Law Practice Management Section (LPM) has resources to help women achieve balance in their own busy lives and the practice of law, including its groundbreaking group, the ABA Women Rainmakers. We understand the unique challenges and opportunities women face in the legal profession.

<u>Who We Are</u>
ABA Women Rainmakers is a national forum enabling women to network and develop business opportunities. By understanding how to develop business, women can exert greater control over their careers and integrate their personal lives successfully with the practice of law. The ABA Law Practice Management Section provides the programs, publications, and resources you need to succeed in the *business* of practicing law—including marketing, management, technology, finance, and more!

<u>Resources</u>
Books such as *Women in Law*, *The Lawyer's Guide to Balancing Life and Work*, and *Women Rainmakers' Best Marketing Tips*, 2nd Edition. Programs such as Optimizing Your Career Potential, Mission Accomplished: Scaling Your Personal Everest, Jill be Nimble: Reinventing Your Practice, and Multi-Focus Marketing: Understanding Your Audience.

Join LPM and the ABA Women Rainmakers today and start taking advantage of these valuable member benefits:

• Networking Events
• Education Programs
• Publication
• List Serve Discussion List
• Speaking and Publishing Opportunities

Take a step towards achieving a better balance in your life and join*
both LPM and the ABA Women Rainmakers *today* for only $40
(https://www.abanet.org/lpm/membership/wjoin2.html).

You must be a member of the ABA to join the ABA Law Practice Management Section. You must be a member of the ABA Law Practice Management Section to join the ABA Women Rainmakers. There is no cost to join ABA Women Rainmakers.